PAUL'S
NEW
MOMENT

PAUL'S NEW MOMENT

Continental Philosophy and the
Future of Christian Theology

John Milbank
Slavoj Žižek
Creston Davis
with Catherine Pickstock

BrazosPress
a division of Baker Publishing Group
Grand Rapids, Michigan

© 2010 by John Milbank, Slavoj Žižek, and Creston Davis

Published by Brazos Press
a division of Baker Publishing Group
P.O. Box 6287, Grand Rapids, MI 49516-6287
www.brazospress.com

Printed in the United States of America

Library of Congress Cataloging-in-Publication Data

Milbank, John.
    Paul's new moment : Continental philosophy and the future of Christian theology / John
    Milbank, Slavoj Žižek, Creston Davis, with Catherine Pickstock.
        p.   cm.
    Includes bibliographical references and indexes.
    ISBN 978-1-58743-227-9 (pbk.)
    1. Christianity—Philosophy. 2. Philosophy and religion. 3. Continental philosophy.
I. Žižek, Slavoj. II. Davis, Creston. III. Title.
BR100.M49 2010
261.5′1—dc22   2010023576

10   11   12   13   14   15   16   7   6   5   4   3   2   1

To the memory of Jeff Wittung

Contents

Acknowledgments

We would like to thank Michele Hunt for her work on this project. In addition, we thank Georgi Georgiev, Joe Hughes, and Caleb Jones for their help with the IT side of this project.

I (Creston) would also like to thank my students in the spring 2010 continental philosophy seminar at Rollins College, along with my colleagues Mario D'Amato and Vidhu Aggarwal at Rollins College for their stimulating conversation and friendship. I would also like to thank Rodney Clapp and Arika Theule-Van Dam at Brazos Press for their brilliant support of this project! Finally, I would like to acknowledge how significant Jeffrey Hoffheins has been to my life. From youth to adulthood, you have truly shown me the way.

Introduction

At a point when the capitalist world is coming apart at the seams, we may pause and ask ourselves: what has happened to serious leftist protests against the unjust and dehumanizing logic of global capitalism? For the last few decades, any attempt to criticize the inner dark logic of capitalism has been simply dismissed as passé (or un-American). But now, as we perch precariously on the brink of total financial-capitalistic collapse, we may wonder why and under what cultural conditions true critiques from the Left have been systematically marginalized into non-existence. Has not the academy utterly failed to name and identify the perils of greed built into the very heart of the structures of capitalistic commodification? Can anyone, or any discipline, speak up?

We think there is a discipline or field of study that does possess the resources to mount an uncompromising stance against capitalism and its supplement, neoliberalism. That discipline is theology. Of course, the very meaning of the term "theology" is far from being universally agreed on (even among the authors of this book). But for the purposes of our thesis, we need only agree that theology (and the Christian tradition) serves as a wellspring capable of funding a materialist politics of subjective truth. Unlike liberalism, theology has a positive truth-claim, namely, that God's disclosure happens most fully in the Event of Christ's death on the cross. So this Event forever shatters a world defined by passive indifference, diluting "truth" to the common denominator, and clarifies the stakes of a materialist life. Consequently this positive stance is not founded on an eternal, unchanging idea but in a fragile, contingent Event in time and space.[1] Further, this Event gives the ontological

---

1. Marcus Pound makes this point in his *Žižek: A (Very) Critical Introduction* (Grand Rapids: Eerdmans, 2008).

1

coordinates of a stance *for* something and not simply a stance that is picked out of the choices already determined ahead of time. So in the end, this positive theological stance radically shatters the liberal view of freedom as highlighted by Lenin. Lenin, as Žižek has shown, cuts through the clutter when he posits a decisive distinction between *actual* and *formal* freedom, which helps to clarify how sharp Christianity's stance is compared to that of liberalism. Liberalism can only ever provide formal freedom, which is freedom to choose between options—except that these "options" are themselves never chosen by a subject but are already predetermined. Thus in formal freedom one has a choice to live one's life within predetermined coordinates (that is, you can buy this deodorant and not that one, and so forth). But Lenin is clear about the fact that this type of freedom amounts to nothing but a trick—or, in Marxist terms, ideology. It is ideological because we think we are free, but in reality we function more like robots in a demonic laboratory. By contrast, actual freedom is the freedom to choose an entirely new set of coordinates. This matches well with Christianity's claim to the Incarnational Event, inasmuch as its truth-claim is not determined by a set of predetermined a priori coordinates but is an unabashedly positive event not capable of being absorbed into the domesticated ideological fabric of our world. In short, and siding with Paul, we propose that Christian theology contains within it an irreducible revolutionary possibility that ruptures with the predetermined coordinates of the world and offers an entirely new kind of political subject altogether. In this way, too, the positive side of this thesis is that theology provides a critical stance against the basic assumptions and ruling ideologies of this world.

By contrast, take the standard version of the Left today, which can be seen in Chuck Palahniuk's brilliant 1996 novel, *Fight Club*. The novel depicts a young man recently out of college who works as an automobile product recall specialist. His job consists of doing cost-benefit analyses on the basis of which he either recalls the defective vehicles or does not. His profound dissatisfaction with his job turns him into an insomniac. Through this and other experiences, he begins to perceive the true logic of the profit-making machine and what this logic turns his own personhood into. One part of his personality sees his work as a sign of success that eventually gives him the "nesting syndrome," the condition whereby one's identity is possessed by consumerist practices to the point where authenticity is voided from the world. The main character learns to resist this ghastly corporate logic by developing an unconscious personality that desires only chaos (and not pure rationality). Eventually this chaotic personality founds Fight Club. Fight Club is an underground organization where men gather together to fight each other with nothing but their bared fists. The idea here is to create the conditions in which one can truly and actually feel a naked, unmediated reality. So the pain felt from a blow to the face cuts through the mirage of the fake world of corporate capitalism.

This novel gives us the inner workings of the leftist critique of capitalism by revealing capitalism's true character of abstraction and fake truth. In contrast to what is fake, pretend, and "successful," Palahniuk shows how the glitter of life can be overthrown by getting back to the bedrock of the real, which for him is coterminous with blood, pain, and violence. The revolutionary strategy for bringing down capitalism happens through the process of raising an army of "space monkeys," increasing revenue by selling expensive soaps (whose ingredients are harvested from liposuction dumpsters) to the rich, and ultimately making bombs destined to blow up financial corporations—the cornerstone of capitalism.

In the wake of the global financial meltdown, the leftist critique found in *Fight Club* seems totally superfluous. Within the literary horizon of *Fight Club* we witnessed capitalism by opposition: capitalism opposes the fake (Ikea) with the real (he sleeps on a dirty mattress), the abstract (distant smiles in the office, suits, ties, and the like) with the concrete (a bloody fist bearing down), and the lie (American Dream) with the truth ("we are all equally insignificantly organic"). But notice the hidden premise that undergirds the entire text, discovered when we finally get to the unadulterated "real" concrete existence: concrete existence is composed of violence and is nothing less than a living nightmare. But is not this very premise exactly the same one that underlies capitalism? Is this not exactly what Hegel meant by his insight that the opposite of a thing contains within it the kernel truth of that opposite thing?[2] This truth is borne out perfectly in light of the financial meltdown because capitalism does not need militant revolutionaries in order for it to collapse—the truth of capitalism is that it will, as Marx rightly stated, collapse under its own terms. The real terrorists—the real destroyers of capitalism—are not the "space monkeys" in underground organizations like Fight Club or even hardcore Marxist revolutionaries; they are, rather, the graduates of the MBA programs, bankers, and mortgage brokers who frame the meaning

2. G. W. F. Hegel, *Phenomenology of Spirit*, trans. A. V. Miller (Oxford: Oxford University Press, 1977), secs. 178–96.

of value solely and reductively in terms of money, private property, and the heedless extractions of natural resources from the earth.

This raises the basic question: is there any alternative to capitalism? And with this a further question is raised: what are some of the philosophical and theological resources that can help articulate a countervailing life-world that functions within the matrix of late capitalism? In other words, how do we follow the biblical injunction to live in the world, but not of the world (see, for example, John 17)? The standard interpretation of this injunction today takes the form of two different views. The first, fundamentalist view is simply to detach the material world from one's eternal "soul." Thus the tension is neutralized. The world will finally vanish and does not ultimately matter. In that sense the world really does not exist after all but is more like a passing illusion. The other and opposite interpretation comes from the liberal camp, which proposes that there is no real difference between the world and the Christian community of resistance. The problem with the liberal understanding is that the tension between being "in" the world and not being "of" the world is neutralized precisely by valorizing the world as if it is all there ever is and ever will be. But notice that these two apparently different interpretive horizons (fundamentalist and liberal) are united at a deeper, more secret level, for they each extract the struggle of Christian resistance either by giving up the world (fundamentalist) or by giving over the world (liberalism) to the powers.

In contrast to this dualism, which in reality hides a secret monism, this book's main imperative is to challenge the American bourgeois interpretation of Christian faith that simply hands over the world to the corporation without a fight. We want to locate and characterize the point of tension established between the prepositions "in" (the world) and "of" (the world). Our thesis begins by examining the basic contours of contemporary philosophy to see if there are resources for the struggle we are announcing.

Contemporary Philosophy

According to Alain Badiou, contemporary philosophy takes on three different orientations:[3] *hermeneutical philosophy* (Heidegger and Ga-

---

3. Of course, Badiou says there are many different types of positions that emerge from combining aspects of each of these three orientations ("Philosophy and Desire," in *Infinite Thought: Truth and the Return to Philosophy*, trans. and ed. Oliver Feltham and Justin Clemens [London: Continuum, 2003], 31).

damer), in which the task of philosophy is the act of interpreting, that is, uncovering *meaning* in a linguistically obscure horizon of existence; *analytic philosophy* (Wittgenstein and Carnap), in which the task of philosophy is the policing of the *rule* of language, which is reduced to the question of what can be said coherently and/or meaningfully in propositional form that alone can distinguish truth from falsehood; and *postmodern philosophy* (Derrida and Lyotard), in which the task of philosophy is a decisive act of destabilizing the foundations of modernity, of truth, and of the pure actions of thinking and the political subject.[4] The attempt of each of these three rival tasks of philosophy to exert its own procedural "paradigm" amounts to little more than the exertion of naked power in the "market of ideas." This attests to the reality that philosophy is no longer concerned with the quest for the truth of the world and so is reduced to a limited sphere, which only ensures the uninterrupted flow of capitalist markets. Truth as a philosophical category thus becomes enslaved to the unthinking markets of capitalism: philosophy at the service of the robber barons. Truth's instantiation is thus brutally reduced to the exercise of pure and arbitrary power in various domains of the world.

In our contemporary world, true philosophy is dead. Philosophy is dead because it no longer believes in itself, in truth, in a world in which reflection is supported. The death of contemporary philosophy suggests that philosophy's original desire, which (and we follow Alain Badiou) is to instantiate the truth of Being-in-the-world, must find a way of traversing its contemporary conditions if its true destiny is to be preserved. This suggests that other theoretical and practical possibilities may provide some resources to which philosophy can appeal in order to circumvent its present ill-fated condition. In other words, for philosophy to survive its present conditions it must appeal to other fields of knowledge external to itself. But when we canvass the various disciplines and their concomitant theoretical structures today, we are confronted with a barren wasteland of options. Truly we witness little short of a bankrupt conceptual (and thus practical) domain of thought, Marxism notwithstanding.

4. Ibid., 29–42. See also Peter Hallward, "Editorial Introduction," in "The One or the Other: French Philosophy Today," ed. Peter Hallward, special issue, *Angelaki: Journal of the Theoretical Humanities* 8, no. 2 (2003): 1–32. Hallward argues that philosophy as a discipline is "in retreat, a despondent branch of learning defeated by its unsustainable ambition and subsequently rearranged by needs external to its own needs borrowed or imposed by government, pedagogy, science, history" (1).

In both John Milbank and Slavoj Žižek's first major arguments, *Theology and Social Theory* and *The Sublime Object of Ideology* (each published almost two decades ago), they unabashedly and equally identified the dead end of thinking in the Western tradition. Bourgeois liberalism had finally arrived at epistemological and existential structures that could no longer survive an attack on their own foundations. For Milbank, secular knowledge was exposed for what it truly was (baseless and thus not knowledge at all), and for Žižek, the outright dismissal of Hegelian dialectical ontology in the twentieth century finally proved once and for all that philosophy avoided taking any risks and so eventually dies on the vine of security and enslavement to the brutal conditions of capitalism and postmodern irony (which is a double-speech testimonial to a groundlessness of language[5]). Thus is the condition of our time, and our thesis is an attempt to break out of this ironic, postmodern deadlock by putting down stakes so that one can actually risk the Absolute in the face of the shifting sands of relativism.

Again, for philosophy to survive it must risk a commitment to something more than the materialization of our present coordinates, something beyond the shifting sands of the postmodern that announces the end of both thought and action. Thus we turn to Christian theology as a way to establish an embodied and incarnated struggle for truth. Moreover, this trend that moves from philosophy to theology (for to save philosophy one must, as Hegel and Benjamin rightly saw, move into theology) reverses what was for a long time considered unfashionable and even taboo. In the zenith of the high modern era of the eighteenth century, religion was considered a species of opiate that ran radically against reason not simply to the point of the irrational[6] but also to the extreme of ideology and false consciousness.[7]

At the end of modernity, after the collapse of any alternative ideology to global capitalism or empire,[8] philosophy confronts its own terminal point and so is forced to seek out alternative resources, even if these

5. I am indebted to Rodney Clapp for this expression.

6. W. K. Clifford, *Lectures and Essays* (London: Macmillan, 1986).

7. Karl Marx and Friedrich Engels, *The German Ideology*, ed. and trans. C. J. Arthur (New York: International Publishers, 1970); Max Weber, *The Protestant Ethic and the Spirit of Capitalism*, trans. Talcott Parsons (London: Unwin, 1930). For a nice analysis of this from a theological point of view, see Daniel M. Bell Jr., "Only Jesus Saves: Toward a Theopolitical Ontology of Judgment," in *Theology and the Political: The New Debate*, ed. Creston Davis, John Milbank, and Slavoj Žižek (Durham, NC: Duke University Press, 2005), 200–227.

8. Michael Hardt and Antonio Negri, *Empire* (Cambridge, MA: Harvard University Press, 2000).

resources require philosophy to go where it has feared to tread for centuries. The survival of true philosophy has been forced to hazard the ultimate risk: it must return to a theology in order to return to itself and its ultimate destiny. We say philosophy "returns" to theology because, from its historic inception onward, philosophy was inextricably bound up within the theological register. This can be seen in how the ancient philosophers, from Thales to Parmenides, appealed to the divine as a means by which their quests for truth were guided. The joint nature of theology and philosophy can be further seen by how these two fields of knowing finally split under the pressure of a reified force of reason sundered from both history and the divine. To understand the world, to imagine Being-in-the-world, as Martin Heidegger famously put it, was absolutely impossible without the operation of the religious as a presupposition to existence as such. And as we interpret philosophy that makes this ultimate risk to return to its true destiny through the theological, the very composition of philosophy will inexorably change. So the question that brings this book into focus is: to what degree will philosophy need Christianity in order to survive both the death of philosophy and liberalist and fundamentalist Christianity? To understand this, our thesis states that Christian theology possesses the requisite ontological resources that deliver a revolutionary politics grounded in the Incarnational Event of God becoming human. Indeed this Event of God becoming human is so earth-shattering that it enacts something akin to the psychoanalytic concept of trauma, in that the very means by which an event is birthed forever throws everything so far off balance that even our very conception of this Event is rendered forever irreparable.[9]

The crisis that philosophy confronted at the dawn of the twentieth century was the logical end of modernity's false move that denied the existence of something beyond the reduction to a singularity of meaning, which finally sundered the world into a dualism between mind and the material world. This dualism, moreover, was the rudimentary problem that Hegel attempted to resolve. With few exceptions, the past century of philosophy has simply confirmed the death of philosophy and offers no resources from within its restrictive structure that could revitalize it. At the same time, twentieth-century forms of theology have

---

9. For an excellent analysis of theology and trauma, see Marcus Pound's work, especially *Theology, Trauma, and Psychoanalysis* (London: SCM, 2007). The trauma of the Incarnation is irreparably in this world—we are forever thrown off balance.

been just as guilty of falling prey to the false split or dualism between the secular (immanent reason) and the religious (pure dematerialized transcendence). From Barth to Tillich and from Niebuhr to present-day theologians, theology either jettisons reason's truth in creation (and so sunders the Logos from the intellect) or becomes a polite apologist who unwittingly justifies pragmatic secular violence in the name of theology. And this is not even to mention how both sides of twentieth-century theology play into the same trap into which philosophy was lured. To put it brutally, this theological divide in the twentieth century can be described in terms of two fundamental camps. There is the Barthian side, and there is the Tillichian side. Barth falls into the theological death trap because his thinking is not moored to ontology but is instead mediated by fragmented communities sundered from a Pauline universalism via his limitation of the a priori of revelation into which God must conform in order to be! Tillichian theology, which is premised on a lukewarm dialectical ontology, forgets that it is the core truth of any dialectical structure, namely, the place for the exception, that founds its own truth. This is why Tillich could never be a thinker of a militant Incarnational Event, because everything ultimate is dissolved into a dialectical morass of "oneness." So Barth cannot resist the totality of capitalism because it shrinks back into a security (revelation/communities) that finally subverts itself from within, and Tillich has no point of irruption from without. Thus both are finally subsumed within the ideology of empire. In this way, theology on these twentieth-century terms is, like philosophy, dead.

This book claims that not only does theology provide the rich resources that enable philosophy to overcome the crisis of its own death, but theology can also actually give us the coordinates of freedom in the face of a pure determinist capitalistic horizon. Indeed, in many ways, twentieth-century theology has hidden theology's radical stance from itself and has committed something tantamount to cosmic false consciousness. Our thesis, which is aimed at nothing short of emancipating theology from the clutches of bourgeois liberalism, will unfold by drawing on one figure and two different themes.

The first part will draw on the figure of St. Paul, whose vision of the Event of the cross and resurrection radically breaks with reified forms of knowledge and political structures. Thus Paul's radical thought, which breaks from the law, grounds our thesis in a particular Event that opens up a radically new life-world. It is this distinctively Christian Event that finally reveals the intrinsic and subversive nature inherently bound up in Christian theology. Our thesis will unfold in the following three ways: first, there is Paul, who gives us the coordinates for a theology of liberation; second, there is the liturgy, which puts the radical nature of Pauline theology into action; and finally, there is the question of how theology relates to the logic of mediation (vis-à-vis Alain Badiou) and the death of philosophy as well as to the future (especially the doctrine of predestination and apocalypse).

Part 1, "On Paul," is divided into three chapters. In the first chapter, Milbank sets the stage by positioning Paul with and against Agamben and biopolitics. In doing this, he further extends a devastating critique of modern liberalism, which he asserts is dominated by secular categories. Paul, Milbank argues, breaks with the collusion of secular logic by offering an alternative vision of the resurrection that returns justice to this world. In the second chapter, Žižek follows Milbank in further extending the nature and critique that the figure of Paul unleashes. Žižek articulates his clearest and most sustained treatment of Paul and, as an atheist materialist, arrives at rather surprising conclusions that Christianity must confront or be carried off in the winds of indifference. Part 1 concludes with a chapter in which Davis reads St. Paul as a revolutionary who gives Christianity the coordinates for a gospel of love and service rather than an imperialist set of doctrines that too often finds itself in bed with the principalities and powers of this world.

In the second part, "On the Liturgy," we move from clarifying Paul's theoretical stance to fleshing it out in more concrete, materialist terms. In this way, this section of the book reveals the need to rethink the relation between transcendence and immanence, not in terms of abstract theory but in terms of actual practice. Said differently, this section unites Paul's vision of the scandalous cross with an embodied action. Thus the relation between infinity and finitude needs to be reconceived as an action and not as reductive abstraction left to theologians or philosophers; indeed, is not this one of the many problems that plagued twentieth-century theology, where theology was simply divorced from practice? In this section, however, something of an "internal" debate surfaces within the book, as would be expected. The debate centers around the entire nature and validity of the liturgy itself. And here we have two sides: On the one side are Pickstock and Davis, who argue that the liturgy is the supreme action that intensely unites creation with the Creator. As Pickstock argues in chapter 4, the impulse to worship precedes philosophical reflection about God, and yet the liturgy concludes and completes our highest abstract reflections and action. With the theme of the liturgy clarified in chapter 4, Davis links Paul with the liturgy in chapter 5 by arguing that Paul's subject is finally completed within the unfolding liturgy, whereby the subject becomes substance with the divine as such. On the other side of the debate is Žižek, who, in chapter 6, questions Christian liturgy as being little more than a type of paganism that seeks to bring rival cosmic forces and powers (i.e., good and evil) into a balanced harmony with each other. More than this, Žižek even questions the idea of worship as atoning for humans' lack (i.e., sin) by paying off Satan through the "price" of Christ's death. In this way, he questions God's omnipotence and by extension our worship of a God who, on Christian terms, has lost his power in the act of atonement.

In the third and final section, "On Mediation and Apocalypse," Žižek and Milbank spell out the details of their own (very different) theological procedures. In chapter 7, Žižek sketches out his atheistic theology by engaging the doctrinal notions of predestination and apocalypse. He does this by exploring a wide variety of philosophical and theological positions from neuroscience to Pascal's wager, and from the logic of salvation to the future of theology and the end of the world. In chapter 8, Milbank fleshes out his theology by engaging Alain Badiou. More specifically, he questions Badiou's view of mediation—that is, how things and events relate to each other. In the final analysis, Milbank argues that Badiou's view of mediation is not theological enough, and so Badiou's entire project is called into question exactly because it finally cannot produce a political subject of the Event. Milbank argues that only through an orthodox theological ontology can one finally produce what Badiou (and other Marxist materialists) desire. By finishing the book with Milbank's engagement with Badiou we, in a manner, return to the beginning of the book, especially in regard to thinking through the idea of Paul vis-à-vis the Event. That is to say, by understanding how trinitarian mediation (à la Milbank) relates to Paul's Incarnational Event, we are better able to understand what is at stake for the future of theology and its concomitant political subject for our time.

To better understand how our common thesis coheres, it may be helpful to briefly introduce the basic positions of each author. Doing this gives a depth not only to our common thesis—that is, the stakes of the very meaning of Christian theology today in light of our main character, Paul of Tarsus, and our themes of liturgy, mediation, and the future of the church—but also to the counterthesis that runs just below our common one, namely, the debate afoot about the very meaning of the term "theology" in both its orthodox and its atheistic variants. As you will immediately see (if you haven't noticed already), these authors could not be more different: John Milbank and Catherine Pickstock are orthodox Christian theologians whereas Slavoj Žižek is a radical atheist materialist. Creston Davis was a student of both Milbank and Žižek and is influenced by the structures of both thinkers.

Positions

Milbank

Milbank was the first to refute what Charles Taylor now calls the "subtraction theory" of secularization, that is, the view that secularization simply removed religious elements to reveal a "secularity" that had been lurking all along. Milbank argues that secularity was a historical anomaly that had to be positively imagined and constructed; indeed, for Milbank, "once, there was no 'secular.'"[10] Whereas Milbank did this for the history of ideas, Taylor has done this for the history of events and cultural practices in his work *A Secular Age*.[11] Milbank argues that these intellectual constructs of the secular rested on preferences for some types of theology rather than for others, especially nominalism/voluntarism and revived gnosticism. In the first instance, he suggests that it was a certain kind of (dubious) theology itself that first invented a space that was secular, a space drained of "enchantment" and sacramental significance. Other, later modes of secularity (i.e., liberal modernity) purporting to be neutral in religious terms were, he demonstrates to the contrary, built on assumptions incompatible with orthodox Christian teachings. These assumptions were also arbitrary in character, not truly objectively warranted.

Next Milbank shows that nearly all secular theories of politics, economics, and society assumed an inevitability of violence and that violence is primary and a given ontological reality for human beings. From this he strongly argues that this is in contrast with Christianity, which assumes that being is in itself peaceful and only contingently interrupted by fallenness (the state of sin). Redemption therefore believes in and works for the ultimate restoration of ontological peaceableness and harmony achieved through final justice. This trust in an ontol-

10. John Milbank, *Theology and Social Theory: Beyond Secular Reason* (Cambridge, MA: Blackwell, 1991).

11. Charles Taylor, *A Secular Age* (Cambridge, MA: Harvard University Press, 2007).

ogy of peace is unique to Christianity and breaks with the ontological agonistic assumptions of classical antiquity, to which modern social theory returns in new, "post-" Christian ways. So Milbank argues that modern secularity, from the vantage point of Christian orthodoxy, was a mixture of the heterodox, the neopagan, and the antireligious. And he argues that the humanism of secular modernity is bound logically to become postmodern nihilism.

Milbank goes on to submit that from an internal theological point of view the notion of "secular reason" was rather dubious. From a secular perspective, secularity was only an existential choice for the heretical, the neopagan, or even the nihilistic. Put differently, he argues that once the claims to a rational foundation of modern social theory have been deconstructed and all religious commitments (heretically Christian, neopagan) have been abandoned, then the only logical secular position is a Nietzschean, nihilistic one. From this he asks if this view is no more rationally objective than a Christian one. Both views see finite reality as indeterminate and aporetic, but nihilism opts to see this as a sign of the unreality of reason and the chaotic springing of all from a Void. By contrast, Christianity opts to see this as a sign of the "borrowedness" of finite reality, as created from an infinite plenitudinous truth. So while the choice between the two is rationally undecidable, only Christianity, according to Milbank, allows differences to coexist peaceably, and so only this outlook really permits differences to flourish (and the neighbor to appear), because if they compete or are established only through a constant agon—as for Deleuze, Derrida, and the like—they cannot really flourish or even survive.

Clearly, then, in theological terms *Theology and Social Theory* radically broke with most twentieth-century theology in two principal ways: First, it refused to say that theology must conform to secular knowledge, which is regarded as established independently of theology, and it refused a Barthian-style fideism, which says that theology simply expounds the givens of faith and ignores rational deliberations. Second, it broke with the approach of most twentieth-century theology that thinks there is a sphere of secular theologically "neutral" knowledge. In contrast to this, Milbank argues that we should follow Henri de Lubac in seeing that the duality of faith and reason is itself a modern construct.[12] *Theology and Social Theory* thus puts an end to all the assumptions of

---

12. John Milbank, *The Suspended Middle: Henri de Lubac and the Debate concerning the Supernatural* (Grand Rapids: Eerdmans, 2005).

modern Protestant thought about divisions between faith and reason and demonstrates that liberal theology (more built up from reason) and neoorthodoxy (more expounding faith) were both equally modern and indeed "liberal." This applies also to much Catholic theology still taught within early-modern scholastic paradigms, which deny that we have a neutral orientation to the supernatural as a single human end. This further means that the *nouvelle théologie* orientation (of Lubac and others) alone looks forward to a twenty-first-century theology that goes beyond the faith-versus-reason norms established in twentieth-century philosophy and theology.

Žižek

Žižek's thinking, like Hegel's and Milbank's, is so global that it inherently resists summary; indeed to summarize his view(s) is to immediately get it wrong, as with the cliché that reduces Hegel's philosophy to little more than a thesis/antithesis/synthesis structure into which everything must fold in order for it to exist. So for our purposes, I will highlight some seminal points regarding Žižek's foray into Christian theology. Žižek rereads Christianity through the filter of an idiosyncratic Hegelian/Lacanian psychoanalytical perspective. What this basically results in is an open ontology of radical contingency (or lack) figured through Jacques Lacan's central ideas (the big Other, "subject supposed to know," the real, the symbolic, the imaginary orders, etc.). Thus the starting point for Žižek is not contingent upon the authority of the church or God's revelation in Scripture and tradition, nor even a Neoplatonic "sacramentalist" ontology in which the world is a transparent icon leading straight up into God's glory. To the contrary, Žižek's starting point could be said to take place within Paul's stance: "now we see in a mirror dimly" (1 Cor. 13:12); the world is, in the first place, a congealed void of obscurity whose outcome is far from being known. In this way, Žižek's starting point (not unlike the prophets of old) may be pessimistic, but it's also couched in a humble posture unwilling to hijack the future in the name of a predetermined orthodox eschatology (i.e., the ideal of Jesus's returning at the end of time). To assent to a conservative orthodox theology would be effectively stealing away the possibility of love and freedom, which for Žižek are crucial terms for any true materialist theology. For Žižek the world's outcome is radically open: evil may indeed win the day, and so calls one to participate in a materialist struggle in the here and now. This is why Žižek critiques orthodox theology as being not truly Christian at all, precisely because orthodox Christianity is too hubristic to live into a real and concrete materialist history where the outcome is not something to be taken for granted. Žižek will even say that the orthodox Christian theologian John Milbank enacts "a regression to paganism," whereas in Žižek's own "atheism," he says, "I am more Christian than Milbank."[13]

Again, for Žižek the future vision of Christ's return at the end of the world's age prematurely determines the ethics of the present epoch. Moreover, orthodox Christianity is complicit in this dematerialized, even "gnostic," politic (i.e., it doesn't care about the material world, for according to this view it does not need to because Jesus is coming back anyway to save his chosen elect). This is strange because Žižek is often accused of being a gnostic himself, but here the table is reversed when he reveals that it is in fact orthodox "Main Street" Christianity that is gnostic in the sense that it continues existing as if it already knows the outcome of history as such. The knowing of the outcome before it actually takes place puts a twist on the meaning of one of Lacan's key notions, namely, "subject supposed to know" (*sujet supposé savoir* [S.s.S.]) that he fleshes out in Seminar XI.[14] For Lacan says, "As soon as the subject who is supposed to know [S.s.S.] exists somewhere . . . there is transference."[15] Žižek links this idea to another of Lacan's seminal notions, namely, the big Other (in this case God, who is the one who knows all things and ensures, no matter how nihilistic and secular the world gets, that the end result will be guaranteed, namely, salvation). Thus what happens is that the very belief in God's work in history (as the big Other who will redeem all things—like the end of a cliché Disney film) radically neutralizes a materialist struggle in the present. In other words, the belief in God here is tantamount to a disbelief in one's very materialist existence in the present, which then cancels out the very ability to struggle for liberation and truth—the heart of the gospel itself. Žižek writes:

> Such a displacement of our most intimate feelings and attitudes onto some figure of the Other [i.e., God or the cliché view of Jesus's romantic return] is at the very core of Lacan's notion of the big Other; it can affect not only feelings but also beliefs and knowledge—the Other can also believe and know for me. In

13. Slavoj Žižek and John Milbank, *The Monstrosity of Christ: Paradox or Dialectic?* ed. Creston Davis (Cambridge, MA: MIT Press, 2009), 249.
14. Jacques Lacan, *The Four Fundamental Concepts of Psychoanalysis: The Seminar of Jacques Lacan, Book XI*, ed. Jacques-Alain Miller, trans. Alan Sheridan (London: Hogarth Press and Institute of Psycho-Analysis, 1977), 232.
15. Ibid.

order to designate this displacement of the subject's knowledge onto another, Lacan coined the notion of the *subject supposed to know*.[16]

This gets to the heart of Žižek's critique of orthodox Christianity, which contains an inherent perversion at the core of its existence. Why? Because on Christianity's own terms it commits its own negation—or in Pauline terms, a scandal that turns the entire world upside down. This happens when God in Christ utters the horrifying words, "Father, why hast Thou forsaken me?" This is the darkest hour within Christianity because the narrative offers up a meaning that is unthinkable, namely, that God the Father is not safely up there in heaven ensuring that all things will work out to his own glory. And here the "system" and "institutionalization" of Christianity crack open, revealing its perverse core—a truth that there is no big Other, no paternal God, but nonetheless one continues believing in God. This is Žižek's idea of "disavowal." A disavowal takes place when one fully knows better (indeed, even the Christian story of Christ dying on the cross demonstrates this truth), but the Christian continues to believe precisely because it is absurd. This sounds very close to the famous phrase often attributed to Tertullian: *Credo quia absurdum* ("I believe because it is absurd"). In *On the Flesh of Christ*, Tertullian says:

> The Son of God was born: There is no shame, because it is shameful.
> And the Son of God died: It is wholly credible because it is incredible.
> And, buried, He rose again: It is certain because it is impossible.[17]

But let us be clear here: Žižek is a total atheist. So he thinks that someone like Tertullian (or Milbank) is simply turning a fetishized disavowal (i.e., the reality that there is no God) into a "paradox" (in which the truth retains its integrity deep within) in order to continue believing in the victory of Jesus.

Žižek's intervention into Christian theology unapologetically names orthodox Christianity as simply ideological in the sense that the church's theology merely helps support the status quo of "Main Street" liberal capitalism. But Žižek sees in the figure of Paul someone whose version of the Christ-event on the cross is something that cannot be domesticated but that inherently upsets the status quo on every level of the cosmos. This is why Žižek thinks that Christianity alone is the religion that can found a true materialist struggle—not by systematically containing and

16. Slavoj Žižek, *How to Read Lacan* (New York: Norton, 2006), 27.
17. 5.4, translation slightly modified.

covering over its radical nature (i.e., orthodox theology) but rather by living into this struggle in the here and now. This is why Žižek begins and ends his materialist theology with Paul, who says: "For our struggle is not against enemies of blood and flesh, but against the rulers, against the authorities, against the cosmic powers of this present darkness" (Eph. 6:12 NRSV). And Romans 12:2: "Do not be conformed to this world, but be transformed by the renewing of your minds" (NRSV). The Christian church, according to Žižek (following Althusser), has indeed conformed to this world—it does not pose a front to the unforgivable injustices that capitalism has unleashed upon us that Paul calls us to struggle against and to overthrow in the name of love.

Davis

Creston Davis studied under both Milbank and Žižek, so his thinking, though still at an underdeveloped stage, can be seen as something of a synthesis of both. He first encountered Žižek and Milbank while he was a student of Stanley Hauerwas and Kenneth Surin at Duke University in the late 1990s. Davis was drawn to the logic found in both Milbank's *Theology and Social Theory* and Žižek's *Sublime Object of Ideology*, both of which not only identified the dead-end logic of neoliberalism with clarity and panache but also went beyond the conservative critical stance by offering a way past the deadlock of capitalism through communal or collective possibilities. What Davis perceived was not the differences in the very premises that define both Žižek's and Milbank's thought structures but rather the similarities. Davis's point of departure was the Incarnation itself (and its aftermath), and from this vantage both Milbank's and Žižek's structures synthesize in terms that resist either an epistemological foundation or a postmodern deference of meaning. This book's thesis could be restated as the identification of the similar and converging premises that line up in both Žižek's and Milbank's thought. Davis has worked with Milbank and Žižek on a number of writing projects, including editing *Theology and the Political: The New Debate* and *The Monstrosity of Christ: Paradox or Dialectic?* He has completed, with Žižek and Clayton Crockett, a book entitled *Hegel and the Infinite* and is working on a book on truth.

Milbank and Žižek

Finally it may be helpful to briefly narrate how Milbank and Žižek first met each other, a meeting that immediately sparked an intellectual fire that burns brightly even after several years. In September 2002 Davis organized an international conference, "Ontologies in Practice," in which he invited Žižek to discuss theology with Milbank. After Milbank gave his lecture titled "Materialism and Transcendence," Žižek stepped on stage in Old Cabell Hall at the University of Virginia and began a debate that mesmerized everyone for several hours. The basic parameters of the debate circled around the relationship between politics, ontology, and theology. After that event it was clear that something special had happened. In the midst of this debate, a critique would emerge between these two thinkers that began to challenge nearly all the underlying assumptions that informed the areas of theology, sociology, politics, and philosophy, to name a few. This synergistic encounter has acquired a direct debate posed in oppositional terms that materialized in *The Monstrosity of Christ*. But in this book the oppositional stance between Milbank and Žižek is overcome by the articulation of a common thesis that confronts the crisis of theology today, namely, the monstrous Event of God becoming man!

With this common thesis in place we can observe that it both enhances and advances a new theological critique against capitalism (and neoliberalism) from the standpoint of theology premised on an Event (and not premised on an abstract ideal or a sick, lukewarm dialectic or a reductionist view of language). In this regard this book extends the work of both Milbank and Žižek on their own terms, and especially in terms of the other's work. Perhaps, at the end of the day, one might still need to choose between either Milbank's or Žižek's position, but this book also presents a new option, namely, that one may not need to make such a choice after all.

PART 1

On Paul

1

Paul against Biopolitics

John Milbank

The Modern Biopolitical

Today we live in a neo-Weberian moment. Capitalism, since it requires for its very operation (and not as mere ideological concealment) a belief in abstract fetishes and the worship of the spectacle of idealized commodities, is a quasi religion.[1] But in the early twenty-first century, capitalism appears to need to buttress itself with the approval and connivance of actual religion. Fundamentalist and evangelical Protestantism of certain stripes plays this role, and increasingly a segment of the Catholic Church also—so-called Whig Thomists, most notably in the United States and in Italy.[2]

This chapter originally appeared in a slightly altered form as "Paul against Biopolitics," *Theory, Culture & Society* 25, nos. 7–8 (2008): 125–72.

1. See Walter Benjamin, "Capitalism as Religion," in *Selected Writings*, vol. 1, *1913–1926*, ed. Marcus Bullock and Michael W. Jennings (Cambridge, MA: Harvard University Press, 1996), 288–91; Philip Goodchild, *Capitalism and Religions: The Price of Piety* (London: Routledge, 2002).

2. See Tracey Rowland, *Culture and the Thomist Tradition: After Vatican II* (London: Routledge, 2003), esp. 42ff. In Italy, this current is mainly represented by Forza Italia politician Marcello Pera, who forwards a characteristic neoconservative mix of neoliberal economics with a "Straussian" insistence on the role of lay Catholics in the educative and cultural spheres and proposals for a pan-Christian "civil religion." He is also an apologist for the State of Israel. Although Pope Benedict has cowritten a recent book with him focusing on the evils of moral relativism, he has, by contrast, always clearly distanced himself from the neoliberal advocacy of the pure market. See Marcello Pera and Joseph Ratzinger, *Without Roots: Europe, Relativism, Christianity, Islam* (New York: Basic Books, 2006).

Why should this be the case? Why do we now have the sacred in a double register? Perhaps the answer has to do with the extremity of neoliberalism (mutated into neoconservatism) as such. As Walter Benjamin and later Michel Foucault argued, liberalism concerns the biopolitical,[3] for liberalism promotes an imagined self-governing of life through a certain capture and disciplining of natural forces of aggression and desire within the framework of a cultural game, governed by civil conventions and instituted laws. In this conception, life is as much a cultural construct as is law, although the naturalness of life, thought of as innately self-regulating, is always insinuated. Yet the life that biopolitics both unleashes and governs is also conceived as intrinsically wild and untameable and dynamically creative, since it has to do with the expression of egoistic passions. Both in politics proper and in economics, liberalism rejoices in an order that is supposed to emerge naturally from the clash of passions themselves. This may, as in contract theory, imply a point of rupture in which the clash is diverted from anarchic war to a regulated agonistic game, or else, as in the more sophisticated perspectives deriving from the Scottish enlightenment, it may imply a precontractual tendency of passion to balance passion, resulting in an unplanned and regulated order, political as well as political-economic.

But in either case a threshold is invoked, whether this be one of contractual rupture or of almost imperceptible transition from anarchy to spontaneous agonistic self-ordering according to a hedonistic calculus of long-term "interest," rather than mere unreflective "passion," within a sequence of emergent and yet all-the-same tacitly or explicitly recognized cultural norms. In either case it is deemed that, by nature, a simultaneously competing and cooperating (through natural mutual sympathy) human multitude erects an artificial framework that will channel this spontaneity for further mutual benefit. Life itself is seen as generating contract and law. Contract and law are seen as disciplining life, but only in order to further it.

---

3. Benjamin, "Critique of Violence," in *Selected Writings*, 1:236–52, esp. 237. Benjamin here points out how Darwin reinforces Hobbes: prior to the political, living things are seen as having a "natural right" to deploy violence, and life and violence are seen as practically coterminous. It is, however, Foucault who defined precisely the biopolitical paradigm in the sense that I am discussing it here. See Michel Foucault, *Naissance de la Biopolitique* (Paris: Éditions du Seuil/Gallimard, 2004). It is finally Giorgio Agamben who makes the crucial connection between biopolitics and the political philosophy of Carl Schmitt. (Ultimately it is a Hobbesian legacy that binds all this together.) See Giorgio Agamben, *Homo Sacer: Sovereign Power and Bare Life*, trans. Daniel Heller-Roazen (Stanford, CA: Stanford University Press, 1998), 126–36.

In practice, however, there is nothing stable about this paradox. To the contrary, the regulative framework for economic competition periodically proves irksome to certain of the competitors. When, at the ceaselessly reemerging limit, it frustrates their endeavors, they will resort to the illegal or the quasi legal: to fraud, to deceit, to sheer seizure, sometimes involving military means. Primary accumulation does not stand only at the origin of the capitalist process enabling it to commence; rather, the built-in tension of this process itself requires a periodic return to the initial instance.[4] In this way the claim that contract adequately channels and furthers the aims of purportedly natural egoistic life is given the lie: this life perpetually outruns the law, and the purest capitalist order is always host to government by crime augmented by spectacle, as the history of the United States repeatedly attests.

But this anarchically excessive element appears not only on the side of fantasized life but also on the side of the abstract economic fictions themselves. Since notions of money, profit, and capital are purely nominal, they contain an excess of potential signification over any realized referential content. Money may come as a price tag, or it may be invoked simply as a price. Thus the dynamism of capitalism consists not just in the unleashing of egoistic creativity but also in the piling up of abstract resources of wealth that are entirely unreal and yet, since their nominal force is everywhere acknowledged, entirely real in their effects.

For capitalism to work, however, the abstract has to reconnect with living, egoistically driven cultural reality all the time: money must finally be reinvested in material processes, even if these also become ceaselessly more rarefied, as in the case of an information economy. In this case, nevertheless, signs are still semimaterial entities, while electronic networks, however microscopic and seemingly intangible, remain entirely material. But because the regulation of life within liberalism must remain a formal one without substantive commitments, the sheerly abstract remains in truth (and not merely ideological appearance) the ultimate strange goal of capitalist production, with the consequence that there will arise recurrently a failure to link this nominal sum back to material life. Hence periodic crises of overproduction and overaccumulation ensue.[5]

In this way, anarchy lurks not just in life outrunning contract but also in contract outrunning life. Moreover, these twin excesses collude in

4. See David Harvey, *The New Imperialism* (Oxford: Oxford University Press, 2003), 26–34, 98–112.

5. Ibid. See also Harvey's *Limits to Capital* (Oxford: Oxford University Press, 1982); Giovanni Arrighi, "Hegemony Unravelling-I," *New Left Review* 32 (March–April 2005): 23–80.

such a way that the formal pursuit of nominal goals on the one hand, and real living violence on the other, collapse into one. So, for example, an excess of financial assets with nowhere to go will encourage the more or less violent seizure of new resources for production and new scope for the intrusion of markets (as one can see happening in several parts of the globe at the present time).

These biopolitical paradoxes manifest themselves in the political sphere proper, as well as in the economic one. In modern times, laws typically proceed from a sovereign power granted legitimacy through a general popular consent as mediated by representation. Insofar as such a procedure is taken to be normative, it can be seen as embodying a Hobbesian "natural law" for the derivation of legitimate power from the conflicts endemic to human life. But this is quite different from saying that the sovereign power is answerable regarding equity to a law of natural justice, grounded in an eternal divine law—as, for example, in Aquinas. No, the logic of legality is, in the post-Hobbesian case, entirely immanent and positivistic. Yet just for this reason, as traced by Carl Schmitt, Walter Benjamin, and today Giorgio Agamben, paradoxes of the biopolitical result.[6] Just as life and contract are supposed to harmonize but cannot always, and in the end cannot at all, save negatively and catastrophically, so likewise with life and law. For because the formal framework of law is absolute and is taken to proceed from universal consent, an absolutely sovereign power must be erected in order to enforce this law. But then one can ask, does sovereignty really proceed from a "prior" instance of instituting multitudinous life, or rather from the "post" instance of artificial control of human life that stops it from running amok and in Hobbesian terms converts it from being a "multitude" into the semblance of a "people"?[7] Once the multitude has, supposedly in its own interests, authorized sovereign power, it has likewise, in that same moment, become a people only by renouncing this authority in the very act of first constituting it through exercise. The problematic of alienation is endemic to the very notion of political representation.

Moreover, in granting authority in general to the sovereign center, a people cannot in principle anticipate all the emergencies that the sovereign power will have to deal with. No number of plebiscites could cope with this conundrum, for even the selection of and posing of

6. Benjamin, "Critique of Violence"; Carl Schmitt, *Political Theology*, trans. George Schwab (Cambridge, MA: MIT Press, 1985); Giorgio Agamben, *State of Exception*, trans. Kevin Attell (Chicago: University of Chicago Press, 2003).
7. Thomas Hobbes, *De Cive*, 12.8.

questions for referenda lie in principle (save for an infinite regress) outside democratic control. Therefore that shadowy, unruly life that is projected by the sovereign light of liberalism on the screen of nature constantly throws up new threats and disorders that legislation will have to deal with.

At the same time, as with the economy, anomic threats derive from both sides of the divide. Since unlimited power has been granted to the sovereign center in order to preserve a formal order of regulated self-interest, a pure logic of power for its own sake is bound to take over. The supposed representative guardian of sovereign authority will excessively pursue the interests of its own exercise for its own sake. Division of powers installed at the center in order to mitigate this tendency can do so only to a certain degree, and ultimately, since the balancing occurs precisely at the center, it ends up *reinforcing* the unlimited power of the center by rendering the center itself the sight of a constant power struggle.[8] And since it is the executive that tends constantly to exceed in spirit the letter of authorization by which sovereignty is supposedly bound, there will also be a continuous tendency in the long term for the executive to usurp the sovereign authority by capturing the sovereign moment itself. Such a process, Agamben argues, has been under way ever since the French Revolution and accelerated throughout the twentieth century: democratic immanence itself demands an unlimited central power unconstrained by any imagined natural transcendence, and for this very reason this power tends to outrun mass control.[9] For no extrademocratic law of natural justice may be invoked by pure democracy to bind within the bounds of democratic answerability the democratically engendered excess to democracy. (Despite recognizing the state of exception as a characteristically modern political phenomenon, Agamben also points to Roman theoretical and practical equivalents, particularly in the condition of *iudicium* that was a suspension of the law following on a decree of *senatus consultum ultimum*.[10] Although Agamben does not make this clear, one can relate this foreshadowing of the modern to the relatively formalistic and "protoliberal" character of the Roman *imperium*, which had lost the tight cohesiveness of the *polis* and tended increasingly to make the protection of individual liberties paramount.)

8. See John Milbank, "The Gift of Ruling: Secularization and Political Authority," *New Blackfriars* 85, no. 996 (March 2004): 212–39.

9. Agamben, *State of Exception*, 1–31.

10. Ibid., 41–51.

Finally, the anarchy of political life and the anarchy of political law come together, because the formal system of laws never provides a complete guarantee of order and must always be supplemented and defended. This supplementation and defense involves an overriding of the very principles of these laws themselves. Hence today we get an increasing suspension of civil liberties in the name of the defense of those liberties—a process that can perhaps never be curtailed, first of all because the self-interest of power will be reluctant to concede once more an advantage that it has already gained, and second because the very resort to perpetual global quasi-military police action tends itself to engender perpetual global civil war. This resort inevitably meets with a further development in terroristic ingenuity that will in turn call forth yet further emergency legislation or secret executive action. And since, in a democracy, the policing power will covertly lay claim as a citizen-defending body to an unrestricted right to do whatever is necessary in the name of such defense and will tend to enjoy absolutely unrestricted access to all information (unrestricted by local or aristocratic privilege), democratic policing, as Walter Benjamin argues in his "Critique of Violence," tends more to the totalitarian than did the policing of absolute monarchies (which remained somewhat more constrained by what Benjamin describes as the "elevating" influence of the crown and also by social hierarchy).[11]

So there is an innate tendency within liberalism to engender permanent executive rule and unrestricted policing in the name of a continuous emergency, because at the heart of modern, unrestricted sovereign legal authority lies the right to resort to something not legislated for, something paradoxically extralegal. Symmetrically, as Benjamin indicates in relation to Schmitt's reflections, the democratic will of the people makes sense only as a permanent latent right to rise up in bloody revolution. The latter also, as Agamben shows, typically appeals to an extraordinary authority of the existing positive law itself.[12]

How, then, might this relate to the neo-Weberian moment and the doubling of the religious? Perhaps it is the case that the more abstract capital and abstract law come to order and govern by being permanently in excess of constitutional legitimacy, and the more the formal salve against violence coincides with a constant use of police violence now merged with military violence—since home and abroad are increas-

11. Benjamin, "Critique of Violence," 243. These remarks, like so many others that he makes elsewhere, reveal Benjamin as uniquely capable of breaking free of the straitjacket of mere "left-wing" thinking operating as a new sort of piety.

12. Ibid., 239–40; Agamben, *State of Exception*, 28–29, 52–64.

ingly treated as one—the more the excess comes close to being a visible embarrassment. The more also it becomes difficult to view this excess as a bland, white mystery, a remarkably productive Void, not unakin, as Slavoj Žižek argues, to the Void of "Western Buddhism," from Schopenhauer through to Heidegger, whose temporalized being is identical with nothingness.[13] Such elite mysticism, which is echoed in a mass consumerist gnosis (as portrayed in Don DeLillo's novel *White Noise*), becomes, one might suggest, insufficient for general consensus where the indeterminate abstractness of law and capital assumes increasingly the positive and personal guise of deliberate violence.

In these circumstances, a new appeal to a positive transcendence is correspondingly made. While the law of the market is still seen as emerging from the logic of life as such, such life engendering such law is seen as itself embodying an order laid down by God regarded as the ultimate primary accumulator. In this way, a constitutive capitalist excess to its own rule-governed market norms is finally underwritten by a positive transcendent instance. What I am positing here is a kind of Schmittian addition to Marxist political economy. This parallels David Harvey's insistence that primary accumulation is not simply initial but is rather a "spatial fix" that must be constantly re-resorted to at the point where the signification of capital (the capitalist economic symbolic and the capitalist cultural imaginary in Lacanian terms) threatens to lose all relation to the material real that capitalism always encodes yet still requires as a *different* sort of truly natural excess that it must constantly colonize and recruit but does not of itself engender (by contrast with the cases of capitalized life and abstract capital itself).[14] Just as primary accumulation is constantly resumed, in such a manner that an old-fashioned, as it were kingly or feudal, violence is ceaselessly regenerated by the apparently "postmilitary" agon of the market itself, so likewise a personal god is periodically reinvoked as opposed to the usual immanent abstract fetish of generative capital. (The latter is perhaps loosely underwritten by a vague bourgeois "Buddhistic" sentiment that reads the cosmos in effect as a mystical marketplace in which the guiding hand is less hidden than virtual and yet less prior than emergent, with dynamic processes themselves as their own implied but null transcendental ground.)

13. Slavoj Žižek, *On Belief* (London: Routledge, 2001), 12–13, 15, 26; Žižek, *The Puppet and the Dwarf: The Perverse Core of Christianity* (Cambridge, MA: MIT Press, 2003), 13–33.
14. Harvey, *New Imperialism*.

The same applies to the political order: as Schmitt concludes, the doctrine of modern sovereignty is a secularization of (one should add, late medieval voluntarist) theological authorizing of absolute rule. For Schmitt, the grounding of secular sovereign power in the right to assume exceptional authority in the case of exceptional circumstances involves an appropriation (and later a problematic secularization) of the divine right to overrule his own commands, rooted in his *potentia absoluta*.[15] However, Agamben is right to argue against Schmitt that the appeal to exception cannot lie within the law as an emergency power allowed by the law; instead, since sovereign power authorizes the law, and yet the sovereign power is legally constituted, the exception that proves its rule lies aporetically both within and outside the law as the *anomie* that haunts all positive law as such.[16] In this way, a constitutive excess escapes the field of formal authorization and, as with the case of resumed primary accumulation, an authorizing by void form gives way to a direct authorizing by personal decree and personally commanded violence. If, therefore, the immanent secular sphere of political power is defined by a positivity regulated by formal rules, then an aporetic fracture of such rules implies that Schmitt was most right when he implied that the circumscription of the secular is never finally secure.

A supposedly "premodern" political theology may always be reinvoked in an emergency, and perhaps will be continuously reinvoked by a rule that proclaims a continuous state of emergency. This could possibly explain why Bush's new American order was linked with his deliberate reinvoking of "old-fashioned" American religion. Where legal authority once more assumes a manifestly armed guise, the danger that this guise will give it an anarchic appearance may render it necessary to look for legitimation in terms of an absolute transcendent personal authority. The God of monotheism may not authentically be armed, but he has often been rendered so when invoked to underwrite the authority of "single" sovereign powers on earth.[17]

For conservative evangelical Christianity in our day, it is consequently supposed that there would be anarchy without a constant police war on human sin waged by a sovereign power. The apparent anarchy of the policing power as such can be overlooked, because what, in human

---

15. Schmitt, *Political Theology*; John Milbank, *Theology and Social Theory*, 2nd ed. (Oxford: Blackwell, 2006), 9–25.

16. Agamben, *State of Exception*, 32–41.

17. See Regina Schwartz, *The Curse of Cain: The Violent Legacy of Monotheism* (Chicago: University of Chicago Press, 1997), passim.

terms, might appear to be "just one more power" (Augustine's unjust political authority as a "robber band") has in fact been authorized by the infinite power of God to impose at least some sort of order on potentially absolute disorder.

Yet while, in the fashion just delineated, a certain mode of religion can be seen as justifying and massaging the endemic excesses of neo-conservatism, it is inversely the case that the same mode of religion sees its own values as being promoted by this political and economic tendency. In the case of both the economic and the political, the specifically religious doubling of secular quasi religion (capitalism itself) ensures that the sphere of life is brought under divine law but also drained of all spiritual significance. What happens in the political and economic spheres concerns the best that can be made of interactions between fallen creatures pursuing essentially selfish motives, but the supposed real religious advantage of liberalism is that it renders the individual supreme, in the sense of the hidden inner life of the person and his or her private salvific destiny, regarded as untouched by social processes. One now gets Catholic as well as Protestant versions of this. Liberal, biopolitical systems are then seen in religious terms as being ultimately authorized by their promotion of that religion, namely, Christianity, which purportedly (and truly, in many dominant versions) makes the isolated individual into the site of the highest value.

At the same time, there is some place for the church here, considered in a Kantian fashion as the social organization that combats the very corruption of individual purity by socially generated, yet socially damaging negative emotions.[18] More specifically, the church is regarded as a safety valve for biopolitical excesses: as a supplementary economizing of the abstract surplus to the material political economy itself, much as Kant thought that the church engendered a "general moral will" that would exceed in purity the Rousseauian general political will. Hence the church becomes perversely that place where egotism is diverted from criminal recourse into subtle modes of spiritual pride, the place where both excessive emotional drives and excessive accumulated capital can be redirected toward the recruitment of new souls for heaven in the world to come.

While, in one sense, this is a sort of sacrificial burning off of a material surplus that allows it to ascend vaporously to heaven, in another

18. John Milbank, *Being Reconciled: Ontology and Pardon* (London: Routledge, 2003), 12–17.

sense this process reconnects the abstract surplus with material space and time in the form of living human beings themselves. American conservative evangelical Christianity in its most recent modes is precisely a new mutation of the slave trade. Pursuit of profits and the salvation of souls become so seamlessly fused in the mode of a new "church enterprise" (involving huge material and abstract capital resources) that here effectively the "born again" become themselves the produced, exchanged, and capitalized commodities. A new evangelical church's measure of success, both in spiritual and in financial terms, is precisely its "ownership" of so many souls (and thereby indirectly bodies) or potential to own so many more souls. Of course the notion that these souls are really owned by Jesus, and so held by men only through a sort of proxy, is the alibi ensuring that this enslavement does not appear to be such.

At this point the circle is closed: the religious safety valve that drains off an endemic excess itself legitimates a new mode of excess that provides a further outlet for overaccumulated capital. This is the production and exchange of human "spiritual slaves," who, through imbibing the "gospel of free enterprise," are ideally tailored to be good producers and consumers within those disciplined limits that paradoxically best ensure a continued drive to the excessive. It is in this fashion that one can see how the doubling of the religious involves something in addition to the offering of a safety valve in the face of late capitalist extremity.

It is *itself* an aspect of this extremity, insofar as it resolves a standing aporia concerning capitalism and slavery. Capitalism in the eighteenth century restored, after the demise of "feudalism" (a hopelessly inadequate term), the practice of slavery by meshing the capitalist market with newly found ancient, prefeudal slave economies in Africa. This appears to be in conflict with the liberal understanding of the self as the negatively free subject of ownership who therefore cannot himself be owned. However, in this instance, one must once more consider the paradoxes of the biopolitical. If one's starting point is the naturally free living individual, then only by exacted necessity will this individual not naturally instrumentalize and objectify other human subjects. And indeed, the leash of contract, whereby one must accord other people the dignity of self-possessed freedom, only restrains and does not abolish this natural (according to biopolitical construction) tendency of the subject to objectify other subjects. Thus within the liberal capitalist order, all subjects remain, formally speaking, free, and this formal freedom normally grants them the actual right, for example, to refuse employment or to resign from a job. Yet in de facto terms, such refusal or resignation can be in many instances not a real option at all, since it might leave the subject facing death, literally. The absolute real degree of control over workers exerted by capital and its subordination of them to the status of mere instruments of production, or to that of consumers able to realize the profit-value of commodities, means that workers can indeed be properly described as "wage slaves." Today, the increasing proletarianization of intellectual labor (lack of job security, routinization of tasks, exponential increase of working hours) means that one can speak equally of "salary slavery" among the middle classes.

Nevertheless, a contradiction in principle exists between the liberal definition of one's own selfhood as a negatively free ego and the equally liberal potential reduction of all other selves to objects that might instrumentally serve one's own egotistic needs. This is the hinterland of "life" that liberalism evokes, from Hobbes onward. While the emergence of legal contract demands a recognition of the other as the mirror of one's own freedom, its very artifice tends only to qualify and mitigate a "natural" situation that is not thereby really suspended. This is even more the case when the Hobbesian/Lockean model of explicit imposed contract gives way to the Scottish political economic model of a process of contracting that itself emerges "naturally" through the mutual limitation of one ego by another: a process that for the Scots gave rise to political government and law *just as much* as to economic contract and markets.[19]

In this way, the self of liberal capitalism is aporetically at once an absolute negative subjective freedom and something always in principle reducible to a mere objective set of bodily functions. It is indeed, after Agamben, always potentially the outcast *homo sacer*, since the liberal guarantee of "natural" rights depends on upholding an artificial contract, and this contract, because of its very artificiality, can always in principle be suspended, and indeed must remain always partially in suspense, since it exists only to channel and manage a precontractual "living" state of affairs. Racism can be seen as one way of managing this aporia: only white people possess full subjectivities; other races can be relatively objectified. But neo-evangelical Christianity "resolves" this aporia far more neatly. The ideal white, American or quasi-American self is at once absolutely free in its submission to salvation and yet also absolutely the "slave" of Christ and so of the whole evangelical

19. See Dugald Stewart, *Collected Works*, 11 vols. (Edinburgh: Constable, 1854), 2:248.

machinery that now operates just like a business corporation. This self has absolutely and freely sold itself into slavery: as still formally free it entirely belongs to the corporation it serves and is dedicated not just to maximizing the profits of the corporation but also to maximizing these profits in terms of the capture of, and investment in, other selves who will likewise come (precisely as "subjects") to belong irrevocably to the organization in the manner of pure commodities, save for the ever-lurking chance of apostasy.

In this way, then, neo-evangelical religion assists the extremity of advanced capitalism by fulfilling the commodification also of people, but without abandoning their formal freedom as subjects.

Such an assertion should not, however, be read as a sociological explanation by functionality, because the Weberian collusion of capitalism with certain modes of Christianity can always be read the other way around. It is precisely the Protestant (and also Jansenist) reduction of the this-worldly to a merely instrumental significance for the pursuit of material ends, or else to a ledger-book register of spiritual privilege, which has helped to create the space within which a pure capitalism can so successfully flourish. Thus the fact that the most capitalist country in the world, the United States, is the most imbued with this "Weberian" version of the Calvinist legacy is not at all accidental. So likewise today, the "commodification of people" that evangelism permits can also be read, in theological terms, as a more perfect fusion of the spiritual logic of mission with the keeping of a material register of divine favor and disciplinary spiritual striving. The new "doubly religious" mutation of capitalism is at the same time a new mutation of Protestant Christianity, which tends to take back within its own logic the quasi religion of capital that it had helped to spawn. Therefore if neo-evangelicalism is functional for capital, capital is equally functional for neo-evangelical religion.[20]

This religious phenomenon, however, notoriously endorses a highly puritanical sexual code and a pattern of family living that might appear to be outmoded in terms of the requirements of late capitalism. Indeed, in this phase we are witnessing the capitalization of the sexual sphere itself, as explored by the novelist Michel Houellebecq, whereby more and more "sexual capital" is acquired by fewer and fewer, and all the old constraints and taboos are abandoned.[21] Just for this reason,

20. I am grateful to discussions with Neil Turnbull of Nottingham Trent University and with Philip Goodchild of Nottingham University concerning these issues.

21. Michel Houellebecq, *Atomised*, trans. Frank Wynne (London: Heinemann, 2000). Published in North America as *The Elementary Particles* (New York: Knopf, 2000).

Houellebecq suspects that the current apparent revival of religion will prove to be short lived. Yet it is possible that sometimes exactly the same people are becoming increasingly subject both to puritanical and to libertarian influences all at once: the sexual marketplace and the drama of sin and salvation play off each other, while, more decisively, evangelical religion (especially in its charismatic mode) becomes more and more concerned with a supramoral redemption that starts to have as little regard in practice for sexual behavior as for economic and political depredations. (Donna Tartt's novel *The Little Friend*, set in the Bible Belt, shows in certain episodes how the "born again" may be far from immune to chemical and sexual libertarianism or decadence.)

All the above considerations tend to suggest that, while the churches under such a regimen appear to temper the egotistic, this very tempering in the end only augments it. The anarchy of market and state is not really ecclesially qualified in any genuine sense. Instead, while it may seem that the churches are granted a new role in educating us into a compensating virtue and civility by Bush, Blair, and Berlusconi, in truth they become thereby quasi-capitalist corporations ultimately serving the ends of immanent abstraction and local branches of the state police working toward the same end. This is just what the Grand Inquisitor offers to the churches in our times.

So biopolitics today reinforces itself with a sacral economy. But is there a secular, immanentist way out of the biopolitical? No. I shall now argue that there can be only an authentically religious route out of the biopolitical.

The Antique Biopolitical

Agamben significantly concedes that medieval modes of governance escaped the paradoxes of the law of exception, since the resort to unlegislated power was here seen as necessary, not in aporetic terms of the exigencies of the law as such but rather in those instances where the written law no longer served justice.[22] Appeal was made, in other words, to a natural law of equity rooted in an eternal, divine law. Presumably Agamben thinks that such an appeal is impossible today. Indeed, he seems to consider, in a Marxist fashion, that some dialectical gain emerges from biopolitics. The gap that opens up between law and life supposedly

---

22. See Agamben, *State of Exception*, 24–25, for his discussion of the Latin adage *necessitas legem non habet* in Gratian and Aquinas.

reveals for him the possibility of a pure human practice that would be a creativity for its own sake, a pure "means" pursuing no end, a practice neither natural nor legislated.[23] Yet in response to Agamben here, one should say that there can be no human practice outside language, and language always assumes rules and projects goals. Elsewhere, indeed, Agamben himself sees a parallel between the law of the exception and the transcendental norms of all discourse.[24] He recalls that Lévi-Strauss showed that there is a permanent excess of the signifier over the signified; hence reference must always appeal paradoxically to an excessive nonreference, just as law must ceaselessly invoke an extralegal life and contract an extraeconomic military egoism.

Agamben even goes further than this: the Heideggerean account of our ontological condition is metaphysical Schmittianism. For in the former case Being as such is conceived as anarchic and insubstantive, yet the ontic must constantly instantiate what it also tries to conceal. Although Agamben speaks of a "messianic" deliverance of the ontic from this captivity through a "purer" and redemptive realization of its own abandonment, this seems ontologically incoherent—if beings "are not" of themselves and cannot give rise to themselves, then one must ask in what possible sense they can really leave behind Being itself, or escape its tyrannical vacuity, as atheism must indeed understand it.[25] In

23. Ibid., 64; and Benjamin, "Critique of Violence."
24. Agamben, *State of Exception*, 36–39.
25. Agamben, *Homo Sacer*, 59ff., 182–88; *State of Exception*, 59–60: "Pure violence as the extreme political object, as the 'thing' of politics, is the counterpart to pure being, to pure existence as the ultimate metaphysical stakes; the strategy of the exception, which must ensure the relation between anomic violence and law, is the counterpart to the onto-theo-logical strategy aimed at capturing pure being in the meshes of the *logos*." One wonders here just why Agamben reads premodern Western reflection on being in this empty Scotist and Heideggerean way, and equally why he appears to read all premodern political reflection in this Schmittian fashion that begins with the naturalness of evil. (This was only inaugurated by Machiavelli.) The discussion of Derrida in *Il tempo qui resta* suggests, however, that Agamben entertains the notion that the messianic hope is for something that breaks with the ontological-ontic trap of endless reinvestment and postponement of Being, given its "original" voidness that never was. See (in the French translation) Giorgio Agamben, *Le temps qui reste*, trans. Judith Revel (Paris: Rivages, 2000), 162–64. Likewise, in *Homo Sacer* (60) Agamben speaks, deploying Kafka, of a messianic deliverance from the law of exception and from a reading of ontology in terms of a relation between Being and beings that constantly "bans" or evacuates the latter in the name of a *logos* or "law" of that pure Being that is in itself sovereign vacuity. This deliverance, however, seems only to arise through a yet more-extreme degree of embracing abandonment, such that no relation any more pertains between Being and beings. Yet how is it possible for beings to be, purely of themselves, anymore than it is possible for human cultural beings not in any sense to invoke a *nomos*? If we were to "shut the door" on being (Is there a Levinasian echo here?) and the law, then we would in reality be yet more absolutely under their sway. The solution is surely

this way, as Slavoj Žižek following Jacques Rancière suggests, Agamben ontologizes the concentration camp, since this *schema* would seem to imply that we are, all of us, by virtue of our human existence and not by virtue of biopolitics alone, *homo sacer*, reduced by nature to a condition where our rights as a human animal are always threatened with suspension by the very power that grants them to us, reducing us to the level of "bare life" that is not even accorded the dignity of condemnation (this being the case for the inmates of Auschwitz, as today for those of Guantanamo Bay and the secret torture prisons of Europe).

So since we are speaking and existing creatures, in what terms can pure practice be enacted for Agamben, other than those of apocalyptic refusal? Sometimes he invokes the response of Walter Benjamin to the Schmittian problematic: a good revolutionary violence will no longer exercise a pagan, mythical economy of blood whereby some perish on behalf of others but will rather, as "monotheistic" violence, once and for all abolish the whole aporetically conjoined logic and regime of the law and the exception, just as Yahweh caused the Levitical company of Korah, jealous of Moses's priesthood, to be swallowed whole into the ground, leaving not a trace behind.[26] But so almost literally apocalyptic is Benjamin's vision here that he intimates nothing as to how his recommended postapocalyptic playful reading of the law-now-become-a-dead-letter (this is how he, and Agamben in his wake, reads Kafka) will issue in a just social practice among existing, living, and speaking creatures.[27]

---

not to make still more extreme Heidegger and Schmitt's lack of mediation but rather to rethink the possibility of mediation (between Being and beings, Justice and its instances)—which means, of course, to think within the terms of Catholic theology.

26. Slavoj Žižek, "Against Human Rights," *New Left Review* 34 (July–August 2005): 115–31. In the end, though, Žižek, again following Rancière, disappointingly defends human rights, reading their formalism as pure negativity and therefore as translatable into hope—but for what, might one ask, save for something whose positivity cannot itself derive from the notion of rights? He is right to defend universalism and the need to appeal to the ideal but fails to consider that there may be modes of universalism other than those of human rights that appear to be inexorably tied to the contradictions of the biopolitical. See also Jacques Rancière, "Who Is the Subject of the Rights of Man?" *South Atlantic Quarterly* 103, nos. 2–3 (2004): 307–9.

27. Derrida is properly critical of Benjamin's apocalypticism at this point, arguing that while "justice" transcends law and cannot, unlike law, be deconstructed, it nonetheless must always seek expression in the legal, without which it would remain a dead letter. See Jacques Derrida, "Force of Law: The 'Mystical Foundation of Authority,'" in *Acts of Religion*, ed. Gil Anidjar (London: Routledge, 2002), 230–98. However, Derrida never states that law truly "expresses" justice, taken as a transcendent value. On the contrary, he regards justice as "impossible" or as a transcendental regulatory horizon beyond the "being" of law. Of course "impossible" does not exactly mean "unreal," because the invocation of justice is precisely what allows us to de-

I eventually want to suggest that, by contrast, only St. Paul points us authentically beyond the order of the biopolitical. Nevertheless, classical antique notions of natural law, to which Paul appealed, do so to some degree. For if one believes there is a real, substantive, eternal good that can be echoed in time, then the excess of authority over law becomes the excess of equity over law, the fulfillment of law in exactly appropriate judgment whose very temporal unrepeatability indicates the extratemporally abiding.

However, antique politics knew its own form of the biopolitical, as the term *zoon politikon* in Aristotle shows us. Here indeed life as such (*zoē*) was not valued, but rather higher intellectual life (*bios theoretikos*)— a life informed *intrinsically* by judgment and justice, since it is truly an extramaterial *psychic life* (by contrast to the case of the modern liberal conception, for which human life, as basically animal life, accidentally generates nomic order that in turn governs life extrinsically,

---

construct legal systems as aiming for a justice that they also (inevitably) betray and thereby to modify them or to substitute a revolutionary new legality. However, for Derrida as for Schmitt (and here Derrida does not question a "modern" horizon), the instituting moment of law, since it must be aporetically in excess of legality, embodies a necessary violence and arbitrariness that continues to contaminate the practice of law thenceforward. In consequence, while justice can only be realized as law, it is also always betrayed by it. It appears to follow that the occurrence of "impossible" justice (as of impossible gift) that, for Derrida after Levinas, would be an infinite concern for every other beyond the imperatives of distribution and restitution can occur only "between" law and justice as an ambivalent double negation. Justice could therefore be real as what disturbs and provokes to change, but it could never be "present" as an instance of justice that, as a perfect finite instance of equity, would participate in justice as an eternal transcendent value. Derrida's vision therefore remains one of negative dialectics and not of authentic mediation. Essentially he presents a "gnostic" vision of necessary ontological and cosmic violence that can be only temporarily refused. One should accept neither this "gnosticism" nor Benjamin's and Agamben's apocalyptic refusal of a gnostic predicament but rather embrace the Pauline notion (see below) of the possibility of an unbetrayed though limited incarnation of justice in a *different* economy of exchange that exceeds the contractual and fixed limits of legality. In this respect Theodore Jennings, in his interesting book about Paul and Derrida, is wrong to think I fail to realize that for Derrida justice and law are necessarily associated with each other despite their heterogeneity: see Theodore W. Jennings Jr., *Reading Derrida/Thinking Paul* (Stanford, CA: Stanford University Press, 2006), 204n8. Rather, it is the *nature* of this association that I contest: for Derrida it *must* contain a dialectical and treacherous dimension whereby law loses justice by trying to institute it; for me this is not necessarily the case. Instead, the inflection of law by equity may analogically embody, without betrayal, the infinite truth of justice. He is also wrong to think that I "slip" from the aneconomic into the economic. On the contrary, I explicitly question the notion that the infinite and the excessive lack "measure" even if this be one that exceeds any preconstituted *mathesis*. This is why I consistently argue that exchange as asymmetrical and nonidentically repeated can exceed contract and sustain the gratuity of gift. By contrast, Derrida was forced in his own "gnostic" terms to say that, while gift must always be linked to exchange (as justice to law), it is nonetheless always contaminated by exchange that it must therefore resist to the same degree that it must also embrace it.

as though it were alien to its own notion). Nevertheless, antique politics involved the governing of "mere life" (*zoē*)—of animals, slaves, women, and children—by male aristocratic hyperrational, higher-psychic, and political life (the cultural life for which the Greeks reserved the term *bios*).[28] And even in the case of those fully intelligent Greeks fitted to be citizens, governance also involved the self-governance of mere life within themselves, a rule over their unruly bodies and passions, over the internal "slave element."

Thereby this antique biopolitics *also* gave rise to its own inherent tensions. There was, nevertheless, as just stressed, no liberal concept of self-governing life. Modern thought, by contrast, is stuck between the idea of an order that emerges spontaneously, on the one hand—that is, the rule of life—and the idea of a centrally imposed order, on the other—that is, rule by a centralized legal authority enjoying a monopoly (in principle) on the exercise of violence. Left-wing critiques do not themselves tend to escape this duality: either they speak of a more absolute state management, perhaps for a transitional interim, or else they suggest a utopian exceeding of both state and market. But in the latter case there is often an ironic appeal to something like the former, Hayekian model of the market itself: all freely expressed desires and urges are to be "naturally" and spontaneously coordinated. This is the case with Michael Hardt and Antonio Negri's "multitude," as Malcolm Bull has shown: here we have an implausibly unmediated contrast between personal expressions, on the one hand, and an "inhuman" but beneficent coordination, on the other.[29]

Premodern thought, to the contrary, did not conceive of agency solely in terms of individual freedom or in terms of explicit representative sovereign action—leaving a consequent problem of the apparent spontaneous patterning of the unplanned. This was because it did not think of an act as primarily an expression of freedom or as something "owned" by the individual or the sovereign's will or motivation. Instead, it paid more attention to the fact that every act is always pre-positioned within a relational public realm and in turn cannot avoid in some way modifying that realm beyond anything that could in principle be consented to by the other, since the full content of any act is unpredictable. In consequence, the outgoing of an action was seen, by Aristotle for example, as having

28. Agamben, *Homo Sacer*, 1–12.
29. Malcolm Bull, "Limits of Multitude," *New Left Review* 35 (September–October 2005): 19–40.

the character of a gift (assuming that normative action is appropriate action), a specific contribution to the social present and the social future that extended from the narrow society of immediate friends to the entire network of friends that composes a polity.[30] As a gift, it was also part of an entire sequence of gift-exchanges, of outgoings and returns between friends and finally between parts of the whole political community. This rendered action-as-gift in some sense "interested," but only insofar as it was not merely "blind" like the modern liberal paradigm of interested action but rather had some sort of approximate onlook toward the entire social outcome. Action as gift, unlike action as pure freedom, tends in this way to undercut the opposition between sheerly planned and sheerly unplanned collective social products. For action as gift envisages and anticipates, albeit in an imprecise way, something of the nature of likely responses to one's own action and the kind of total process this action will serve to build up. This is because action as gift has to consider who is a suitable and potentially grateful recipient

30. For Aristotle, the most defining action of the human animal is political, and the *polis* is composed of the bonds of friendship that establish a concord at once more fundamental and more ideal than that of justice. Friendship itself nonetheless ideally consists in a balanced interchange of the good between equals (and here the measure of appropriate return should be the extent of the generosity of the donor), less ideally in an exchange of the useful (where the measure of appropriate return should be the benefit to the recipient) and in unequal relationships (where the exchange of benefits should also be unequal), constituting that reciprocity (*antipeponthos*) on which every community is based and that extends beyond the constant interchange of friendship to a more general exchange of benefits. Thus the defining human action for Aristotle is donation. Because it is an offering of friendship and because a friendship already involves community, action-as-gift for Aristotle lies between modern individual *action*, on the one hand, and modern political/economic *structure*, on the other: it occupies something like the mediating position of Anthony Giddens's "structuration." Hence within his section on friendship, largely taken up with discussing appropriate exchanges of benefits, Aristotle includes a discussion of the different types of political constitution: political association itself for him corresponds to the highest kind of friendship because it concerns the generally human and therefore the good as such; more-debased forms of polity tend to demean the political with the aims of lesser, more-utilitarian forms of association that correspond to the lesser modes of friendship and the baser modes of exchange. The higher friendship is reciprocal, but nevertheless it is more important here to give than to receive, and the quality of generosity in the gift counts higher than the benefit conferred. Indeed, the highest virtue for Aristotle lies not in the exchange of friendship but in the single exercise of magnanimity. This corresponds to the way in which for him monarchic polity stands above even aristocracy. See Aristotle, *Nichomachean Ethics* 1133a3–5; 1157a3–9; 1157a35–36; 1159a10–32; 1162a30–1163a20. Much later, within the early Christian era, Seneca wrote: "How else do we live in security if it is not that we help each other by an exchange of good offices?" (*De beneficiis* 4.18.1–2). See also Jean-Luc Nancy, "Decision, Desert, Offering," in *The Experience of Freedom*, trans. Bridget McDonald (Stanford, CA: Stanford University Press, 1993), 142–47; Marcel Mauss, *The Gift: The Form and Reason for Exchange in Archaic Societies*, trans. W. D. Halls (New York: W. W. Norton, 1990).

who will deploy a gift well; it has also to consider what sort of gifts should be given to what sort of people, and in this way it already bears the freight of a consideration of ideal social roles and their intercoordination. Hence, for Aristotle the hierarchically supreme social role and *locus* of virtue was precisely that of the "magnanimous" man, the great-hearted and yet judicious giver and forebear.[31]

This is paralleled by premodern conceptions of thought and language. Here the relationship between the excessive signifier and the defined signified is not anarchic, since "gift" is implicitly taken as the third term between sign and thing within an order of meaning deemed to be fatally or providentially governed.[32] A gift, in order to be a gift, must be a thing and no mere sign; yet it must also exceed this thingness in terms of meaning if it is to convey to the recipient the message of generosity, and therefore it must be a thing whose adoption as a sign exceeds in turn its mere thingness. Here we have Lévi-Strauss's excess of the signifier, but this does not require, as he supposed, any mythic and ideological obfuscation of its apparent anarchy if the excess of sign over thing is seamlessly taken to be a "Maussian" reading of all meaning as promise of further donation in an unending spiral that encompasses nature as well as culture.[33] In this case, the excess of the signifier is taken to be not a problematic abstract and traumatic Void

31. Aristotle, *Nichomachean Ethics* 1123a31–1125a20. The supremely virtuous quality of "magnanimity" is described by Aristotle in relation to the exercise of the virtue of liberality.

32. Lévi-Strauss tried to reduce Mauss's gift to sign, but really Mauss, by describing the archaic gift, described the point of cultural articulation between sign and thing. On the relation between gift and sign, see Jean-Joseph Goux, "Seneca against Derrida: Gift and Alterity," in *The Enigma of Gift and Sacrifice*, ed. Edith Wyschogrod, Jean-Joseph Goux, and Eric Boynton (New York: Fordham University Press, 2002), 148–61.

33. See Jacques T. Godbout and Alain Caillé, *The World of the Gift*, trans. Donald Winkler (Montréal: McGill-Queen's University Press, 2000). In Marcel Hénaff's magisterial and very important book, *Le Prix de la vérité: Le don, l'argent, la philosophie* (Paris: Éditions du Seuil, 2002), he argues that the function of ritual gift-giving is one of mutual recognition of personal honor and dignity through the presentation of gifts as symbols. This is certainly the case, but it is questionable to assert that this function is not also an "economic" one. Indeed he himself seems to discuss many instances (for example, the exchange of women, exchanges with the animal world, medieval exchanges within and between fraternities, early modern Spanish construal of profit and usury as gift) where ritual presentation has to do *intrinsically* and not just incidentally with economic distribution. He appears at times wrongly to assume both that "an economy" is basically concerned with subsistence and that the gift-exchange of sacred and symbolic items is not also in some instances of (materially or socially) useful items. And he also on the whole ignores that segmentary societies granted a certain agency to the gift-object itself. All these interpretative biases are bound up with a reduction of gift to sign. Yet it is prima facie clear that a gift cannot be only a sign; rather, the unique thing about a gift is that it must be both meaningful sign *and* usable thing and that both functions perfectly keep pace with each other.

but rather a reserved treasury of ever more-possible generosity, positively traumatic on account of its inconceivable plenitude.[34]

No tensions, therefore, arose in antique thought between order understood as central imposition and order understood as spontaneous impersonal coordination. In consequence, there was considered to be no permanent lurking excess of the central will-to-power, on the one hand, or of the merely "living" individual will, on the other. In the same fashion, there was deemed to be no anomic lurking excess of meaning over its concrete investment—and this can be ideological occlusion only if one takes (without reason) the "given" nihilistic overcoding of the signifier-signified relationship to be normative instead of the overcoding in terms of "gift" that reads the ineliminable excessive absence as ontologically reserved plenitude.

But at the same time, one *can* detect somewhat analogous tensions to those of modernity in antique thought, between the act of giving and the cycle of gift-exchange. In Aristotle, as Bruno Blumenfeld stresses, rule by law implies an oscillation between ruling and being ruled.[35] Law is what I, as citizen, may apply, and at the same time it is that which I must in turn be ruled by. It is therefore a mode of political gift-exchange, given that law confers the benefits of order and justice. Moreover, to give law is also to give a capacity to give, since to apply the law to the other is also to assist him or her to apply the law if occasion arises—it is to give that person potentially a share in ruling, to give the gift of rule.[36]

However, such mutuality lies within bounds and may not extend very far into equity where situations arise that are so unique that they do not fall within the oscillating sequence of precedent and anticipation. (In the latter case, for one citizen to apply the law in this given instance may be to recall his or her own undergoing of the law on previous occasions, or to reliably assume that it might be similarly applied to him or her on some future one.) It also tends to exclude the noncitizens or any measures of sheerly disinterested welfare. Where a purer disinterest is in later Roman times (which often foreshadow modern liberalism) recommended as the supreme duty by Seneca in his *De beneficiis*, it nevertheless seems to escape the political and the social, since a pure gift given regardless of the likely response of the recipient is seen by Seneca to be socially irre-

34. This can be related to the later Lacan's discussions of trauma and feminine sexuality. See Jacques Lacan, *Le Séminaire 20: Encore* (Paris: Éditions du Seuil, 1975).

35. Bruno Blumenfeld, *The Political Paul: Justice, Democracy, and Kingship in a Hellensitic Framework* (London: Continuum, 2001), 65–69.

36. See Milbank, "Gift of Ruling."

sponsible (if personally worthy), while every dutifully required proferred sign of gratitude is regarded by the Stoic sage as in some measure reducing gift to contract.[37] There is therefore a certain "aporia of gratitude" in Seneca that is remarkably "Derridean": responsible giving should be to the grateful, but giving with an eye to the gratitude of the recipient contaminates the purity of the gift. A true gift is therefore irresponsible and even, perhaps, too much like "throwing something away" to qualify as a gift after all, while a responsible gift undoes gratuity by giving only under a specified condition. Insofar as Seneca resolves this he seems to do so by anticipating modernity and privatizing the gift, while denying to public contract a fully ethical status.

By contrast, a *political* apparently pure and one-way gift as a practice of disinterested welfare, "provision for widows and orphans," descends to us, as longstanding scholarship shows, not from the egalitarian *polis* but from the oriental despotisms that Israel imitated but qualified.[38]

Yet the Greeks were fascinated by such despotisms, sometimes because they seemed to permit a more radical generosity as welfare, but more especially because of their greater scope for the practice of equity.[39] For Aristotle, the latter goes beyond the law and therefore requires an absolute authority not bound by the law's instituted norms. This is why he had a certain admiration for Alexander the Great. Yet at the same time, his habitually guiding fear of any sort of imbalance, and in this case the loss of the role of middle-class mutual limitation through the reciprocal application of legality, leads him to suggest that the exceptionally good and powerful man who might effectively rule alone should generally be ostracized from the city.[40]

In this way, then, the equivalent to the modern biopolitical tension between pure life and contract/law lies, in antique politics, between a one-way gift that may intervene equitably on behalf of the vagaries of

---

37. Seneca, *De beneficiis* 2.31.2–5; 5.3.2–3. In the latter place, Seneca affirms that he who shows gratitude is equal to the giver, even if he cannot make adequate return. This is a more democratic account than Aristotle's celebration of the magnanimous man who counts it to his honor never to owe a debt of gratitude for nonreturned gifts.

38. See Hendrik Bolkestein's classic treatise *Wohltätigkeit und Armenpflege im vorchristlichen Altertum* (Utrecht: A. Oosthoek, 1939). This line of specifically Dutch research (initially conducted quite independently of the Maussian tradition) has been followed up by Willem Cornelis van Unnick. See, for example, his article "Eine Merkwürdige Liturgische Aussage bei Josephus (*Jos. Ant.* 8, 111–113)," in *Josephus-Studien*, ed. O. Betz et al. (Göttingen: Vandenhoeck & Ruprecht, 1974), 362–69.

39. Blumenfeld, *Political Paul*, 120–276, esp. 251.

40. Aristotle, *Politics* 3.1284a10–1287a32; Blumenfeld, *Political Paul*, 64–84.

life and a gift-exchange that concerns a more regular and egalitarian game of balance between those whom life has relatively well-blessed. This tension was implicitly recognized by the "Hellenistic Pythagoreans" writing around the time of the New Testament, since they characteristically endeavored to blend the exchange of the *polis* with the unilateral equity of the *basilea* in accordance with a real pertaining situation in which many semifree cities had fallen under the overall suzerainty of distant monarchs. If anything, it was the rule of the latter that these Hellenistic thinkers tended to favor.[41]

But, one can contend, St. Paul thinks outside the horizon of *both* antique *and* modern biopolitics.

The Politics of Resurrection

Like the ancient Greeks, Paul espoused natural justice, and like the Hellenistic thinkers, he linked it with the invocation of a supreme divine King who exceeded the law as himself embodying a "living law"— *nomos empsychos*, as the Pythagoreans had it.[42] The key difference is that Paul considered natural justice not just in relation to life but also in relation to resurrection.

Agamben is right: the ontological dimension of politics is inescapable. But if one takes life to be only biological life restricted to immanence, then life is subordinate to death. The backdrop-life assumed by secular liberalism is a life defining itself negatively over against death and scarcity—it is the pursuit of my life rather than yours, the prolongation of the life of some at the expense of the life of others, since that is what the unfair extraction of profits from workers and consumers and greater political privilege ultimately amounts to.

It is precisely this life that lives to preserve itself and grossly to augment itself that must supplement itself with law and contract: self-protective and self-augmenting devices, mutually consented to. They are therefore essentially reactions in the face of the overwhelming fact of death—they seek for a futile while to economize death or to delay its arrival.

But St. Paul begins with a vision of a resurrected man. This discloses for him another and more original life—a prefallen life without death that has now been restored in its original possibility not by economizing

41. Blumenfeld, *Political Paul*, 189–276.
42. Ibid., 187, 235–36.

or resisting death but by enduring it to the end. In consequence, justice now lies before the law, not *only* in the sense of exceptional equity but also as a hidden excess of ever-renewable autogenerating pneumatic life that gratuitously renews and redistributes the good (1 Cor. 15:42–50). In the face of this indefectible abundance, law is not needed, because there is no death and no malicious will that deals in death.[43] Nor is there any longer a life bounded by death ("the flesh," *sarx*), since we have, in Christ, already proleptically undergone such a death. Being already dead (one should take this literally) we can no longer sin, because this is only a possibility for that life that is always weakened by death and the defensive passions that rage against mortality (Rom. 6:7: "For he who has died is freed from sin"). Within the new resurrected life without such passions, malice can no longer be deemed inevitable or even comprehensible, since there is nothing that it could possibly snatch or gain from plenitude save the malicious and pointless pleasure of inventing the very notion of a gain at the expense of others through the institution of death and scarcity. And this institution, of course, renders possible a reverse visiting of malice by others upon the originally malicious one. (For all the above, see Rom. 7:4–6: "You have died to the law through the body of Christ [the *ekklēsia*], so that you may belong to another, to him who has been raised from the dead in order that we may bear fruit for God. While we were living in the flesh, our sinful passions, aroused by the law, were at work in our members to bear fruit for death. But now we are discharged from the law, dead to that which held us captive, so that we serve not under the old written code but in the new life of the Spirit.")[44]

The more-original goodness for Paul, therefore, does not act reactively or defensively in the face of death, suffering, and evil, even where those negativities affect another person. Rather, it simply distributes its own instance in a constantly creative fashion, always engendering a more intense life rather than shoring up existing life against death. (This point is well made in slightly different terms by Alain Badiou in his book on St. Paul.)[45] Nevertheless, in a world into which sin and

43. Blumenfeld deals with this briefly in *Political Paul*, 342.

44. See also Rom. 3:19–26; 4:13–24; 5:12–21; 6:5–8; 8:1–11.

45. Alain Badiou, *Saint Paul: La fondation de l'universalisme* (Paris: Presses Universitaires de France, 1999), 70 (attacking Hegelian dialectical readings of Paul): "La grace . . . est affirmation sans negation préliminaire, elle est ce qui nous vient en césure de la loi. Elles est pure et simple *rencontre*"; and 69–78. It is with this affirmation that Badiou, unlike Derrida and even Deleuze, truly realizes the *soixante-huitarde* ambition to break with negative dialectics.

death have irretrievably but contingently entered (and have distorted, through a metahistorical event, the ontology of life), requiring in their mutual complicity some sort of biopolitical economy intended to restrict their instance (law attempting to control a death-bound and semimalicious life that remains in consequence always alien to the perpetuity of law itself), the more-original goodness is accessible only through suffering. That is to say, it is accessible only through enduring to the limit (Rom. 8:17–23) the full negative consequences of sin, death, and the law, which reinforces sin and death by falsely assuming their irreducible ultimacy and so offers in the face of their violence a counterviolence (which alone defines the violence of sin *as* transgressive violence) rather than a removal of their ontological grip. (Rom. 4:15: "For the law brings wrath, but where there is no law there is no transgression"; 5:13: "Sin indeed was in the world before the law was given, but sin is not counted where there is no law.") Hence Christ on the cross suffered death, the ravages of human malice, and the attempt by *nomos* (Roman and Jewish) to control and economize this malice for the sake of the seemingly best achievable welfare of the political community.

According to Paul, to be a citizen of the *ekklēsia* is constantly to repeat this founding trauma. Normally, in any human society, founding traumas must be at least partially covered over because of a collective memory of inaugural guilt or inaugural shame. Both original crimes and original defeats have to be massaged by memory. Moreover, a strong contrast is usually made between a founding violence and sorrow and a later peaceful, pastoral civility that the initial sacrifice has made possible. Yet in the case of the *ekklēsia*, all this is reversed. Now to be a citizen is, ideally speaking, constantly to repeat the founding trauma in all its horror. Even though Christ's death was the final sacrifice and therefore the least repeatable, precisely for this reason it must be constantly dwelt within and constantly re-actualized. For it was not a suffering of death in order that others need not die, nor that their death pangs should be lessened. Rather, it was a revelation that within a death- and evil-dominated world, drastic and pointless sacrificial suffering is apparently

---

For in Derrida (here followed by Theodore Jennings), grace as gift arrives only in its negative "interruption" of that economic exchange to which, nonetheless, it must also submit. For Badiou, by contrast, "grace" initiates a positive "truth-process" that escapes the oppressive logics of "situations." Since this truth-process nonetheless involves a "fidelity to the event" that links event with event through time, it also involves a positive "mediation" that is not the Hegelian synthesis achieved through mutual negation. (The latter is retained by Derrida, but without the synthesis.)

the last word. Since the fallen human city and the fallen cosmos are all-encompassing, they must be met in the end with a lonely gesture of passive refusal (Rom. 6:10–14). Thus Christ did not die on the cross merely instead of us; rather, having uniquely suffered the death of the innocent, he calls on all human beings to partake of this death, and in a measure to repeat it.

However, *all* can now be suffered precisely because, beyond the cycle of life and death, there has been disclosed by the passage through the cross another, more-living, actively receptive, and participatory life that knows no death (Gal. 2:19–20: "I through the law died to the law . . . the life I now live in the flesh . . ."). This is the more original life that does not spring from death or alternate with death but is autogenerated. For life itself, as Leibniz and Bergson later saw, is not involved in an oscillation with death, in the way that "lives" are involved in an oscillation with "deaths." Life as such knows no death, is more original than death, and survives every death; indeed, as Leibniz argued, life as process knows only metamorphoses, not extinctions, such that of a dead creature we can only really say that it has ceased to appear as living, not that its life, its share in life, has ceased "to be."[46]

It is this transcendental life that Paul could conceive of as eternal and as rendering possible resurrection. Since this life informs all the organic creation, it is more basic than that modern self-governing life that guards itself egoistically against death, or any antique debased "mere" life that assumes the slavery of human passions to greedy and defensive impulses that presume scarcity.[47] While we are to suffer limitlessly on behalf of others and our own integrity, this suffering permits us negatively to resume contact with a wholly positive order of mutual ecstatic giving. Within this plenitudinous order there is nothing left to be resisted in the face of death or scarcity, and therefore all unruly passions can potentially be entirely purged away, such that only the ecstatic donating passion of *agapē* ("the surpassing road," as Blumenfeld so well translates the *hyperbolē hodos* of 1 Cor. 12:31)[48] remains, along with the practice it informs of unrestricted, superabundant generosity (2 Cor. 9:8: "God is able to provide you with every blessing in abundance, so that you may always have enough of everything . . . for

46. See Alain Badiou, *Logiques des mondes: L'être et l'événement 2* (Paris: Éditions du Seuil, 2006), 343–48.

47. On the question of assumptions of plenitude versus assumptions of scarcity, see Schwartz, *Curse of Cain*, 33–38, 80–83, 116–19, 173.

48. Blumenfeld, *Political Paul*, 204.

every good work"; v. 11: "You will be enriched in every way for great generosity, which through us will produce thanksgiving to God"; and see in general vv. 6–15). This order then composes a higher organism, the resurrected body of Christ collectively participated in. This *ekklēsia* is undying because it is not composed of sacrifices in the face of death for the sake of the endurance of a finite edifice that must one day collapse. Rather, in Benjamin's and Agamben's terms, it is composed only of "pure means," of ecstatic living offerings of divinized bodies according to a "logical worship" (*logikē latreia*, Rom. 12:1),[49] whose superfluous potential can always be resumed, in any circumstances. Yet the realization of an infinite ecstatic community is itself here seen as the penultimate true *telos* and as possible only within an ontological reality lured by an infinite transcendent harmony: God, who is the ultimate goal-beyond-goal of all human life, surpassing all contrasts between ends and means.

Of course, Paul's solution here is incredibly drastic and to most people today must appear to pay an impossible price. He insists that we can found a just community only on the basis of a wholly counterfactual invocation of an undying reality. In this way—despite the fact that such developments were strongly anticipated by the Hellenistic Pythagoreans, particularly the Pseudo-Archytas—he fuses together in the most radical manner achieved hitherto salvific, cosmic, and political categories and equates political freedom with psychic and corporeal salvation.[50] This means both that the classical antique notion that the highest life is to be discovered only within the civic order is not abandoned by Paul[51] and, equally and inversely, that a practice of detachment from the flesh bound to death, and an entering into a divinizing pneumatic sphere, is newly made the very condition for citizenship.

The linking element between these two themes is the body. It is the body that both connects the spirit and soul to the public political sphere and remains itself conjoined to the spiritual since it is a living reality only on account of its infusion by psychic power.

---

49. Blumenfeld (ibid., 388–89) comments that this near oxymoron was characteristic of the "Baroque" character of Hellenistic culture.

50. Ibid., 124–39, 248. The parallel between Paul and Pseudo-Archytas plus Diotogenes is also discussed by Agamben (*State of Exception*, 70–71). Agamben notes that this parallel extends at times to linguistic usage, citing *chōris nomou dikaiosynē* at Rom. 3:21 compared with *aneu nomou dikaiosynē* in Diotogenes.

51. Blumenfeld, *Political Paul*, 355.

One could argue that it is just for this reason that Paul now stresses the body/city analogy, where Plato and Aristotle had much more emphasized the soul/city analogy.[52] For the latter two thinkers, it was a matter of analogical (mathematically proportionate) comparison between two separate realms, but for Paul it is a matter of an analogy made possible only through the relational mediation that bodily interaction brings about and that ensures the civic is itself constituted by the psychic and vice versa. (The same contrast then extends to the mode of invocation of a further analogy of soul and city to the cosmos both in the ancient Greek and in the Pauline case; in the latter instance, Christ's work of shattering all boundaries between the Creator and the creation and between life and death has ensured that the cosmic is now effectively one with the psychic and the political.)

So even though the existing Roman-Greek political order is both recognized and secularized by Paul, the new, more fundamental political order of "the church" that he insinuates within this regime, like a benign parasite, is theocratic in a quite unprecedented sense. For now it is only the adherent of a mystery cult who can be a full-fledged citizen, only the person who participates in the more fundamental pneumatic life and who starts to transfigure his body in the direction of wholly purified passion who is capable of true civic virtue.

One could say that, for ancient Greek thought, it was already the case that there can be justice within a political *bios* only because human beings have nonmaterial and even, for certain thinkers, immortal souls: something that responds to imperatives other than those of purely organic survival, growth, and material flourishing. And against secular liberalism, one should continue to affirm that only a belief in the soul provides any barrier against the various modes of political fascism. But to this Paul adds the precondition for a more democratic version of the ancient politics of the city, namely, corporeal resurrection. For if the body also is immortal, then the body is also potentially the site of a perfect harmony and goodness. This means that the once "baser" passions and the once subordinate categories of humanity can now fully participate in political processes: *all* of one's life as an individual (erotic, domestic, and economic as well as politically deliberative) can now become part of political life, while all stages, genders, and ranks of human life are fully brought within the scope of the highest friendship and love (*agapē*), which is political in the most precise sense (1 Cor. 13).

52. Ibid., 383.

There are several decisive practical consequences of the notion of a theocratic order founded on resurrection life—that is to say, an original life before and without death, regained through an absolute endurance of death.

Oikos *Merged with* Polis

First of all, the tendency of Hellenistic political thought to merge categories of *oikos* and *polis* (because of its strong bent toward personal, patriarchal rule) is taken still further. Because there is no more "mere" human life and true human life is now defined more as the ecstatic exercise of love (*agapē*) than as intellectual self-control or personal excellence (Paul rarely uses the word *aretē*, as Blumenfeld points out), women, children, and slaves can now be, through baptism, fully citizens of this new sort of polity (Gal. 3:27–29).[53] Indeed, in some sense Paul intimates that all living things, and even all things contained within the cosmos, will one day be fully included within this new and final political order (Rom. 8:18–23; Phil. 2:10).

The Overcoming of Law and Death by Trust and Life

In the second place, there is for Paul no longer any law/life duality precisely because there is no longer any life/death duality to be econo-mized. Law, Paul suggests, colludes with fallen death-bound reality, including its malicious drives, because it can only resist it in an endless bad infinite and must thereby assume the force of its imperatives. (And one should argue here, following Jacob Taubes and Dieter Georgi, that Paul, in a characteristically Hellenistic Jewish fashion, is thinking of *nomos* as such and hence of Roman and Greek as well as of Jewish law.)[54] Moreover, since the law can only hold back and not overcome, it is ceaselessly improvised and approximate and must be endlessly revised. Law is therefore inherently diverse: law always means many

53. Ibid., 112–20, 151.
54. Jacob Taubes, *The Political Theology of Paul*, trans. Dana Hollander (Stanford, CA: Stanford University Press, 2004), 23ff. Theodore Jennings also rightly insists that Paul is offering a critique of law as such—Roman, Greek, Jewish, whatever—and not just of Jewish law, still less of Jewish ritual law only, as it has too often been recently the fashion to claim. (Such a stress at once wrongly downplays the supercession of the Jewish law tout court by the gospel *and* belittles the logic of the Jewish ritual law that, of course, Paul considers would continue to be observed by some Christians.) See also Dieter Georgi, *Theocracy in Paul's Praxis and Theology*, trans. David E. Green (Minneapolis: Fortress, 1991), 33–40.

competing law codes, as Paul esoterically acknowledges when he ascribes law not to the direct command of the *one* God but to the mediating agency of the *many* angels and demons: "the law . . . was ordained by angels through an intermediary. Now an intermediary implies more than one; but God is one" (Gal. 3:19–20). Hence the ultimacy of the law (as reactive) is for Paul incompatible with monotheism because of its incurable relativity that follows from the fact that it can only limit but never cure (2 Cor. 3:6; Gal. 3:5).

By contrast, Paul wishes politics to be an overcoming practice of psychic medicine rather than a disciplinary police procedure. In speaking of such a practice, he exceeds in advance the apocalyptic perspectives of Walter Benjamin. For the gesture of refusal is in Paul intertwined with a new positive mode of association sustainable through time. This new sort of polity will be governed not by *nomos* but by *pistis*, which means variously something like "trust" or "persuasion" or "fidelity."[55]

Hence according to Romans 3:25–26 (to retranslate), "God set forth . . . a propitiation through trust in his blood [*not* "an expiation by his blood, to be received by faith" as the RSV has it, thereby concealing that the context here is eucharistic] . . . in his holding back of hostility [*anochē*] in order to indicate [*endeixin*—a legal term of demonstration of evidence] his justice in the current critical time [*kairos*] in [*eis*—not "for"] the one [i.e., any ecclesial person] who is himself just and is made to be just out of [*ek*—not "of"] the trust [*pisteōs*] of Jesus."

The latter phrase suggests that justification occurs through a participation in Jesus's *own* exercise of trust, not through "faith in Jesus," as the RSV has it, and indeed Galatians clearly implies that *pistis* is an eternal hypostasis that has now been "revealed" and that has "arrived" with Jesus (Gal. 3:23–25). Thus it is legitimate to conclude that Jesus is, in one respect, the arrival in time of the "personhood" of faith.[56]

55. See Blumenfeld, *Political Paul*, 307, 335. Blumenfeld does not consider the point that in the rhetorical context *pistis* means "persuasion." However, it may come to the same thing: to trust someone is essentially "to be persuaded by" them, while to be persuaded by a speaker's rhetoric involves an element of trust in the person and in what he or she has to say. See James L. Kinneavy, *Greek Rhetorical Origins of Christian Faith: An Inquiry* (New York: Oxford University Press, 1987).

56. My revised translation of the Romans passage above is less drastic than Blumenfeld's, which does perhaps at this point border on the tendentious (see Blumenfeld, *Political Paul*, 335). Nevertheless, his basic reading can still stand in the face of my rendering. See also Georgi, *Theocracy*, 37, 43, for a further argument that *pisteōs Iēsou Christou* in Galatians (esp. 2:16 and 3:23–25) means the "faith of Jesus" and that *pistis* is even hypostasized to become identi-

It should, however, be said here that Paul also speaks of the rule of trust and of natural justice as constituting a more fundamental mode of eternal law (see Rom. 2:13; 3:31: "Do we then overthrow the law by this *pistis*? By no means! On the contrary, we uphold the law"; 7:22; "I delight in the law of God, in my inmost self"; 8:2; Gal. 6:2). And often within Judaism itself, as Giorgio Agamben points out, the most primal uncreated law is taken to be equitable justice (the *Torah de Atzilut* for the Kabbalah) and as prior to notions of injunction or prohibition.[57] As Jacob Taubes has argued, from a Jewish perspective, Paul's critique of the law is not necessarily "un-Jewish" nor to be seen as the main bone of contention between Judaism and Christianity.[58]

All the same, the Jewish sense of "pure law" that is an authority before the law belonging to a lone absolute and impenetrable unity can sometimes, as with the messianism surrounding Sabbatai Sevi— whose apostasy to Islam was read within some Jewish mystical circles as paradoxically salvific—revert into the pure antinomianism that Paul avoids, with its thematic of the redeeming sin (in which terms one would have to read Judas, not Jesus, as the redeemer, as in the famous story by Borges). A similar phenomenon can be traced at points in Islamic history itself, where the pure divine one is normally taken as mediated by the unity of law and the political terrain but can also be exceptionally read, as in Ismaili Shi'ism, as the mediated unity of the lone—and possibly "terroristic"—prophet, whose authority exceeds that of the law as so far given.[59] In Franz Kafka's *The Castle* also, the pure law has become terrifyingly senseless. Hence rather than an appeal to a sense of an infinite primary equity—that is strongly linked with the Christian sense of analogical eminence and the trinitarian going out of the One itself toward the expressed diversity of *logos* or *nomos*—Judaism and

---

cal with Jesus. This sort of possibility is now too quickly dismissed by exegetes, because they rightly reject Bultmann's belief in a pre-Christian Gnosticism, a belief that Georgi still espouses. However, this still leaves entirely open the possibility that Gnosticism later developed (usually in unfortunate, heterodox ways) many themes of philosophical gnosis already present in Paul. Indeed, I would contend that anyone who dismisses too quickly a gnostic reading of Paul has not read Paul carefully enough.

57. Agamben, *Temps qui reste*, 83. See also Regina Schwartz, "Revelation and Revolution," in *Theology and the Political: The New Debate*, ed. Creston Davis, John Milbank, and Slavoj Žižek (Durham, NC: Duke University Press, 2005), 102–27.

58. Taubes, *Political Theology of Paul*, passim.

59. For Judaism, see Gershom Scholem, "Redemption through Sin," in *The Messianic Idea in Judaism* (New York: Shocken, 1974). For Islam, see Henri Corbin, *Histoire de la philosophie islamique* (Paris: Gallimard, 1986), 140–54; Christian Jambet, *La grande resurrection d'Alamût: Les formes de la liberté dans le shî'isme ismaélien* (Paris: Verdier, 1990).

Islam can invite a "left-Schmittian" recoil *both* from the provisional-
ity of written law *and* from the frightening reserve of the unknown
legislating power whose authority is constituted only by its capacity to
legislate exceptions to its own legislating. The radical response here then
takes the form of "shutting the door of the law," as with Kafka, or of
responding to the absolute divine ineffability with a "religiously atheist"
and apocalyptic invocation of an equally unknown but hoped-for purely
human future.[60] Such an oscillation between a basically gnostic extreme
pessimism and an apocalypticism that dangerously suggests no positive
political project can perhaps be traced in the secularized Judaism of
Marx's philosophy and in certain handlings of Freud's psychoanalytic
legacy.[61] In Lacan especially, the symbolic "law of the father" becomes,
in a logical development, entirely inscrutable, while the imaginative
economies that seek to channel and mitigate it are equally arbitrary;
love seeking an exit to "the real" tries to escape both and cannot escape
either: its paradoxical affirmation of an excess to the "all" still binds it
absolutely to an all whose authority can regard the escapism of desire
only as a distracting pathology of alienation to be extirpated.[62]

So even if Taubes is right and Paul's own self-understanding is that
he is a "second Moses" who follows through on the latter's threat to

60. Agamben also seems to endorse such a stance (see *Temps qui reste*, 72). As noted earlier,
he entertains a variant of Benjamin's apocalyptic refusal that here takes the form of reading
Paul's *kairos* as that time out of time that is purely our own in which we represent time, following the linguistic theories of Gustave Guillaume (ibid., 108–15). But this seems to remove the
question of the decisive time from the unfolding social and historical context (which is surely
itself constituted *as* primary time by the sequence of such "representations" of time—or "re-
capitulations" to use Paul's own term invoked by Agamben—by every living and moving thing
and, to be sure, by psychic creatures the most intensely). But his consequent reflections on the
influence of Paul's prose and notion of recapitulation on Christian poetics is fascinating (see
ibid., 130–40).

61. See note 27 above, where I suggest that Derrida represents the "gnostic" pole of this
oscillation while Benjamin and Agamben represent the apocalyptic one.

62. Hence Žižek's bizarre invocation of the human condition as a kind of tortured pursuit of
romance that arises only within and yet against a "Stalinist" totality—to which we nonetheless
appeal to liberate us from such torture and so return us to the public realm—does indeed seem
to develop the logic of Lacanianism to its limit. He apparently criticizes Taubes and Agamben
for reducing Paul's love beyond the law to a Kafkaesque excess of an inscrutable authority within
the law itself (in which space the possibility of an excessive mercy without reason would also
lie) in the name of a Lacanian love as "not all." Yet he then goes on to make it clear that this
Lacanian surpassing of the logic of the exception is only itself opened up by this very logic: the
aporetic gap within it is taken by desire to be the missing particular and elected "real" that it
seeks. Hence for Žižek redemption and fall, God and godlessness, coincide. But such gnosticism
is not the true meaning of Paul. See Žižek, *Puppet and the Dwarf*, 92–122. Also Agamben, *Temps
qui reste*, 169, where he speaks of a "messianic state of exception" in Paul.

turn to "another people" in the face of the Hebrews' recalcitrance (thus rendering him a kind of early Sabbatai Sevi), this still does not imply, as Taubes suggests, an appeal to the pure vagary of the divine will or the Kafkaesque specter of a commandment without reason. Just for *this* reason, Paul (as Taubes himself stresses) never suggests that God has gone back on his promises to Israel, only that for the moment the prime shoot of Israel has become paradoxically the wild Gentile branch that has been grafted into the domestic plant, itself now temporarily exiled from the divine garden (Rom. 11:17–24: the metaphors here are notoriously stretched to catachrestic breaking point).[63] And indeed the moment of the eschaton, of universal resurrection, is to coincide with the final reconciliation of these two branches, which are *both* (it must logically follow) branches at once of Israel and of the new *ekklēsia*. (See Gal. 6:15–16: "Neither circumcision counts for anything, nor uncircumcision, but a new creation. Peace and mercy be upon all who walk by this rule, upon the Israel of God.") In the same way that the "justice of trust," or more accurately "just solidarity through trust" (*dikaiosynē pisteōs*), means for Paul in part the inclusion of the Gentiles, so also it means a long-term trust in the final uniting of Gentile with Jew. After Paul has denied in Galatians that one can compel the Gentiles to live like the Jews, he immediately invokes the principle of justification through the faith of Jesus (2:14–16); and if, as I have argued, this has to do with justice, trust, and fidelity, then Paul must be invoking a new community of a reenvisaged Israel that is bound together by justice rather than by the law. He may well be here invoking Psalm 142, where King David, hiding in a cave from his persecutors, begs to be restored to the society of the "righteous." Thus for Paul, as for the Old Testament, to be saved is to be freed from a captivity that excludes one from the community of justice—yet now all human beings, even pagans, can be thought of as kings held in captivity, waiting to be restored to their own true kingdom of righteousness.[64]

But all this suggests that the trust that exceeds the law is very far from an invocation of the exceptionally anarchic and the unsettlingly threatening, on the Schmittian model that Taubes here invokes (albeit that he desires to detach against Schmitt the Kierkegaardian notion

63. See Taubes, *Political Theology of Paul*, 50–51, 62–70, 84–85; see also 74: "Benjamin differs from Paul, however, in the thought of the autonomy of that which he calls the profane." Precisely.

64. See Georgi, *Theocracy*, 36n9.

of the divine exception from that of the political exception).[65] To the contrary, it is precisely a trust that God is just to an eminent and infinite extent that we cannot begin to fathom and a trust that this justice will eventually so triumph that a harmony of peaceful order will embrace not just Jews and Gentiles (who will at last discover just how their various customs may cohere) but also all God's creatures.

However, this primacy of trust follows from Paul's scandalous institution of a polity founded wholly on the counterfactual. In a world wholly encompassed by death, suffering, and egoistic defensive reactions to these realities, justice is possible only on the basis of trust that there is something more primary than the necessarily tyrannical economy and laws that all these assumed transcendental circumstances give rise to. We trust in, "have faith in," God as the source of an undying life that is a never-exhausted gift: "The . . . Lord . . . bestows his riches upon all who call upon him" (Rom. 10:12). In trusting God we trust also that the current negative order is a violation and that "in the end" the order of gift must be restored. It then follows that to trust others as potentially good—as potential sources of gratuitous life (which Paul's missionary and political practice endlessly attests)—is to trust their own trust in God and in eschatological finality (2 Cor. 9:6–14).

It may appear that trust is a weak recourse compared to the guarantees provided by law, courts, political constitutions, checks and balances, and so forth. However, since all these processes are administered by human beings capable of treachery, a suspension of distrust, along with the positive working of tacit bonds of association, is the only real source of reliable solidarity for a community. Hence to trust, to depend on others, is in reality the only reliable way in which the individual can extend his or her own power, his or her own *conatus*, that is, the legitimate reach of one's own capacities, and also the only reliable way to attain a collective strength.

Paul's horizon at this point is Jewish and prophetic rather than Greek: he has founded a community that lives always in expectation of the arrival of the new. It therefore continues to be crucial for him that to the Israelites belong "the promises," yet the irony is that they have often failed to realize that trust in the promises and trust in trust itself are more basic to the realization of justice and law than instituted law— thus the Gentiles, lacking the prophetic promises, have yet sometimes succeeded more in attaining to a blind trust that has ushered in a certain measure of good polity (Rom. 9).

65. Taubes, *Political Theology of Paul*, 65–76.

In keeping with this eschatological perspective, for Paul "the solidarity achieved through justice" (*dikaiosynē*) can never be simply a "Greek" matter of fair spatial distribution (though it certainly remains that), because in a world of time and change and pneumatic inspiration we can never fully anticipate (though we can and must to some degree) the future scope of that "share" that a particular individual or body has been accorded; no measure is forever fixed. It follows that the Greek principle of distributing more to the virtuous (even though the definition of virtue has now been revised) now becomes still more exigent: justice is realizable only if we accord trust to the trustworthy, trust to those who trust that it is possible for further good to arrive and are constantly on the watch for it.[66] Hence the *ekklēsia* is defined by Paul as a *koinōnia*, and he extends its Greek meaning of "partnership" or "community of interests" to include "collection" in applying it to his new international support system that now creates a real, functioning cosmopolitan community of interests, or "sharing of trust."[67] The term *ekklēsia* itself originally meant within Greek culture "the governing assembly" of the city, and it had already been occasionally applied by

66. In *Reading Derrida/Thinking Paul*, 19–96, Jennings uncritically adopts Derrida's Levinasian view, opposed to that of Aristotle, that transcendental justice exceeds distribution altogether. One can agree that it exceeds any fixed or once-and-for-all distribution, but to say that it exceeds distribution or "economy" as such is to espouse an essentially liberal and individualist, or what Badiou calls a "democratically materialist" (for which there are only bodies and words and no "truths" to be shared in), rather than a socialist perspective. For here justice becomes an infinite attention to the infinite otherness of every other, taken one by one. But if, as is the case, people exist only in relations, then one cannot "do justice" to one person without having regard for that person's relations with others and the way these relations "distribute"—according to whatever measure, however "lesbian" or flexible this may be—what people share in common. And one can go further. Even an egalitarian measure that desires that all may fulfill their potential individually and collectively must still seek to place *good* resources in the hands of the *virtuous*; justice means that the "valuable" is placed in the hands of the "valiant," as John Ruskin put it. For to squander resources in the hands of those who prove lazy, corrupt, or incompetent or to permit people regularly to waste their powers and wealth on worthless objects and goals (the norm of our liberal society) is to remove true human benefits from the human majority. Conversely, an egalitarian distribution of resources according to need and capacity requires a considerable consensus (as Badiou realizes) concerning human "truths" or desirable ends. By contrast, if there are only bodies speaking words, then the only consensus will be that we should liberate the desires of the body. Since these are inherently diverse, there can be no question of their fair distribution and therefore no socially agreed on limit to the capitalization of desires by some at the expense of others. Derrida was a liberal, and this is exactly why he appeals to the American left, which is usually a liberal left (although the United States of America also now harbors many of the most authentic socialist and distributist thinkers). See Alain Badiou, preface to *Logiques des mondes*, 9–17.

67. See Blumenfeld, *Political Paul*, 110–11; Hénaff, *Prix de la vérité*, 417–26.

Hellenistic Judaism to the gathering of the elders of Israel. Its application to an entire new polity as such by Paul implies that in some sense
all are now elders, all are now governors within a process of continual
mutual governance.[68]

This is an exchange that builds up "the plenitude of good things in
Christ" (Philem. 6, my translation), which is at once an exchange of
spiritual matters (Phil. 2:1) and of spiritual matters for material and vice
versa (Gal. 6:6). It is the trustworthy members of the community who
in turn trust God and so trust others who share this trust. There is in
consequence both a hierarchy of trust and a circulation and exchange
of trust, and this alone sustains a dynamically just distribution: "For
by the *charis* given to me I bid every one . . . to think [of himself] with
sober judgment, each according to the measure of *pistis* which God
has assigned him [by division (my translation)]. For . . . we, though
many, are one body in Christ, and individually members of one another.
Having gifts [*charismata*] that differ according to the *charis* given to
us" (Rom. 12:3–6).

The translation of *dikaiosynē pisteōs* as "justice of trust," as suggested by Blumenfeld, or perhaps better as "just solidarity through
trust" (following Dieter Georgi), should be preferred to the translation
"justification by faith," since the first two chapters of Romans make
it crystal clear that Paul's fundamental perspective is a (perhaps primarily Greek) "naturalistic" one. Paul believes that all people everywhere should have been able (and by implication have sometimes been
able) to acknowledge the true God and that all people everywhere are
saved according to their obedience to the unwritten justice of God—
in other words, according to ethical works (!) in the broadest sense:
"For he will render to every man according to his works" (Rom. 2:6);
"it is . . . the doers of the law who will be justified [or "rendered just,"
dikaiōthēsontai]" (Rom. 2:13).

Whenever Paul discusses *dikaiosynē pisteōs* (as recent scholarship
has time and again stressed) the context is always, as has already
been indicated, the question of the Gentile-Jewish relationship.[69] In

68. See Georgi, *Theocracy*, 57. In qualification of Georgi, however, I am grateful to Markus
Bockmuehl of the University of Oxford for the point about a Jewish precedent for the use of
this word.

69. For a summary, see Douglas Harink, *Paul among the Postliberals: Pauline Theology beyond
Christendom and Modernity* (Grand Rapids: Brazos, 2003). Harink also correctly stresses that
"justification" in Paul is the divine action of really making just, not of imputing justice; that
"the faith of Christ" is primarily such and not "faith in Christ"; and that *ekklēsia* is a political

declaring that salvation is "by faith," Paul is insisting that the Gentiles have never been outside God's plan, by suggesting that the prelegal recourse of Abraham (whom no one can doubt belongs intrinsically to the divine schema of salvation) to faith was open to them also. If, nevertheless, he has already declared that the Gentiles are redeemed because they "do by nature what the law requires," then this appears to suggest that it is indeed by faith that one is essentially able to be just, that is to say, ethical under the governance of the law of nature. This reading is confirmed by Paul's further explication that Gentiles outside the law judged according to their works are more precisely granted eternal life according "to their awaiting [*hypomonēn*, suggesting a staying behind, a staying firm to await something in a battle] of the good work [*sic*] in seeking glory, honor, and incorruption" (Rom. 2:7; my translation). This "endurance in seeking" sounds close to the quality of *pistis*: the good man is precisely he who trusts that God will so let it fall out that there are, indeed, good works to be performed, or that he will be able to fall into trustworthy relationships with other human beings.

For the Gentiles to follow natural justice in this way is to be "a law to themselves" (Rom. 2:14), which is precisely the quality of autonomy that Paul attributes to members of the church under grace and which for him is most of all embodied in Christ himself as the fulfillment of the law (1 Cor. 2:15–16). As the "living law," Christ, as we have already indicated, is presented by Paul in terms somewhat close to descriptions of Hellenistic divine kings, who exceeded the law in terms of natural equity.

This entire chain of echoes therefore strongly implies that to be "just by faith" and to exercise a sovereign equity beyond the written law lie very close together in Paul's mind. (And *dikaiosynē* always meant "justice" or a "binding together in justice" in the contemporary Greek or Judeo-Greek context and never "imputed salvation," while any suggested likely Hebrew equivalents tended to have a similar primary focus

---

project. However, he fails to see that Paul criticizes law as such, including the entirety of Jewish law, and he cannot bring himself to admit that Paul is, indeed, albeit subtly, supercessionist in relation to Israel—and correctly so, since Christianity *is* the project of a concrete universalism that alone fulfills the "promises" to Israel, outside of which humanity can now see that it has no meaning whatsoever. While, indeed, the continued witness of Israel itself involves elements of insight that must one day be integrated within the church if it is to attain to its full eschatological universality (this being more or less what Paul declares in Romans), the danger of Judaism degenerating into a subtly racist *cultus* needs to be openly recognized. Nor can one agree with Harink or with Jennings that Paul is straightforwardly "opposed" to Roman imperialism.

and certainly never implied anything imputational.)[70] What is then added beyond the inherited Abrahamic or good Gentile perspective is an appeal to a purer equity based on the reemergence of a *purer nature*: the resurrection life that does not in principle require the restraint of instituted written law at all. (Paul directly links the universal natural perspective of creation ex nihilo with that of resurrection in Rom. 4:17: "God . . . who gives life to the dead and calls into existence the things that do not exist.")

The remaining point at issue, then, is what exactly Paul means by denying that one is saved by works of the law. Here one can suggest that he means at least the merely reactive and not originally donating or curative works of justice.[71] Perhaps also (following Blumenfeld's fascinating suggestion) he evokes, in an Aristotelian lineage, the performance of roles in a merely socially imposed dutiful way that is not informed by a spirit that would pursue, in an integral fashion directed toward the common and highest good, every mode of virtue (which would now mean for Paul every mode of *pistis*) in every possible situation and on every possible arising occasion.[72] The latter sort of works are conceiv-

---

70. See Blumenfeld, *Political Paul*, 415–51; Harink, *Paul among the Postliberals*, 25–67.

71. Jennings, in *Reading Derrida/Thinking Paul*, is absolutely right to suggest that for Paul justice beyond the law is grace as gift and that this is what faith "trusts in." He is further right to argue that our "justification" involves a participatory sharing in the divine gift such that for us, "to be just" is to give, without limit or reserve. However, he goes wrong in following Derrida and simply opposing (in an all-too-modern and indeed liberal capitalist manner) the free unilateral gift to ceremonial gift-exchange, as first uncovered by Marcel Mauss and others. This means that he simply ignores all the evidence that Paul thinks about our salvific giving in very reciprocal and exchangist terms—for a discussion of this, see below, in my main text. Indeed, for all his refusal of grace as imputation, Jennings remains highly Protestant in thinking of the gift as entirely self-denying, on the one hand, and as indifferent to the merits of the donee, on the other. Likewise Protestant, and here liberal Protestant, is his playing down of Paul's founding of a new religious polity (the *ekklēsia*) involving specific *dogmata* and sacraments and institutional practices. Thereby he renders Paul's cosmopolitanism implausibly pan-religious and disconnected from his Christology. Moreover, this same rendering overlooks the fact that the "church" for Paul is, if not a fully utopian project, at least a reforming one that sets no limits to its hopes of overcoming injustice. Jennings, by adopting Derrida's "gnostic" pessimism, by contrast thinks that justice will always be corrupted by the legal systems it requires for its implementation, just as the "religious" aspiration to pure gift will be unavoidably corrupted by market exchange and state bureaucracy. He fails to see that Paul has invented the *ekklēsia* as a noncontractual economy and a nonlegal practice of human transformation. Finally, Jennings's preference for regarding forgiveness as negatively indifferent to repentance rather than as a positive process of reconciliation requiring both repentance and processes of penitence is also all too Protestant. He does not see that Catholic (i.e., Christian) penance is as removed from the mere "equivalence" of punishment as gift-exchange is removed from the mere equivalence of contract.

72. Blumenfeld, *Political Paul*, 336. See also Aristotle, *Nichomachean Ethics* 1.1097b25– 1098a20. These suggestions are certainly more plausible than those of scholars like J. D. G.

ably for Paul those that proceed from our being "created in Christ"—
so belonging to his body, the *ekklēsia*—and which thereby belong to a
single divine "poem" or "workmanship" (*poiēma*, Eph. 2:8–10).[73]

The Division and Hierarchy of Gifts

In the third place Paul, again in the wake of the Hellenistic Pythagoreans (and ultimately Plato more than Aristotle), associates justice with
the division of labor (1 Cor. 12:4–7) and tends to downplay the role of
the Aristotelian "all-round" elite man of virtue in favor of a sense of
general all-informing virtue (of the kind just invoked) as achieved via
collective interaction of different functions (which was also *one* aspect
of the Stoic vision).[74] He explicitly says that the same God operates
through all the diverse human social operations in the *ekklēsia*, which
all by divine gift "manifest the spirit" for the sake of a collective *sym-
pheron*, or symphony—a term that in the Pythagorean legacy had at
once musical and political connotations. (Blumenfeld even suggests
that we should read glossolalia in the context of the Greek legacy of
thinking of political peace in musical terms as a kind of daring atonality that can be incorporated into the surprising new ritual harmonies
granted by *charis* that help to "build up" the peace and harmony of
the community.)[75]

But this uniting division is now according to various degrees of the
possession of trust: *pistis*. Divine *charis*, he says, gives us gifts of *pistis*,
but he immediately makes it clear that this means a "measured" (which
is to say "politically economic") distribution of various different social
roles within the body of the church (Rom. 12:3–8; Eph. 4:7–13). These
roles concern modes and hierarchical degrees of the exercise of trust
("having gifts that differ according to the grace [*kata tēn charin*] given
to us," Rom. 12:6), which also concerns something like the "holding
in trust" without limits of the well-being of others. These roles are described in Romans 12 as being ones of prophecy, serving (in the diacon-

---

"Jimmy" Dunn (who appear to have spent their lifetimes reducing the great apostle to banality)
that works refer merely to ritual observances or even to the following of the letter of the Jewish
law alone. See Harink, *Paul among the Postliberals*, 37–38.

73. Ephesians may not be by Paul himself, but it certainly emerges from his school of
thought.

74. Blumenfeld, *Political Paul*, 95–107, 184–85, 385–86.

75. Ibid., 127. One can note that Paul declares, "I will sing with the spirit and I will sing
with the mind also" (1 Cor. 14:15). Paul appears to share in common with the Pythagorean
philosophers a liking for comparisons between musical and political harmony.

ate), teaching, exhortation, "sharing in simplicity" (ascetic guidance?), and performing acts of mercy. They are described in 1 Corinthians 12 as being the *logos sophias*, the *logos gnoseōs*, the gift of *pistis*, "gifts of healing," "operations of powers" (*energēmata dynameōn*), discerning of spirits, kinds of tongues and interpretation of tongues, and later in the same chapter as being apostleship, prophecy, teaching, operation of powers, gifts of healing, "assisting," "organizing of exchanges" (*antilēmpseis* means "exchangers" and suggests an economic role), "governing" (metaphorically "piloting"), speaking in tongues, and interpretation of tongues (see also Eph. 4:11–13).

Paul's placing of "prophecy" at the top of the hierarchy in Romans, and "wisdom" and "gnosis" as next in order (corresponding possibly to "apostleship" and "prophecy," and so perhaps concerned with an eternally hidden order and that which is to come; see also 1 Cor. 2:6–7), significantly underscores the way in which for him the visionary anticipation of a hidden eternal present and an eschatological future in which the resurrected life will be "all in all" is the architectonic foundation for the possibility of justice. The world awaits a final historical event already commenced that will be also the final disclosure of the metahistorical secrets of eternal outgoings from God. Just occurrences in historical time are just only to the measure that they prefigure and make apparent this apocalyptic dimension, while the eternal metanarrative mysteriously and from all eternity includes the event of overcoming evil that has only been enacted in human time, on the cross. In the latter event, Christ trusted in an eternity of trusting justice that, nevertheless, only his fidelity both guaranteed and restored. To a lesser degree, and with an absolute assurance, the members of the body of Christ must also undergo this passage through an incomprehensibly vertiginous mystery that yet has about it a familiar ring: trust when enacted secures the very reality and stability of trustworthiness that it at first could only "trust" in. So the gospel augments a circumstance that we already simply intimate: trust as act in time presupposes itself as eternal reality, yet the unshakenness of this reality through the course of all time is established only through the act of trust and reestablished only when trust is restored. The New Testament accordingly teaches most fundamentally an extraordinary circular mutual dependence between an "oriental" and "gnostic" permanent apocalyptic secret and an "occidental" and "exoteric" contingent historical event, even if this has seldom been realized because of respective Eastern and Western biases.

But trust, as we have just seen, also circulates more mundanely throughout the ecclesiastical hierarchy and can involve the exchange of spiritual for material gifts. Ultimately, the hope that is inseparable from trust and that people are capable of in different degrees will give way to the fulfilled reign of *agapē*, of which all are equally capable (Rom. 12:9–13; 1 Cor. 13)

The Monarchic Blended with the Democratic

In the fourth place, there is the question of how the resurrected Christ exerts his rule, and of the blend in Paul (again following Hellenistic thought) of the democratic with the monarchic. He does not explicitly speak of Christ as *basileus* (perhaps because he is no ordinary sort of king), but he does speak of him in many terms that emphatically denote rulership over a *basileia*, and he clearly identifies him as a king when he says that he was "descended from David according to the flesh" and "designated Son of God in power"—implying that he is the unique heir to the divine paternal monarchy (Rom. 1:3–4). Crucial here, as Blumenfeld argues, is the link in Hellenistic Pythagorean thought between the idea of equity exceeding the law and the monarch who as a "living law" rules in constant exception to the law but with reference of course to natural, eternal justice.[76] But here the idea of Christ's "grace" as distributing to us a kind of one-way equity, whatever our circumstances might seem to be, is in a certain tension with the idea that the divine gift is precisely of a circulation of trust within the body of Christ.

To mediate this issue, one needs to become more aware of the sheer peculiarity of what Paul proposes. The Greeks had spoken already of the rule of a godlike king and had earlier with more circumspection said that such a potential individual ought rather to be ostracized from the city. But Paul announces nothing less than the eternal rule commencing here and now on earth of a dead, executed man, ostracized from the Jewish, Hellenistic, and Roman communities! One is inevitably reminded here of the theme of the "king's two bodies," which Ernst Kantorowicz found in the Middle Ages but which Agamben points out had far earlier exemplifications in the Roman period. On Agamben's account, if, in certain circumstances, the living sovereign power alone upholds law in the mode of a personal *auctoritas* (as opposed to more impersonal *imperium*), then it is for this reason that the death of the

---

76. Blumenfeld, *Political Paul*, 189–276.

sovereign constitutes a moment of crisis—either one of potential anarchy or else one of possible augmented and now magical influence of the
apotheosized emperor—which is ideologically dealt with by the fiction
of an undying monarchic body often represented by an artificial effigy
that doubles as the dead body of the deceased sovereign.[77] This effigy
(the *colossus*) does not (as Kantorowicz supposed) represent in terms
of concrete metaphor the undying abstraction of legal authority but
rather represents the excess of sovereignty over such authority. (Related
to this, Agamben argues, is the idea that the killing of a sacred king
is not exactly homicide because it is *more* than homicide.) Death is
seen as actually releasing and in a sense augmenting this excess, since
its psychic or pneumatic character is precisely a power over all merely
"zoological" life, a power to return all such life to a "bare" condition
of a death that carries no regular religious (sacrificial) or legal (mur-
derous) connotations.[78] The death of the sovereign himself is seen,

77. Agamben, *State of Exception*, 23; Agamben, *Homo Sacer*, 91–103; E. H. Kantorowicz,
The King's Two Bodies: A Study in Mediaeval Political Theology (Princeton, NJ: Princeton
University Press, 1957).
    78. This is how Agamben understands the Roman figure of *homo sacer*, who is somehow
abandoned to death outside the law rather than put to death by the law or sacrificed for expia-
tory purposes. It is in this way that such a figure prefigures the liberal subject, which outside
the artificial sway of contract loses its humanity—as at Guantanamo Bay. Whether Agamben
exaggerates this prefiguring can nonetheless be debated: in particular the issue of whether *homo
sacer* is really imbued with some elements of *extraordinary* sacrifice. (See Milbank, *Being Reconciled*, 92.) The denizens of Guantanamo Bay are perhaps a wholly new sort of entirely arbitrary
victim, given that in post-Hobbesian biopolitics there is supposed to be a constant threat of all
to all and this threat must be constantly kept alive and constantly shown to be "dealt with." In
the current more-global area, where the authority of the nation-state has become problematic
(or else has become excessively extended), it becomes all the more the case that the threat is
continuous and never goes away and therefore that there must perpetually be "nonplaces" where
those deemed to threaten the entire biopolitical system—and therefore are neither criminals nor
warriors—can be dealt with in the absence of all normal legal restrictions. Perhaps the antidote
to this was proposed by Hobbes's contemporary Thomas Browne: "Every man's hand might slay
us," he declared, "so we should constantly be grateful to every man who stays his hand against
us." And for a fictional reflection on this English Baroque topos, see Michael Cox, *The Meaning of Night* (London: John Murray, 2006). Cox appears to suggest that the willingness to kill
an identified man (which always involves in some sense a seizing of an identity or the vengeful
cancellation of a stolen identity, as is the case in this novel) requires also a willingness to kill
the unidentified man, the human as such—in part because no one is ever fully identified and
in part also because the pursuit of identity will engender an indifference toward the unidentified, the absolute stranger. His villain-hero who has first literally killed an unidentified victim
in order to have the courage to kill his real, known enemy and displacer, finally renounces a
belief in pagan fatality, an ancestral concern with bloodline, a desire to restore true identity, and
even a revolutionary overturning of all social identity, by returning to Christian belief in exile.
The implication seems to be that only the recognition of the divine in humanity as such, as the
capacity for gift or mercy, which cannot be fully "identified"—a capacity that the hero has been

Agamben argues, as a kind of paradoxical ultimate zero-degree of the
exercise of his own power. This power, once released by death, must
either be neutralized by being relocated in a *colossus* that is burned or
buried alongside the actual body of the emperor (as in ancient Rome),
or else it must be talismanically passed on to the king's successor (as
in medieval France and England).

In the case of Christ, however, Paul evokes not a second body whose
power is to be neutralized or recaptured but the real dead body of a
divine man, which is now somehow brought again to life. This concurs
with the fact that Paul sees in Christ not simply one godlike ruler but
the incarnate rule of God himself, which has alone overcome the sway
of death and reactive rule in the face of death. It follows that only
Christ is fit to rule the human cosmopolity and also that Christ, once
incarnate, having now achieved the divine-human fusion, cannot really,
even though "ascended," desert the physical cosmos. Hence the "fiction"
(be it true or not) of his resurrection must be one that is to be forever
upheld. However, there is also a further contrast: the Roman-derived
theme of the king's two bodies suggests a certain uneasy interval between the instituting will-to-law and the rule of legality itself. Without
the former, the latter may crumble, or with too much of the former
the latter may become debased. Yet in the case of Christ, who is the
incarnate *Logos*, there is no such interval. Christ does not primarily
authorize the new law to which he stands in excess; he simply is this law
in its fulfillment. And this means that his death is not so much aporetic
as rather outrightly catastrophic: it does not open out a problematic
gap between law and sovereignty but dramatizes the disappearance of
both, since on this conception law is less authorized by personal will
than it is thought of as something that can be personified and concretely
exemplified *only* in a living life, since "justice" has no meaning outside
the realm of living spirits. It would follow from this that the medieval
christocentric construal of kingship combined both Kantorowicz's and
Agamben's readings: the undying body of the king was the undying
body of equity that must be at once the spirit of the written law itself
and a power of judgment that belongs to persons alone.

In consequence, there can be justice for Paul only if we all act as sur-
rogates for the king who is resurrected and yet also semiremoved and

---

abundantly shown by some, despite being wronged by others—prevents the practice of that
abjection that is constitutive of liberal modernity. Jacques Derrida also, in the more antiliberal
moment of his thought, suggested that a recognition of the divine in man alone secures human
justice in a way that "human rights" cannot possibly do.

absent. Christ can reign on earth only if we all become kings (a theme later echoed in Christian Gnostic texts),[79] which means that his one-way top-down equity has now been democratized and itself circulates (1 Cor. 4:8). Thus while the husband is to exercise authority (*exousiazei*) over his wife's body (according to a supposed "order of nature" that Paul was not revolutionary enough to question), nevertheless the subordinate wife is *also* to exercise authority over her husband's body. Likewise Paul astonishingly suggests (1 Cor. 12:24–25) that our genitalia are *not* socially concealed because of shame but rather because, by christological kenotic reversal (that we only now fully understand in the light of the *euangelion*), we give greater honor (*timē*, which is also lordship, "the prerogative of a king") to that which in itself possesses the least honor (and is most to be ruled over: the drastic implication is that in the purified, already-resurrected body, it is safe for the passionate genitals also to rule the head).[80]

So we are all to act equitably all the time, beyond and outside the regulations. This is precisely why it is crucial for Paul to found a community based on something in excess of regulation, for so to act requires social space and mutual permission; otherwise the exceeder of the norms would be simply a transgressor and would be locked up. Therefore within a community that systematically organizes processes of mutual trust, penance, forgiveness, and reconciliation and that consistently operates sanctions of shame and dishonor,[81] there increasingly comes

79. See, for example, *The Apocalypse of Adam* 82.19–21: "But the generation without a king over it says that God chose him [the "Savior," probably Jesus Christ] from all the aeons. He caused a knowledge of the undefiled one of truth [God, not the gnostic demiurge who is the Creator] to be in him." Georgi sees this as a "Jewish Gnostic" text, but it is much more likely a post-Christian one, as Simone Pétrement first argued. The text does not mention Jesus explicitly, since it takes the form of a supposed prophecy, yet it ends with an identification of "the secret acquaintance of Adam" with "baptism" or "Iesseus-Mazareus-Lessedekeus, the living water." It earlier speaks of a savior sent from the true God who performs signs and wonders in defiance of "the powers and their rulers"—this sounds very like Paul—and who is then "chastised in the flesh" by this ruler. Also like Paul is the mention of Adam and Eve's fearful and servile relationship to the Creator God (in Paul the equivalent is the cosmic powers who are the source of the law) and the "dead things" that they learn about after their banishment from glory. Finally, it is fairly clear that the work is indebted to the clearly Christian *Apocryphon of John*—an alternative supposition would involve positing a series of wholly unknown works. See Simone Pétrement, *A Separate God: The Origins and Teachings of Gnosticism*, trans. Carol Harrison (San Francisco: HarperCollins, 1984), 433–36.

80. Dieter Georgi plausibly identifies a strain of coarse humor and parody in Paul: see Georgi, *Theocracy*, 49, 54.

81. See Blumenfeld, *Political Paul*, 311–12. He mentions that these sanctions were also central for the Pseudo-Archytas and Diotogenes.

to be no need to "go to law" against each other. (Rom. 1:16; 1 Cor. 6:4–5, 7: "If then you have such cases, why do you lay them before those who are least esteemed by the church? I say this to your shame. . . . To have lawsuits at all with one another is defeat for you. Why not rather suffer wrong?")[82]

If democratic circulation is now informed by monarchic equity, then, inversely, Paul democratizes monarchy. Christ ruled only because he was *doulos*, a slave, obedient to the Father and to the needs of his human brothers and sisters (1 Cor. 1:27). This means that Christ the supreme giver was such only because he was also, as the divine Son, the supreme, infinite recipient, something also mediated to him by human acts of favor (like the anointing of his feet—symbolically, for Jewish tradition, his genitals—by Mary Magdalene). In this way Christ's supreme, unilateral rule was also involved in a certain kind of gift-exchange—and in such a fashion that, as Blumenfeld puts it, Paul thereby contrives to "save the political game."[83] For this "game" (as Aristotle described it) with the Greeks, as we saw earlier, concerned the essentially reciprocal rule of law. The exercise of a supreme, sovereign equitable good seemed to exceed this game, engendering a further problematic within the antique notion of the biopolitical: the more one has superceding "sovereign" equity, the less it seems one can have social equality. Paul, however, resolves this problematic. The most hierarchical rule is supreme precisely by virtue of its greater degree of kenosis: to attend to particular needs is truly to receive a gift from the seemingly purely needy themselves. Inversely, the mutual application of justice, since it is now an exchange of positive gifts in mutual trust (nonidentically repeated and asymmetrically reciprocal) constitutes a continuously magnanimous bestowal of equity

82. It may, however, be possible to argue here that in "going beyond the law" Paul is only *accentuating* the dominant tendencies of all antique legal and political systems, which had more to do with persuasive rhetoric, ideal exhortation, narrative instances, hyperbolic warnings, public shaming, and magico-religious sanctions than they did with formal consistency and an expectation of regular enforcement as pertains with modern (roughly post-sixteenth-century) law systems. Thus the fact that many Jewish laws were always "dead letters" (we know of *no one* ever executed for working on the Sabbath, for example) may not at all—as is too often claimed—distinguish it from *nomos* or *lex*: they also were fundamentally exhortatory and underwritten by divine sanction. Moreover, the extreme migration of the *torah* from something enforced to something merely studied most probably has to do with the context of the rabbinic era, where Jewish communities increasingly became islands within an alien legal sea. I am indebted to discussion with Dr. Caroline Humfress of Birkbeck College, London, on this point.

83. Blumenfeld, *Political Paul*, 342: "Now this is reason for boasting (Romans 5:11), *ecce homo!* Master and slave, ruler and ruled, Christ is Paul's solution to the demand for reciprocity in Aristotle's political construct. Christ saves the political game as well." See also ibid., 183.

by many kings, each to each. Frequently, this exchange is a mutual offering of suffering and its fruits (1 Cor. 4:10; 2 Cor. 1:1–24) while it
is also often a reparation of the exchange process through a forgiving
forbearance in the face of a lapse in charity, generosity, and trust by
one party or another (2 Cor. 2:5–11).

Blumenfeld's understanding of how Paul reconciles the sovereignly
unilateral with the democratically reciprocal in his understanding of
gift and grace is to be preferred to Agamben's reading, which categori-
cally declares that "grace is not the foundation of exchanges and social
obligations" in Paul. I have already cited abundant evidence that, to the
contrary, Paul *always* speaks of *charis* as giving *charismata*, which only
make sense within, and are only given by the Holy Spirit for, a reciprocal political interaction. Agamben does indeed helpfully point out that
the division of love from law recalls the trace of Abrahamic prelaw, of
"magical" pact or covenant (*berith*) that lurks within the Mosaic Torah
itself. However, because such a notion of bond already projects the
notion of something legally binding or "written," the reinvocation of
law as prelegal gift (or as "love") by Paul tends, according to Agamben,
to appeal only to the first "executing" moment of prestation and no
longer to the exchangist counterprestation, since this already implies
"norm": for Agamben, it appears, law is the counterprestation to the
original gift of unilateral love-bonding from a spontaneous donor.
Yet Agamben reaches this conclusion only because, like Taubes, he
approximates love to a kind of exceptional and reasonless mercy or
preference that is therefore situated in the same logical space as the
Schmittian exception that constitutes sovereign power as such. In this
way, Pauline love would still be trapped within a dialectic of law and
love, or of contract and gift. Likewise there would be an unresolvable
duality of unilateral monarchic giving power versus the give-and-take
of democratically accepted legality.[84]

For Paul, however, it would seem that there really can be an exception even to this aporetic bind. He conceives of the reception of grace
and the giving of love as a social practice and economy that is binding
without law (in the sense of written prohibitions and injunctions),
because it works through the spiraling asymmetry and nonidentical
repetition of gift-exchange with an accompanying exchange of sanctions of trust, honoring, shame, forbearance, and forgiveness. Love and
mercy are *not* here exercised without measure, judgment, preferential

---

84. Agamben, *Temps qui reste*, 177–93.

discrimination, or due distribution—all that Augustine would later term the *ordo amoris*. For what is sought is perfect peace through appropriate mutual placing and replacing, not the space for the exercise of excessive and purely negative emotions lacking all order and rhythm.[85] So by reinvoking the precedence of oral prelaw (and so of tacit trust) Paul is not rejecting all the magical binding that is inseparable from this horizon. Indeed, he rather pulls off the tour de force of associating modern written contract with magic in a demonic sense of slavery to a formula. Every fixed formula can only be a curse in the end, since its decree is nonrescindable: "For all who rely on works of the law are under a curse" (Gal. 3:10, 1–14).[86] The older, oral magic of trusting affinity was by contrast flexible and variable, even if it did not of course eschew signs, but since Mauss, we have known better than to associate magic only with an "automatic" process.[87]

The archaically prelegal is, nevertheless, purged by Paul of even its incipient legality, but not in Agamben's terms of a privileging only of the initial, autonomously active sovereign and unilateral pole—which is of course in the Schmittian logic only one pole of the aporetic constitution of legality itself. Instead, it is rather both poles, and therefore exchange itself, that are released from restrictions of narrowly defined social roles and confinements of customary space and time, besides limits to the extent and content of generosity. Exchange is now to expand to a cosmopolitan and even a cosmic extent. If indeed there appears to remain a tension between the "free" sovereign moment in giving and the "bound" moment of obligation to return (which, as noted earlier, seems somewhat to parallel the Schmittian biopolitical aporias), then this tension is rendered benign by Paul in his new understanding of the hierarchically free and unilateral moment as itself only legitimate as service to others, as being always already a response, while inversely the democratically obliged response is never servile but always partakes of the creative freedom of sonship, the birthright of the heir to the throne.

This newly achieved synthesis permitted Paul both to take over and to drastically modify the culture of benefaction that surrounded him. In the political world with which he was familiar, magistracies in the city (earlier independent of personal wealth and possibly remunerated) had

85. This should be put in opposition to Jennings's Derridean reading of Paul.

86. See also Georgi, *Theocracy*, 39–40.

87. See Marcel Mauss, *A General Theory of Magic*, trans. Robert Brain (London: Routledge, 2001).

become confused with "liturgies" (services exacted for the support of the city's military, ritual, diplomatic, and convivial life from wealthier citizens), with the result that, increasingly, only the privately rich could rule, and rule itself was becoming virtually coterminous with benefaction: a spectacle at worst to be admired by most and at best passively received.[88] Paul, however, is himself at least once prepared to lay down his pride as an independent spiritual benefactor who worked for his own living by receiving material gifts of support from the church at Philippi. (See also 1 Cor. 9:1–27 and 2 Cor. 11:8, where he says that he has "accepted support from other churches" in order to support the church at Corinth—suggesting that the Philippian support was not an isolated instance.) These he identifies as themselves equivalent to a spiritual sacrificial offering that thereby redounds more to the spiritual than to the political glory of the Philippians and befits them also to become recipients—this time in relation to God, who "will supply every need of yours according to his riches in glory in Christ Jesus" (Phil. 4:19). Thus the new political primacy of benefaction (the new "ruling by giving" or the dominance of the *euergetēs*)[89] is not so much refused as subverted. An oligarchic paternalism is transformed into a process of reciprocal offering newly regarded as the primary instrument of government. Paul, under Christ, is the supreme legislator and executor for the Gentile churches; nevertheless, he is prepared to be in a servile and grateful relationship to them (even if his other epistles often show prideful hesitancies about his degree of submission).

Yet this is only because receptivity has itself been redefined: thinking ultimately of the trinitarian relation of Christ the divine Son to the divine Father, it has now become paradoxically "original" (since the Father was never without the Son).[90] Christ's initial power is based wholly on a

88. Blumenfeld, *Political Paul*, 101. See also G. W. Peterman, *Paul's Gift to Philippi: Conventions of Gift-Exchange and Christian Giving* (Cambridge: Cambridge University Press, 1997). Peterman, however, overstresses the vertical religious dimension of gift and gratitude in Paul and exaggerates the extent of his critique of euhemerism (benefaction) and gift-exchange. For it is clear that Paul encourages the growth of a mutual support system (sometimes exchanging spiritual for material goods), especially as between the Gentile churches and the Jewish church in Jerusalem.

89. See Paul Veyne, *Le pain et le cirque* (Paris: Éditions du Seuil, 1976).

90. This may sound anachronistic with respect to Paul. However, I would argue that the later orthodox trinitarian and christological formulations are the best interpretations of his various statements on the Father, Christ, and the Holy Spirit and his understanding of the logic of mediation. On the one hand, Paul clearly distinguishes three hypostatic beings; on the other hand, he insists that God can only be mediated by God, and his critique of the law is profoundly linked to just this point. But that is the entire nub of the later orthodox argument.

loving reception, but this is not the normal reception of a gift that helps
a person to hold back the fateful onset of death for a while, or even one
that shores up one's native strength. Rather, it is a gift that establishes
Christ in the first place as Son, and *just for this reason* it is uniquely a
gift that is coterminous with life: "The free gift of God is eternal life in
[his Son] Christ Jesus our Lord" (Rom. 6:23). And it is this gift of life
as such that for Paul we participate in politically: just as Christ is ruler
under the Father only as his constant equal Son and heir, so also we are
not in turn "sons of Christ," but rather we distribute his rule at least
potentially alongside him, as destined ourselves to become fully sons of
the Father. It is for this reason that we are "debtors" (*opheiletai*) not,
like "slaves," "according to the flesh," whereby a repayment of the debt
would merely hold back death for a while, but rather "by the spirit,"
such that in paying back the debt we ever further receive the gift in this
non-zero-sum game of grace (Rom. 8:12–17). For we do not receive as
the divine gift "the spirit of slavery," which would be a terrible protection from utter destruction (slavery being anciently linked to a grim
sort of asylum for foreign prisoners) but rather "the spirit of sonship,"
which is the generative gift of life as such. When a child receives life
from its forebears (naturally and culturally), this is clearly not the sort
of receptivity of something alien that merely shores you up for a time;
rather, it is the active reception of those powers that are most one's
own, even though they remain always (*unlike* mere assistance) *entirely*
derived from elsewhere. (Ultimately this is a matter of the derivation
of our very existence from "being as such.") Thus in this instance the
more one receives, the more one gratefully acknowledges this reception
("pays back the debt") and thereby permits oneself to receive further,
the more also one is radically free, in charge of one's own life and able
oneself to exercise authority. Here gratitude is really without loss, since
the gift of life is free, whereas sin and even the measured sin that the
law sustains has to pay a price for its apparent liberty and in the end
that price is death itself, the entire surrender of a simulacrum of vital-
ity. (Rom. 6:23: "For the wages of sin is death, but the free gift of God
is eternal life in Christ Jesus our Lord.")

   In the same restrictedly economic manner, mere (legal) delegation,
self-assertion, and sacrificial economizing of negative or threatening
powers can only engender a political rule that is fated one day to end;
but the reception without any trade-off through Christ of the paternal
authority renders us actually "heirs of God . . . fellow heirs with Christ"
(Rom. 8:17), inheritors of an eternal rule that cannot ever terminate—

not simply mediators of this rule but actually heirs: that is to say, people to whom an entirety of divine authority to judge is continuously transferred. It follows that it is not going too far to say that for Paul we receive, entirely heteronomously, the gift of autonomous self-rule and the (political) right to judge others: "The spiritual man judges all things, but is himself to be judged by no one. 'For who has known the mind of the Lord so as to instruct him?' But we have the mind of Christ" (1 Cor. 2:15–16; see also 6:3: "Do you not know that we are to judge angels? How much more, matters pertaining to this life!").[91]

So on the christological exchangist model, the dignity of giving is now also the dignity of receiving, and all are kings because all are receiving and devoted slaves, but in a new sense that converts all slavery into liberal sonship. Thus Paul ecstatically proclaims to the Corinthians: "Already you are filled! Already you have become rich! Without us you have become kings! And would that you did reign, so that we might share the rule with you!" (1 Cor. 4:8). If the notion of kingship as deriving from receptive slavery seems akin to the current neo-evangelical reinstitution of slavery described in the opening section of this chapter, the latter is really a parody of this Pauline theme. For in the Pauline case the context of mutual ecstatic offering means that the objective has been subjectivized, imbued with what one might describe as a characterizing power, as the service of slavery is seen as the most regal, personal attribute of all, while inversely, subjective sovereignty is granted always the concrete character of the objective insofar as it resides in the specific enacted gift and not in the reserved open power of negative freedom. The neo-evangelical coincidence of subject and object merely parodies this, because here subject and object do not temper and fulfill each other, but rather the sheer vacuity of empty freedom and the mere abject thingness of a purely manipulable object coincide absolutely.

Paul, Life, and Gift

In each of these four modalities Paul collapses *basileia* into *polis* and vice versa. It is this that enables him, beyond both antiquity and modernity,

91. This contrasts with passages where Paul, like Jesus, tells us "not to judge." Perhaps one should interpret this contrast to mean that we must not usurp the final judgment, while on the other hand, the anticipation of this judgment by the arrival of Christ permits us to share in advance in the authentic divine judgment. This would accord with the fact that the cross of Christ judges all in overturning all normal human judgment.

also to collapse life into law and vice versa. In this way the biopolitical is exceeded because the political norm is taken to be an undying life that is a living positive law of gift that cannot possibly of itself require the emergency legal measure of economic sacrifice.

Within this grand schema we can also see how Paul resolves the Senecan aporia of gratitude. In the face of the prevalence of ingratitude (which Paul tends grumpily to complain of with respect to his own donations; see Philippians in particular), we still do not need to retreat into the pure citadel of motivation and define the essence of the gift as pure intention that remains whether or not the gift has been well received. We can, rather, accentuate the other side of Seneca's vision, which concerned the prospect of virtue more as mutual exchange than as individual excellence and which envisaged a cosmopolis based on gift-exchange in excess of both law and mercenary contract and which accordingly allowed that slaves could give to masters as well as vice versa.[92] Since the "exchange of offices" now for Seneca defined virtue (see note 30 in this chapter), this meant it was precisely in terms of gift-exchange that Seneca extended the possibility of a fully virtuous life to all human beings.[93] Since for Seneca this exchange is unpredictably and unquantifiably equitable, because the measure of equity is now the matching of gratitude to degree of generosity, given all the circumstances of donation, it is on this sort of basis (a Stoic vision with which Paul may have been somewhat familiar) that one can conceive of a *social practice of gratitude*, and hence one can project a society commensurate with *cosmopolis*, namely the *ekklēsia*, where for Seneca this remained a vaguely ideal notion fully realized only by the sage's resignation to cosmic fate. It follows that the Senecan problematic imperative toward responsible giving only to those likely to be grateful can be more unproblematically upheld: for in the *ekklēsia*, unlike all other polities hitherto, those likely to be grateful are (in principle) more publicly identified, since prestige here is tied to trustworthiness and power-to-trust, which involves a constant openness to giving and receiving.

92. Hénaff, *Prix de la vérité*, 337–51, does not really accommodate this "Maussian" aspect of Seneca, focusing only on his anticipation of a modern, "Kantian" unilateral gift that Hénaff too readily sees as the solely "moral" gift.

93. Seneca, *De beneficiis* 3.17.3–19.1. One can note here that gift-exchange happens characteristically either in circumstances of social proximity or else of total cultural strangeness—as when new peoples first encounter each other and mutual generosity proves to be the only way to open negotiations. *In between* these two extremes lies the realm of contracts entered into between those warily familiar with each other.

Nevertheless, Seneca's equal sense that one should give even to the ungrateful and that the grateful might always prove too few can also be upheld.[94] For Paul offers the horizon of eschatological hope that all will one day prove to be grateful, rendering all people the worthy recipients of our gifts and even our apparently misplaced trust. (But clearly there are no rules governing just *when* one should risk giving to the ungrateful.)

It is in terms of this eschatological hope that Paul can, beyond Seneca, restore the primarily *exchangist* sense of gift as always a passage in real objective space and time, incomplete unless it is received with gratitude. Because he trusts that one day this will always be the case, he no longer needs the guarantee of pure motive in order to ensure the absoluteness of gift for the giver. And since gift now abides in achieved and renewed ontological *relation*, the external *sign* of gratitude is, again beyond Seneca, itself an inherent aspect of gratitude and need not involve the degeneration of *munus* (gift) into *commercium*. An exchanged thing-sign need not necessarily be a commodity because it can be imbued with a pneumatic unpredictability of arrival, surprisingness, and yet appropriateness of content.

Finally, one can try to place Paul's vision within the wider context of the whole story recounted by the New Testament. Christ was born in the reign of Augustus Caesar, according to Agamben the first Caesar to base his power solely on a personal, familial, and exceptional *auctoritas* rather than the regular rule of *imperium*.[95] Within the nets of his new *surveillance* (reported by Luke but nowhere else: Luke 2:1–7), he apparently located one Jesus Christ, but instead he was to be himself positioned, along with all humanity, by Christ's infinitely personal and absolute authority. Christ eventually died under Caesar's rule of the rule of the exception,[96] but if St. Paul is right, then *ekklēsia*, as founded by Christ, names the only polity, or at least possibility of a polity, that collectively lives, beyond death, as an exception even to the law of exception, because it replaces the political animal with the pneumatic body of grace-given mutual trust.

This is not, however, a utopian program. St. Paul did not propose to abolish the biopolitical order of the Roman Empire—indeed, as Blumenfeld waspishly says, his proto-Constantinian program rather

94. Seneca, *De beneficiis* 4.26.1–3; 5.1, 4–5.
95. Agamben, *State of Exception*, 74–88.
96. For the modified application of Agamben's ideas to the Passion Narratives and ideas of atonement, see Milbank, *Being Reconciled*, 79–104.

ensured that the Roman Empire is in reality still with us. So he did not
deny that the second best of the exercise of imperative *nomos* in the
face of scarcity, sin, and death would remain necessary.[97]

Yet at the same time, he simply bypassed empire and did something
else—filled it with a new and more primary content, which caused him
to suffer and finally to die at its hands (2 Cor. 11:24–29). This audac-
ity is witnessed to by the fact that Paul and his followers addressed the
churches in Rome, Galatia, Corinth, Philippi, Thessalonika, Ephesus,
and Colossae simply as if he were addressing the citizens of these places
tout court: Romans, Galatians, Corinthians, Philippians, Thessalonians,
Ephesians, Colossians. By insinuating a counterpolity ruled by a legally
slain and divinely resurrected king, Paul uniquely opened the possibility
that the unstable excesses thrown up by biopolitical processes, ancient
or modern, might nonetheless gradually take on some of the character
of a living excess of equity both hierarchically and unilaterally encouraged and democratically and reciprocally exchanged.

Yet is the price to pay too high? That of trust in a counterfactual ab-
surdity? Surely it is better, like Albert Camus' doctor hero in *The Plague*,
stoically to accept death and suffering as ultimate yet to celebrate and
promote human courage and sympathy in the face of this? Yet inevitably,
in that case, the noblest and highest virtue must be considered reactive: the temporary holding back of final disaster. Moreover, if nature
itself is a constant struggle for scarce resources and a backward race
always to see who can die last, then the suspicion must indeed arise
that the law of the exception and the concentration camp is the human
expression of what, from a human point of view, can appear only an
entirely sinister ontology. It may indeed appear ridiculous to speak of
the current state of nature as fundamentally "contaminated by evil,"
yet we can only not do so by a suspension in our souls of all human
recognition of value, including the spontaneous recognition of nature
as being fundamentally "a good gift."[98]

It would seem that, to the contrary, any hopeful political project
requires a sense that we inhabit a cosmos in which the realization of
good and of justice might be at least a possibility. But that means, first

97. Agamben, *Temps qui reste*, 174, makes this point well. See Rom. 13:1–7; 2 Thess. 2:7.
The latter passage suggests that all *nomos* is a temporary *katechon* restraining evil until the
eschaton—this power to restrain, though, remains for Paul thoroughly ambiguous and literally
demonic, as Carl Schmitt's reading of this passage fails to recognize.
98. See F. W. J. Schelling, *Clara, or, on Nature's Connection to the Spirit World*, trans. Fiona
Steinkamp (Albany: State University of New York Press, 2002).

of all, that we must consider the good to be more than a human illusion but rather in some sense an ultimate reality, ontologically subsisting before evil, both human and natural, including the natural negativities of death and suffering. It means also that we must believe, beyond gnosticism, that the good is in some measure able to be embodied within human time, and this means that human life must somehow bear within its biological spark (which itself must logically be prior to death, which is sheer negation) also a pneumatic spark that links it to undying goodness and justice and that enables it in the end entirely to root out those base passions "of the flesh" (according to Paul) that are concerned only with survival, self-satisfaction, erotic possession of, and military triumph over, others.

Against Heidegger, the ontic must be seen as participating in ontological plenitude, just as every act of signification by the living linguistic animal must be seen as participating in an infinite reserve of the signified as well as of the signifier. While it might seem more rationally plausible to project the concentration camp to the infinite, if we were rather to assume that the undying hope of our living, psychically infused animal bodies offers a more primary clue to the nature of being, then we might rather suggest that the investment, by hope, in the counterfactual of resurrection alone permits us to imagine through hope (although this imagining remains to be done) a politics that does not inevitably support regimes of abjection. In this way, for such an imagination, the ontological priority of good implies also the ontological priority of life and the imperative to live, ethically and politically, out of this priority and not within the damage-limitation exercise of legality.

Thus it would be our ethical imperative to associate well that would of itself obscurely call forth the image of an eternal, resurrected humanity. Only the arrival of such a reality in time, however, provides the event that, for *pistis*, confirms the apocalyptic truth of such a restored ontology of undying life and thereby renders possible the project of human social justice.

2

Paul and the Truth Event

Slavoj Žižek

The Truth Event . . .

The axis of Badiou's theoretical edifice is—as the title of his main work indicates—the gap between Being and Event.[1] "Being" stands for the positive ontological order accessible to knowledge, for the infinite multitude of what "presents itself" in our experience, categorized in genuses and species in accordance with its properties. According to Badiou, the only proper science of Being-as-Being is mathematics—his first paradoxical conclusion is thus to insist on the gap that separates philosophy from ontology. Ontology is mathematical science, not philosophy, which involves a different dimension. Badiou provides an elaborated analysis of Being. At the bottom, as it were, is the presentation of the pure Multiple, the not-yet-symbolically-structured multitude of experience, that which is given; this multitude is not a multitude of "Ones," since counting has not yet taken place. Badiou calls any particular consistent multitude (French society, modern art, etc.) a "situation"; a situation

This chapter was originally published in a slightly altered form as "The Politics of Truth, or, Alain Badiou as a Reader of St Paul," in *The Ticklish Subject: The Absent Centre of Political Ontology* (London: Verso, 1999), 127–70.

1. Alain Badiou, *L'être et l'événement* (Paris: Éditions du Seuil, 1988).

is structured, and it is its structure that allows us to "count [the situation] as One." Here, however, the first cracks in the ontological edifice of Being already appear: for us to "count [the situation] as One," the "reduplication" proper to the symbolization (symbolic inscription) of a situation must be at work; that is, in order for a situation to be "counted as One," its structure must always already be a metastructure that designates it as one (i.e., the signified structure of the situation must be redoubled in the symbolic network of signifiers). When a situation is thus "counted as One," identified by its symbolic structure, we have the "state of situation." Here Badiou is playing on the ambiguity of the term "state": "state of things" as well as "state" in the political sense—there is no "state of society" without a "state" in which the structure of society is re-presented/redoubled.

This symbolic *reduplicatio* already involves the minimal dialectic of Void and excess. The pure Multiple of Being is not yet a multitude of Ones since, as we have just seen, to have One, the pure Multiple must be "counted as One"; from the standpoint of the state of a situation, the preceding Multiple can only appear as *nothing*, so nothing is the "proper name of Being as Being" prior to its symbolization. The Void is the central category of ontology from Democritus's atomism onward: "atoms" are nothing but configurations of the Void. The excess correlative to this Void takes two forms. On the one hand, each state of things involves at least one excessive element that, although it clearly belongs to the situation, is not "counted" by it, properly included in it (the "nonintegrated" rabble in a social situation, etc.): this element is presented, but not re-presented. On the other hand, there is the excess of re-presentation over presentation: the agency that brings about the passage from situation to its state (state in society) is always in excess with regard to what it structures. State power is necessarily "excessive"; it never simply and transparently re-presents society (the impossible liberal dream of state reduced to the service of civil society) but acts as a violent intervention in what it re-presents.

This, then, is the structure of Being. From time to time, however, in a wholly contingent, unpredictable way, out of the reach of knowledge of Being, an Event takes place that belongs to a wholly different dimension—that, precisely, of non-Being. Let us take French society in the late eighteenth century: the state of society, its strata, its economic, political, and ideological conflicts, and so on, are accessible to knowledge. However, no amount of knowledge will enable us to predict or account for the properly unaccountable Event called the "French Revolution." In this precise sense, the Event emerges ex nihilo: if it cannot be accounted for in terms of the situation, this does not mean that it is simply an intervention from outside or beyond—it attaches itself precisely to the Void of every situation, to its inherent inconsistency and/or its excess. The Event is the truth of the situation that makes visible/legible what the "official" situation had to "repress," but it is also always localized—that is to say, the truth is always the truth *of* a specific situation. The French Revolution, for example, is the Event that makes visible/legible the excesses and inconsistencies, the "lie," of the ancien régime, and it is the truth *of* the ancien régime situation, localized, attached to it. An Event thus involves its own series of determinations: the Event itself; its naming (the designation of "French Revolution" is not an objective categorizing but part of the Event itself, the way its followers perceived and symbolized their activity); its ultimate goal (the society of fully realized emancipation, of freedom-equality-fraternity); its "operator" (the political movements struggling for the revolution); and last, its "subject" (the agent who, on behalf of the truth-Event, intervenes in the historical Multiple of the situation and discerns and identifies in it signs or effects of the Event). What defines the subject is his or her *fidelity* to the Event: the subject comes *after* the Event and persists in discerning its traces within his or her situation.

The subject is thus for Badiou a finite contingent emergence. Not only is truth not "subjective" in this sense of being subordinated to one's whims, but the subject oneself "serves the truth" that transcends him or her; one is never fully adequate to the infinite order of truth, since the subject always has to operate within a finite Multiple of a situation in which he or she discerns the signs of truth. To make this crucial point clear, let us take the example of the Christian religion (which perhaps provides *the* example of a truth-Event): the Event is Christ's Incarnation and death; its ultimate goal is the last judgment, the final redemption; its "operator" in the Multiple of the historical situation is the church; its "subject" is the corpus of believers who intervene in their situation on behalf of the truth-Event, searching in it for signs of God. (Or, to take the example of love: when I fall passionately in love, I become "subjectivized" by remaining faithful to this Event and following it in my life.)

Today, however, when even the most radical intellectual succumbs to the compulsion to distance himself from Communism, it seems more appropriate to reassert the October Revolution as an Event of truth defined against the opportunistic leftist "fools" and conservative "knaves." The October Revolution also allows us to clearly identify three ways of betraying the truth-Event: simple disavowal, the attempt to follow old patterns as if nothing had happened, just a minor disturbance (the reaction of "utilitarian" liberal democracy); false imitation of the Event of truth (the Fascist staging of the conservative revolution as a pseudo-Event); and a direct "ontologization" of the Event of truth, its reduction to a new positive order of Being (Stalinism).[2] Here one can readily grasp the gap that separates Badiou from deconstructionist fictionalism: his radical opposition to the notion of a "multitude of truths" (or, rather, "truth-effects"). Truth is contingent; it hinges on a concrete historical situation; it is the truth *of* this situation, but in every concrete and contingent historical situation there is *one and only one* truth that, once articulated, spoken out, functions as the index of itself and of the falsity of the field subverted by it.

When Badiou speaks of "this symptomal torsion of being that is a truth in the always-total texture of knowledges,"[3] every term has its weight. The texture of knowledge is, by definition, always total—that is, for knowledge of Being, there is no excess; excess and lack of a situation are visible only from the standpoint of the Event, not from the standpoint of the knowing servants of the state. From within this standpoint, of course, one sees "problems," but they are automatically reduced to "local," marginal difficulties, to contingent errors—what truth does is to reveal that (what knowledge misperceives as) marginal malfunctionings and points of failure are a structural necessity. Crucial for the Event is thus the elevation of an empirical obstacle into a transcendental limitation. With regard to the ancien régime, what the truth-Event reveals is how injustices are not marginal malfunctionings but pertain to the very structure of the system, which is in its essence, as such, "corrupt." Such an entity—which, misperceived by the system as a local "abnormality," effectively condenses the global "abnormality" of the system as such, in its entirety—is what in the Freudo-Marxian tradition is called the *symptom*: in psychoanalysis, lapses, dreams, compulsive formations and acts, and so on are "symptomal torsions" that

2. To make this logic clear, let us mention another of Badiou's examples of truth-Event: the atonal revolution in music accomplished by the Second Viennese School (Schoenberg, Berg, Webern). Here also we have three ways of betraying this Event of truth: the traditionalists' dismissal of the atonal revolution as an empty formal experiment, which allows them to continue to compose in the old ways, as if nothing had happened; the pseudo-modernist imitation of atonality; and the tendency to change atonal music into a new positive tradition.

3. Badiou, *L'être et l'événement*, 25.

make accessible the subject's truth, inaccessible to knowledge, which sees them as mere malfunctionings; in Marxism, economic crisis is such a "symptomal torsion."

Here Badiou is clearly and radically opposed to the postmodern anti-Platonic thrust, whose basic dogma is that the era when it was still possible to base a political movement on a direct reference to some eternal metaphysical or transcendental truth is definitely over. The experience of our century proves that such a reference to some metaphysical a priori can lead only to catastrophic "totalitarian" social consequences. For this reason, the only solution is to accept that we live in a new era deprived of metaphysical certainties, in an era of contingency and conjectures, in a "risk society" in which politics is a matter of *phronēsis*, of strategic judgments and dialogue, not of applying fundamental cognitive insights. What Badiou is aiming at, against this postmodern *doxa*, is precisely the resuscitation of the *politics of (universal) truth* in today's conditions of global contingency. Thus Badiou rehabilitates, in the modern conditions of multiplicity and contingency, not only philosophy but the properly *meta-physical* dimension: the infinite truth is "eternal" and *meta-* with regard to the temporal process of Being; it is a flash of another dimension transcending the positivity of Being.

The latest version of the disavowal of truth is provided by the New Age opposition of the *hubris* of so-called Cartesian subjectivity and its mechanistic dominating attitude toward nature. According to the New Age cliché, the original sin of modern Western civilization (as, indeed, of the Judeo-Christian tradition) is humanity's hubris, human beings' arrogant assumption that they occupy the central place in the universe and/or that they are endowed with the divine right to dominate all other beings and exploit them for their profit. This hubris, which disturbs the rightful balance of cosmic powers, sooner or later forces nature to reestablish that balance: today's ecological, social-psychic crisis is interpreted as the universe's justified answer to humanity's presumption. Our only solution thus lies in the shift of the global paradigm; in adopting the new holistic attitude we will humbly assume our constrained place in the global order of Being.

In contrast to this cliché, one should assert the excess of subjectivity (what Hegel called the "night of the world") as the only hope of redemption: true evil lies not in the excess of subjectivity as such, but in its "ontologization," in its reinscription into some global cosmic framework. Already in de Sade, excessive cruelty is ontologically "covered" by the order of nature as the "Supreme Being of Evil"; both Nazism and Stalinism involved the reference to some global order of Being (in the case of Stalinism, the dialectical organization of the movement of matter).

True arrogance is thus the very opposite of the acceptance of the hubris of subjectivity: it lies in false humility—that is to say, it emerges when the subject pretends to speak and act on behalf of the global cosmic order, posing as its humble instrument. In contrast to this false humility, the entire Western stance was antiglobal: not only does Christianity involve reference to a higher truth that cuts into and disturbs the old pagan order of the cosmos expressed in profound wisdoms; even Plato's idealism itself can be qualified as the first clear elaboration of the idea that the global cosmic "chain of Being" is not "all there is," that there is another order (of ideas) that suspends the validity of the order of Being.

One of Badiou's great theses is that the pure Multiple lacks the dignity of the proper object of thought: from Stalin to Derrida, philosophical common sense has always insisted on infinite complexity (everything is interconnected, reality is so complex that it is accessible to us only in approximations, etc.). Badiou implicitly condemns deconstructionism itself as the latest version of this commonsense motif of infinite complexity. Among the advocates of "antiessentialist" postmodern identity politics, for example, one often encounters the insistence that there is no "woman in general"; there are only white middle-class women, black single mothers, lesbians, and so on. One should reject such "insights" as banalities unworthy of being objects of thought. The problem of philosophical thought lies precisely in how the universality of "woman" emerges out of this endless multitude. Thus one can also rehabilitate the Hegelian difference between bad (spurious) and proper infinity: the first refers to commonsense infinite complexity; the second concerns the infinity of an Event, which precisely transcends the "infinite complexity" of its context. In exactly the same way one can distinguish between historicism and historicity proper: historicism refers to the set of economic, political, cultural, and other circumstances whose complex interaction allows us to account for the Event to be explained, while historicity proper involves the specific temporality of the Event and its aftermath, the span between the Event and its final end (between Christ's death and the last judgment, between revolution and Communism, between falling in love and the accomplished bliss of living together).

Perhaps the gap separating Badiou from the standard postmodern deconstructionist political theorists is ultimately created by the fact that the latter remain within the confines of the pessimistic wisdom of the failed encounter. Is not the ultimate deconstructionist lesson that every enthusiastic encounter with the real thing, every pathetic identification of a positive empirical Event with it, is a delusive semblance sustained by the short circuit between a contingent positive element and the preceding universal Void? In it, we momentarily succumb to the illusion that the promise of impossible fullness is actually realized—that, to paraphrase Derrida, democracy is no longer merely *à venir* but has actually arrived. From this, deconstructionists draw the conclusion that the principal ethico-political duty is to maintain the gap between the Void of the central impossibility and every positive content giving body to it—that is, never fully to succumb to the enthusiasm of hasty identification of a positive Event with the redemptive promise that is always "to come." In this deconstructionist stance, admiration for the revolution in its utopian enthusiastic aspect goes hand in hand with the conservative melancholic insight that enthusiasm inevitably turns into its opposite, into the worst terror, the moment we endeavor to transpose it into the positive structuring principle of social reality.

It may seem that Badiou remains within this framework: does he not also warn us against the *désastre* of the revolutionary temptation to confound the truth-Event with the order of Being, of the attempt to "ontologize" truth into the ontological principle of the order of Being? However, things are more complex: Badiou's position is that although the universal order has the status of a semblance, from time to time, in a contingent and unpredictable way, a "miracle" can happen in the guise of a truth-Event that deservedly shames a postmodernist skeptic. What he has in mind is a very precise political experience. For example, in France, during the first Mitterrand government in the early 1980s, all well-meaning leftists were skeptical about Minister of Justice Rover Badinter's intention to abolish the death penalty and introduce other progressive reforms of the penal code. Their stance was, "Yes, of course we support him; but is the situation yet ripe for it? Will the people, terrified by the rising crime rate, be willing to swallow it? Isn't this a case of idealistic obstinacy that can only weaken our government, and do us more harm than good?" Badinter simply ignored the catastrophic predictions of the opinion polls and persisted—with the surprising result that, all of a sudden, the majority of the people changed their minds and started to support him.

A similar event happened in Italy in the mid-1970s, when there was a referendum on divorce. In private, the Left, even the Communists—who, of course, supported the right to divorce—were skeptical about the outcome, fearing that the majority of people were not yet mature enough, that they would be frightened by the intense Catholic propaganda depicting abandoned children and mothers, and so on. To the great surprise of everyone, however, the referendum was a great setback for the church and the Right, since a considerable majority of 60 percent voted for the right to divorce. Events like this do occur in politics, and they are authentic Events belying shameful "postideological realism": they are not momentary enthusiastic outbursts occasionally disturbing the usual depressive/conformist/utilitarian run of things, only to be followed by an inexorable sobering disillusionment "the morning after"; on the contrary, they are the moment of truth in the overall structure of deception and lure. The fundamental lesson of postmodernist politics is that *there is no Event*, that "nothing really happens," that the truth-Event is a passing, illusory short circuit, a false identification to be dispelled sooner or later by the reassertion of difference or, at best, the fleeting promise of the redemption to come, toward which we have to maintain a proper distance in order to avoid catastrophic "totalitarian" consequences; against this structural skepticism, Badiou is fully justified in insisting that—to use the term with its full theological weight—*miracles do happen.*[4]

. . . and Its Undecidability

We can now see the sense in which the truth-Event is "undecidable": it is undecidable from the standpoint of the system, of the ontological "state of things." An Event is thus circular in the sense that its identification is possible only from the standpoint of what Badiou calls "an *interpreting intervention*"[5]—if, that is, one speaks from a subjectively engaged position, or, to put it more formally, if one includes in the designated situation the act of naming itself. The chaotic events in France at the end

4. In theory, perhaps that main indication of this suspension of Event is the notion and practice of "cultural studies" as the predominant name for all-encompassing approach to socio-symbolic products: the basic feature of cultural studies is that they are no longer able or ready to confront religious, scientific, or philosophical works in terms of their inherent truth but reduce them to a product of historical circumstances, to an object of anthropological-psychoanalytic interpretation.

5. Badiou, *L'être et l'événement*, 202.

of the eighteenth century can be identified as the "French Revolution" only for those who accept the "wager" that such an Event exists. Badiou formally defines *intervention* as "every procedure by means of which a multiple is recognized as an event"[6]—so "it will remain forever doubtful if there was an event at all, except for the intervenor [*l'intervenant*] who decided that he belonged to the situation."[7] Fidelity to the Event designates the continuous effort of traversing the field of knowledge from the standpoint of Event, intervening in it and searching for the signs of truth. Along these lines, Badiou also interprets the Pauline triad of faith, hope, and love: faith is faith in the Event (the belief that the Event—Christ's rising from the dead—really took place); hope is the hope that the final reconciliation announced by the Event (the last judgment) will actually occur; love is the patient struggle for this to happen, that is, the long and arduous work to assert one's fidelity to the Event.

Badiou calls the language that endeavors to name the truth-Event the "subject-language." This language is meaningless from the standpoint of knowledge, which judges propositions with regard to their referent within the domain of positive Being (or with regard to the proper functioning of speech within the established symbolic order): when the subject-language speaks of Christian redemption, revolutionary emancipation, love, and so on, knowledge dismisses all this as empty phrases lacking any proper referent ("political-messianic jargon," "poetic hermeticism," etc.). Let us imagine a person in love describing the features of his beloved to his friend. The friend, who is not in love with the same person, will simply find this enthusiastic description meaningless; he will not get "the point" of it. In short, subject-language involves the logic of the shibboleth, of a difference that is visible only from within, not from without. This, however, in no way means that the subject-language involves another, "deeper" reference to a hidden true content: it is, rather, that the subject-language "derails" or "unsettles" the standard use of language with its established meanings and leaves the reference "empty"—with the "wager" that this void will be filled when the goal is reached, when truth actualizes itself as a new situation (God's kingdom on earth, the emancipated society, etc.). The naming of the truth-Event is "empty" precisely insofar as it refers to the fullness yet to come.

6. Ibid., 224.
7. Ibid., 29.

The undecidability of the Event thus means that an Event does not possess any ontological guarantee. It cannot be reduced to (or deduced, generated from) a (previous) situation; it emerges "out of nothing" (the Nothing that was the ontological truth of this previous situation). Thus there is no neutral gaze of knowledge that can discern the Event in its effects: a decision is always already here—that is, one can discern the signs of an Event in the situation only from a previous decision for truth, just as in Jansenist theology, in which divine miracles are legible as such only to those who have already decided for faith. A neutral historicist gaze will never see in the French Revolution a series of traces of the Event called the "French Revolution" but will see merely a multitude of occurrences caught in the network of social determinations; to an external gaze, love is merely a succession of psychic and physiological states. (Perhaps this was the negative achievement that brought such fame to François Furet. Did not his main impact derive from his de-eventualization of the French Revolution, in adopting an external perspective toward it and turning it into a succession of complex specific historical facts?) The engaged observer perceives positive historical occurrences as parts of the Event of the French Revolution only to the extent that he observes them from the unique engaged standpoint of revolution—as Badiou puts it, an Event is self-referential in that *it includes its own designation*. The symbolic designation "French Revolution" is part of the designated content itself, since, if we subtract this designation, the described content turns into a multitude of positive occurrences available to knowledge. In this precise sense, an Event involves subjectivity: the engaged "subject perspective" on the Event is part of the Event itself.[8]

The difference between veracity (the accuracy and adequacy of knowledge) and truth is crucial here. Let us take the Marxist thesis that all history is the history of class struggle: this thesis already presupposes engaged subjectivity—that is to say, only from this slant does the whole history appear as such; only from this "interested" standpoint can one discern traces of the class struggle in the entire social edifice, up to the products of the highest culture. The answer to the obvious counter-argument (this very fact proves that we are dealing with a distorted view, not with the true state of things) is that it is the allegedly "objective," "impartial" gaze that is not in fact neutral but already partial—that is, the gaze of the winners, of the ruling classes. (No wonder the motto

8. Up to a point, one can also say that knowledge is constative while truth is performative.

of right-wing historical revisionists is "Let's approach the topic of the Holocaust in a cool, objective way; let's put it in its context; let's inspect the facts. . . .") A theorist of the Communist Revolution is not someone who, after establishing by means of objective study that the future belongs to the working class, decides to take its side and to bet on the winner: the engaged view permeates his theory from the very onset.

Within the Marxist tradition, this notion of partiality as not only not an obstacle to but a positive condition of truth was most clearly articulated by Georg Lukács in his early work *History and Class Consciousness*, and in a more directly messianic, protoreligious mode by Walter Benjamin in "Theses on the Philosophy of History": "truth" emerges when a victim, from his or her present catastrophic position, gains sudden insight into the entire past as a series of catastrophes that led to his or her current predicament. So when we read a text on truth, we should be careful not to confuse that level of knowledge with the level of truth. For example, although Marx himself normally used "proletariat" as synonymous with "the working class," one can nonetheless discern in his work a clear tendency to conceive "the working class" as a descriptive term belonging to the domain of knowledge (the object of "neutral" sociological study, a social stratum subdivided into components, etc.), whereas "proletariat" designates the operator of truth, that is, the engaged agent of the revolutionary struggle.

Furthermore, the status of the pure Multiple and its Void is also undecidable and purely "intermediary": we never encounter it "now," since it is always recognized as such retroactively, through the act of decision that dissolves it—that is, by means of which we already pass over it. For example, Nazism as a pseudo-Event conceives of itself as the decision for social harmony and order against the chaos of modern liberal-Jewish-class-warfare society. However, modern society never perceives itself in the first person as fundamentally "chaotic"; it perceives "chaos" (or "disorder" or "degeneration") as a limited, contingent deadlock, a temporary crisis—modern society appears as fundamentally "chaotic" only from the standpoint of the decision for order, that is, once the decision *is already made*. One should therefore resist the retroactive illusion according to which decision *follows* the insight into the open undecidability of the situation: it is only the decision itself that reveals the previous state as "undecidable." Prior to decision, we inhabit a situation that is enclosed in its horizon. From within this horizon, the Void constitutive of this situation is by definition invisible; that is to say, undecidability is reduced to—and appears as—a marginal disturbance of the global system. After the decision, undecidability is over, since we inhabit the new domain of truth. The gesture that closes/decides the situation (again) absolutely coincides with the gesture that (retroactively) opens it up.

The Event is thus the Void of an invisible line separating one closure from another: prior to it, the situation was closed; that is, from within its horizon, (what will become) the Event necessarily appears as *skandalon*, as an undesirable, chaotic intrusion that has no place in the state of the situation (or, to put it in mathematical terms, that is "supernumerary"); once the Event takes place and is assumed as such, the very previous situation appears as undecidable chaos. For an established political order, the revolutionary turmoil that threatens to overthrow it is a chaotic disloca- tion, while from the viewpoint of the revolution, "ancien régime" itself is a name for disorder, for an impenetrable and ultimately "irrational" despotism. Here Badiou is clearly opposed to the Derridean ethics of openness to the Event in its unpredictable alterity. Such an emphasis on unpredictable alterity as the ultimate horizon remains within the confines of a situation and serves only to defer or block the decision—it involves us in the "postmodernist" indefinite oscillation of "how do we know this truly is the Event and not just another semblance of the Event?"

How *are* we to draw a demarcation line between a true Event and its semblance? Is not Badiou compelled to rely here on a "metaphysical" op- position between truth and its semblance? Again, the answer involves the way an event relates to the situation whose truth it articulates: Nazism was a pseudo-Event and the October Revolution was an authentic Event because only the latter related to the very foundations of the situation of capitalist order, effectively undermining those foundations, in contrast to Nazism, which staged a pseudo-Event precisely in order to *save* the capitalist order. The Nazi strategy was, essentially, "to change things so that, at their most fundamental, they can remain the same."

We all remember the famous scene from Bob Fosse's *Cabaret*, which takes place in the early 1930s in a small country inn near Berlin: a boy (in Nazi uniform, as we learn in the course of the song) starts to sing a sorrowful elegiac song about the fatherland, which should give Germans a sign that tomorrow belongs to them, and so on; the crowd gradually joins him, and everyone, including a group of decadent night- lifers from Berlin, is impressed by its emotional impact. This scene is often evoked by pseudointellectuals as the moment when they "finally grasped what Nazism was about, how it worked." One is tempted to add that they are right but for the wrong reasons: it is not the pathos of patriotic engagement *as such* that is "Fascist." What actually prepares the ground for Fascism is the very liberal suspicion and denunciation of every form of unconditional engagement, of devotion to a cause, as potentially "totalitarian" fanaticism—that is to say, the problem lies in the very complicity of the atmosphere of incapacitating cynical decadent self-enjoyment with the Fascist Event, with the decision that purports to (re)introduce order into chaos. In other words, what is false about the Nazi ideological machine is not the rhetoric of decisions as such (of the Event that puts an end to decadent impotence, etc.), but—on the contrary—the fact that the Nazi "Event" is aestheticized theater, a faked event effectively unable to put an end to the decadent crippling impasse. It is in this precise sense that the common reaction to the Nazi song from *Cabaret* is right for the wrong reasons: what it fails to perceive is how our former cynical pleasure in decadent cabaret songs about money and sexual promiscuity created the background that made us susceptible to the impact of the Nazi song.

So how are an Event and its naming related? Badiou rejects Kant's reading of the Event of the French Revolution, the reading that locates the crucial effect of the revolution in the sublime feeling of enthusiasm that the revolutionary events in Paris set in motion in passive observers across Europe, not directly involved in the event itself, and then opposes this sublime effect (the assertion of our belief in the progress of human reason and freedom) to the grim reality of the revolution itself. (Kant readily concedes that horrible things took place in France; the revolution often served as the catalyst for the outburst of the lowest destructive passions of the wild mob.) Badiou sarcastically remarks that such an aestheticization of the revolution, admired from a safe distance by passive observers, goes hand in hand with the utmost loathing for the actual revolutionaries themselves. (Do we not again encounter here the tension between the sublime and the monstrous [*das Ungeheure*]? What appears from a proper distance to be the sublime cause of enthusiasm turns into the figure of monstrous evil once we approach it too closely and get directly involved in it.)

Against this Kantian celebration of the sublime effect on passive observers, Badiou insists on the immanence of the truth-Event: the truth-Event is truth in itself for its agents themselves, not for external observers. On a first approach, it may appear that Kant's position is more "Lacanian" here. Is not the truth of an Event a priori decentered with regard to the Event itself? Does it not depend on the mode of its inscription into the big Other (personified here by enlightened public opinion), which is always a priori deferred? Is not what is properly unthinkable precisely a truth that would directly know itself as truth? Is not the delay of comprehension constitutive? (Therein lies the Hegelian materialist lesson: the Owl of Minerva flies only at dusk.) Furthermore, if a truth-Event is radically immanent, how are we to distinguish truth from its simulacrum? Is it not only the reference to the decentered big Other that enables us to draw this distinction?

Badiou nonetheless provides a precise criterion for this distinction in the way an Event relates to its conditions, to the "situation" out of which it arises: a true Event emerges out of the "Void" of the situation; it is attached to its *élément surnuméraire*, to the symptomatic element that has no proper place in the situation, although it belongs to it, while the simulacrum of an Event disavows the symptom. For this reason, the Leninist October Revolution remains an Event, since it relates to the "class struggle" as the symptomatic torsion of its situation, while the Nazi movement is a simulacrum, a disavowal of the trauma of class struggle. The difference lies not in the inherent qualities of the Event itself, but in its place—in the way it relates to the situation out of which it emerged. As for the external gaze that bears witness to the truth of the Event, this gaze is able to discern that truth only insofar as it is the gaze of the individuals who are already engaged on its behalf. There is no neutral enlightened public opinion to be impressed by the Event, since truth is discernable only for the potential members of the new community of "believers," for their engaged gaze.

In this way, we can paradoxically retain both distance *and* engagement. In the case of Christianity, the Event (crucifixion) becomes a truth-Event "after the fact," that is, when it leads to the constitution of the group of believers, of the engaged community held together by fidelity to the Event. There is thus a difference between an Event and its naming: an Event is the traumatic encounter with the real (Christ's death, the historic shock of revolution, etc.), while its naming is the inscription of the Event into the language (Christian doctrine, revolutionary consciousness, etc.). In Lacanese, an Event is *objet petit a*, while naming is the new signifier that establishes what Rimbaud calls the new order, the new readability of the situation based on decision. (In the Marxist revolutionary perspective, the entire prior history becomes a history of class struggle, of defeated emancipatory striving.)

Truth and Ideology

From this brief description one can already get a presentiment of what one is tempted to call, in all naïveté, the intuitive power of Badiou's notion of the subject: it effectively describes the experience each person has when he or she is subjectively fully engaged in some cause that is "his or her own." In those precious moments, am I not "fully a subject"? But does not this very feature make it *ideological*? That is to say, the first thing that strikes the eye of anyone who is versed in the history of French Marxism is how Badiou's notion of the truth-Event is uncannily close to Althusser's notion of ideological interpellation. Furthermore, is it not significant that Badiou's ultimate example of the Event is *religion* (Christianity from St. Paul to Pascal) as the prototype of *ideology* and that this event, precisely, does *not* fit any of the four *génériques* of the event he enumerates (that is, love, art, science, and politics)?[9]

So perhaps if we take Badiou's thought itself as a "situation" of Being, subdivided into four *génériques*, (Christian) religion itself is his "symptomal torsion," the element that belongs to the domain of truth without being one of its acknowledged parts or subspecies. This seems to indicate that the truth-Event consists in the elementary ideological gesture of interpellating individuals (parts of a "situation" of Being) into subjects (bearers/followers of truth). One is tempted to go even a step further: the paradigmatic example of the truth-Event is not only religion in general but, specifically, *Christian* religion centered on the Event of Christ's arrival and death. (As Kierkegaard had already pointed out, Christianity inverts the standard of metaphysical relationship between eternity and time: in a way, eternity itself hinges on the temporal Event of Christ.) So perhaps Badiou can also be read as the last great author in the French tradition of Catholic dogmaticists from Pascal and Malebranche on. (We need only to recall that two of his key references are Pascal and Claudel.) For years the parallel between revolutionary Marxism and messianic Christianity was a common topic among liberal critics like Bertrand Russell, who dismissed Marxism as a secularized version of messianic religious ideology; Badiou, in contrast (following a line from the later Engels to Fredric Jameson), fully endorses this homology.

This reading is further confirmed by Badiou's passionate defense of St. Paul as the one who articulated the Christian truth-Event—Christ's

9. As Badiou perspicaciously notes, these four domains of the truth-Event are today, in public discourse, more and more replaced by their fake doubles: we speak of "culture" instead of art, of "administration" instead of politics, of "sex" instead of love, of "know-how" or "wisdom" instead of science. Art is reduced to an expression/articulation of historically specific culture and love to an ideologically dated form of sexuality; science is dismissed as a Western, falsely universalized form of practical knowledge on an equal footing with forms of pre-science wisdom; and politics (with all the passion or struggle that this notion involves) is reduced to an immature ideological version or forerunner of the art of social *gestion*.

resurrection—as the "universal singular" (a singular event that interpellates individuals into subjects universally, irrespective of their race, sex, social class, and so on) and the conditions of the followers' fidelity to it.[10] Of course, here Badiou is well aware that today, in our era of modern science, one can no longer accept the fable of the miracle of resurrection as the form of the truth-Event. Although the truth-Event does designate the occurrence of something that, from within the horizon of the predominant order of knowledge, appears impossible (think of the laughter with which the Greek philosophers greeted St. Paul's assertion of Christ's resurrection on his visit to Athens), today any location of the truth-Event at the level of supernatural miracles necessarily entails regression into obscurantism, since the event of science is irreducible and cannot be undone. Today one can accept as the truth-Event, as the intrusion of the traumatic real that shatters the predominant symbolic texture, only occurrences that take place in a universe compatible with scientific knowledge, even if they move at its borders and question its presuppositions—the "sites" of the Event today are scientific discovery itself, the political act, artistic invention, the psychoanalytic confrontation with love, among others.

That is the problem with Graham Greene's drama *The Potting Shed*, which endeavors to resuscitate the Christian version of the shattering impact of the impossible real. The life of the family of a great positivist philosopher who dedicated his whole effort to fighting religious superstitions is thoroughly shattered by an unexpected miracle: his son, the object of the philosopher's greatest love, is mortally ill and already proclaimed dead when, miraculously, he is brought back to life by means of what, evidently, cannot be anything but a direct intervention by divine grace. The story is told in retrospect, from the standpoint of a family friend who, after the philosopher's death, writes his biography and is puzzled by an enigma in the latter's life: Why, a couple of years before his death, did the philosopher suddenly stop writing? Why did he lose his will to live, as if his life was suddenly deprived of meaning, and enter a period of resignation, passively awaiting his death? Interviewing the surviving family members, he soon discovers that there is a dark family secret no one wants to talk about, until, finally, one of the family members breaks down and confesses to him that the shattering secret is the miraculous resuscitation of the philosopher's son, which rendered his

10. See Alain Badiou, *Saint Paul: La fondation de l'universalisme* (Paris: Presses Universitaires de France, 1997).

entire theoretical work, his lifelong engagement, meaningless. Intriguing as it is, such a story cannot effectively engage us today.

Apropos of St. Paul, Badiou tackles the problem of locating his position with regard to the four *génériques* that generate effective truths (science, politics, art, love)—that is, with regard to the fact that (today, at least) Christianity, based on a fabulous event of resurrection, can be counted not as an effective truth-Event but merely as its semblance. His proposed solution is that St. Paul is the antiphilosophical *theoretician of the formal conditions of the truth-procedure*; what he provides is the first detailed articulation of how fidelity to a truth-Event operates in its universal dimension. The excessive, *surnuméraire* real of a truth-Event ("resurrection") that emerges by grace (i.e., cannot be accounted for in the terms of the constituents of the given situation) sets in motion, in the subjects who recognize themselves in its call, the militant "work of love," that is, the struggle to disseminate, with persistent fidelity, this truth in its universal scope, as concerning everyone. So although St. Paul's particular message is no longer operative to us, the very terms in which he formulates the operative mode of the Christian religion do possess a universal scope as relevant for every truth-Event: every truth-Event leads to a kind of "resurrection"—through fidelity to it and a labor of love on its behalf, one enters another dimension irreducible to mere *service des biens*, to the smooth-running affairs in the domain of Being, the domain of immortality, of life unencumbered by death. Nonetheless, the problem remains of how it was possible for the first and still most pertinent description of the mode of operation of the fidelity to a truth-Event to occur apropos of a truth-Event that is a mere semblance, not an actual truth.

From a Hegelian standpoint there is a deep necessity in this, confirmed by the fact that in our century the philosopher who provided the definitive description of an authentic political *act* (Heidegger in *Being and Time*) was seduced by a political act that was undoubtedly a fake, not an actual truth-Event (Nazism). So it is as if, if one is to express the formal structure of fidelity to the truth-Event, one had to do it apropos of an Event that is merely its own semblance. Perhaps the lesson of all this is more radical than it appears: what if what Badiou calls the truth-Event *is*, at its most radical, a purely formal act of decision, not only not based on actual truth but ultimately *indifferent* to the precise status (actual or fictitious) of the truth-Event it refers to? What if we are dealing here with an inherent key component of the truth-Event—what if the true fidelity to the Event is "dogmatic" in the precise sense of unconditional faith, of an attitude that does not ask for good reasons and that, for that very reason, cannot be refuted by any "argumentation"?

So back to our main line of argument: Badiou defines as "generic" the Multiple within a situation that has no particular properties, reference to which would enable us to classify it as its subspecies: the "generic" Multiple belongs to the situation but is not properly included in it as its subspecies (the "rabble" in Hegel's philosophy of law, for example). A multiple element/part of the situation that does not fit into it, that sticks out, is generic precisely insofar as it directly gives body to the being of the situation as such. It subverts the situation by directly embodying its universality. And, with regard to Badiou's own classification of generic procedures in four species (politics, art, science, love), does not religious ideology occupy precisely this generic place? It is none of them, yet precisely as such it gives body to the generic as such.[11]

Is not this identity of the truth-Event and ideology further confirmed by *futur antérieur* as the specific temporality of generic procedures? Starting from the naming of the Event (Christ's death, revolution), generic procedure searches for its signs in the Multitude with a view to the final goal that will bring full plenitude (the last judgment, Communism, or, in Mallarmé, *le Livre*). Generic procedures thus involve a temporal loop: fidelity to the Event enables them to judge the historic Multiple from the standpoint of plenitude to come, but the arrival of this plenitude already involves the subjective act of decision—or, in Pascalian, the "wager" on it. Are we thus not close to what Laclau describes as hegemony? Let us take the democratic-egalitarian political Event: reference to the Democratic Revolution enables us to read history as a continuous democratic struggle aiming at total emancipation; the present situation is experienced as fundamentally "dislocated," "out of joint" (the corruption of the ancien régime, class society, fallen terrestrial life) with regard to the promise of a redeemed future. For the language-subject, "now" is always a time of antagonism, split between the corrupt "state of things" and the promise of truth.

So, again, is not Badiou's notion of the truth-Event uncannily close to Althusser's notion of (ideological) interpellation? Isn't the process Badiou is describing that of an individual interpellated into a subject

11. Of course, Badiou simultaneously mobilizes the association of "generic" with "generating": it is this "generic" element that enables us to "generate" propositions of the subject-language in which truth resonates.

by a cause? (Significantly, in order to describe the formal structure of fidelity to the truth-Event, he uses the same example as Althusser in his description of the process of interpellation.) Is not the circular relationship between the Event and the subject (the subject serves the Event in his or her fidelity, but the Event itself is visible as such only to an already engaged subject) the very circle of ideology? Prior to constraining the notion of the subject to ideology—to identifying the subject as such as ideological—Althusser entertained for a short time the idea of the four modalities of subjectivity: the ideological subject, the subject in art, the subject of the unconscious, the subject of science. Is there not a clear parallel between Badiou's four generics of truth (love, art, science, politics) and these four modalities of subjectivity (where love corresponds to the subject of the unconscious, the topic of psychoanalysis, and politics, of course, to the subject of ideology)? The paradox is thus that Badiou's opposition of knowledge and truth seems to turn exactly around Althusser's opposition of ideology and science: "nonauthentic" knowledge is limited to the positive order of Being, blind to its structural Void, to its symptomal torsion, while the engaged truth that subjectivizes provides authentic insight into a situation.

St. Paul with Badiou

According to a deep—albeit unexpected—logic, the topic of Pauline Christianity is also crucial for Badiou's confrontation with psychoanalysis. When Badiou adamantly opposes the "morbid obsession with death," when he opposes the truth-Event to the death drive and so on, he is at his weakest, succumbing to the *temptation of the nonthought*. It is symptomatic that Badiou is compelled to identify the liberal-democratic *service des biens*, the smooth running of things in the positivity of Being, where "nothing actually happens," with the "morbid obsession with death." Although one can easily see the element of truth in this equation (mere *service des biens*, deprived of the dimension of truth, far from being able to function as "healthy" everyday life, not bothered by "eternal" questions, necessarily regresses into nihilistic morbidity—as Christians would put it, there is true life only in Christ, and life outside the Event of Christ sooner or later turns into its opposite, a morbid decadence; when we dedicate our life to excessive pleasures, these very pleasures are sooner or later spoiled), one should nonetheless insist here on what Lacan calls the space or distance *between the two deaths*: to put it in Badiou's Christian terms, in order to be able to open oneself to the life of true eternity, one has to suspend one's attachment to "this" life and enter the domain of *ate*, the domain between the two deaths, the domain of the "undead."

This point is worthy of more detailed examination, since it condenses the gap that separates Badiou from Lacan and psychoanalysis in general. Badiou, of course, is also well aware of the opposition of two deaths (and two lives): when St. Paul opposes life and death (spirit is life, while flesh brings death), this opposition of life and death has nothing to do with the biological opposition of life and death as parts of the cycle of generation and corruption, or with the standard Platonic opposition of soul and body: for St. Paul, "life" and "death," spirit and flesh, designate two subjective stances, two ways to live one's life. So when St. Paul speaks of death and resurrection—rising into the eternal life in Christ—this has nothing to do with biological life and death but rather provides the coordinates of the two fundamental "existential attitudes" (to use this modern term anachronistically). This leads Badiou to a specific interpretation of Christianity that *radically dissociates death and resurrection*: they are not the same; they are not even dialectically interconnected in the sense of gaining access to eternal life by paying the price of suffering that redeems us from our sins. For Badiou, Christ's death on the cross simply signals that "God became human," that eternal truth is something immanent to human life, accessible to every human being. The message that God had to become human and to die (to suffer the fate of all flesh) in order to resurrect is that eternal life is something accessible to humanity, to all people as finite mortal beings: each of us can be touched by the grace of the truth-Event and enter the domain of eternal life. Here Badiou is openly anti-Hegelian: there is no dialectics of life and death in the sense of the truth-Event of resurrection emerging as the magic reversal of negativity into positivity when we are fully ready to "tarry with negative," to assume our mortality and suffering at its most radical. The truth-Event is simply a radically new beginning; it designates the violent, traumatic, and contingent intrusion of another dimension not "mediated" by the domain of terrestrial finitude and corruption.

One must thus avoid the pitfalls of morbid masochistic mortality that perceives suffering as inherently redeeming: this morality remains within the confines of the law (which demands from us a price for the admission to eternal life) and is thus not yet at the level of the properly Christian notion of love. As Badiou puts it, Christ's death is not in itself the truth-Event; it simply prepares the site for the Event (resurrection) by asserting the identity of God and humanity—the fact that the infinite dimension of immortal truth is also accessible to a human finite mortal. What ultimately matters is only the resurrection of the dead (i.e., human-mortal) Christ, signaling that each human being can be redeemed and can enter the domain of eternal life—that is, participate in the truth-Event.

Therein lies the message of Christianity: the positivity of Being, the order of the cosmos regulated by its laws, which is the domain of finitude and mortality (from the standpoint of the cosmos, of the totality of positive Being, we are merely particular beings determined by our specific place in the global order—the law is ultimately another name for the order of cosmic justice, which allocates to each of us his or her proper place), is not "all there is"; there is another dimension, the dimension of true life in love, accessible to all of us through divine grace, so that we can all participate in it. Christian revelation is thus an example (although probably *the* example) of how we, human beings, are not constrained to the positivity of Being; of how, from time to time, in a contingent and unpredictable way, a truth-Event can occur that opens up to us the possibility of participating in another life by remaining faithful to the truth-Event. The interesting thing to note is how Badiou here turns around the standard opposition of the law as universal and grace (or charisma) as particular, the idea that we are all subjected to the universal divine law, whereas only some of us are touched by grace and can thus be redeemed: in Badiou's reading of St. Paul, on the contrary, it is law itself that, "universal" as it may appear, is ultimately "particularist" (a legal order always imposes specific duties and rights on us; it is always a law defining a specific community at the expense of excluding the members of other, for example, ethnic communities), while divine grace is truly universal, that is, nonexclusive, addressing all humans independently of their race, sex, social status, and so on.

We thus have two lives, the finite biological life and the infinite life of participating in the truth-Event of resurrection. Correspondingly, there are also two deaths: the biological death and death in the sense of succumbing to the "way of all flesh." How does St. Paul determine this opposition of life and death as the two subjective, existential attitudes? Here we touch the crux of Badiou's arguments, which also directly concerns psychoanalysis: for Badiou, the opposition of death and life overlaps with the opposition of law and love. For St. Paul, succumbing to the temptations of the flesh does not simply mean indulging in unbridled terrestrial conquests (the search for pleasures, power, wealth, etc.) irrespective of the law (of mortal prohibitions). On the contrary, his central tenet, elaborated in what is probably (deservedly) the most famous passage in his writings—chapter 7, verse 7 in the Epistle to the Romans—is that there is no sin prior to or independent of the law: what comes before it is a simple innocent prelapsarian life forever lost to us mortal human beings. The universe we live in, *our* "way of all flesh," is the universe in which sin and law, desire and its prohibition, are inextricably intertwined: it is the very act of prohibition that gives rise to the desire for its transgression, that is, fixes our desire on the prohibited object.

> What then should we say? That the law is sin? By no means! Yet, if it had not been for the law, I would not have known sin. I would not have known what it is to covet if the law had not said, "You shall not covet." But sin, seizing an opportunity in the commandment, produces in me all kinds of covetousness. Apart from the law sin lies dead. I was once alive apart from the law, but when that commandment came, sin revived and I died, and the very commandment that promised life proved to be death to me. For sin, seizing an opportunity in the commandment, deceived me and through it killed me. . . .
>
> . . . I do not understand my own actions. For I do not do what I want, but I do the very thing I hate. Now if I do what I do not want, I agree that the law is good. But in fact it is no longer I that do it, but sin that dwells within me. For I know that nothing good dwells within me, that is, in my flesh. I can will what is right, but I cannot do it. (Rom. 7:7–11, 15–18 NRSV)

This passage, of course, must be seen in its context: in the whole of this part of the epistle, the problem St. Paul struggles with is how to avoid the trap of *perversion*, that is, of a law that generates it transgression, since it needs it in order to assert itself as law. For example, in Romans 3:5, 7–8 (NRSV), St. Paul fires off a barrage of desperate questions: "But if our injustice serves to confirm the justice of God, what should we say? That God is unjust to inflict wrath on us? . . . But if through my falsehood God's truthfulness abounds to his glory, why am I still being condemned as a sinner? And why not say (as some people slander us by saying that we say), 'Let us do evil so that good may come'?" This "Let us do evil so that good may come [from it]" is the most succinct definition of the short circuit of the perverse position. Does this make God a closet pervert who brings about our fall so that he may then redeem us through sacrifice—or, to quote Romans 11:11 (NRSV), "have they stumbled so as to fall"; that is, did we stumble (become involved in sin, in the "way of all flesh") because God needed our fall as part of his plan of ultimate redemption? If this is how things are, then the answer to the question, "Should we continue to sin in order that grace may abound?" (Rom. 6:1 NRSV) is affirmative: it is only and precisely by indulging in sin that we enable God to play his part as our Savior. But St. Paul's entire effort is to break out of this vicious cycle in which the prohibitive law and its transgression generate and support each other.

In his *Philosophical Notebooks*, Lenin made the well-known statement that everyone who aims at really understanding Marx's *Capital* should read the whole of Hegel's *Logic* in detail. He then did it himself, supplementing quotes from Hegel with hundreds of *sic*s and marginal comments like: "The first part of this sentence contains an ingenious dialectical insight; the second part of this sentence is theological rubbish!" A task awaiting true Lacanian dialectical materialists is to repeat the same gesture with St. Paul, since, again, everyone who aims at really understanding Lacan's *Ecrits* should read the entire text of Romans and Corinthians in detail: one cannot wait for a Lacanian volume of *Theological Notebooks*, with quotes accompanied by hundreds of *sic*s and comments like: "The first part of this sentence provides the deepest insight into Lacanian ethics, while the second part is just theological rubbish!"[12]

So back to the long quote from Romans: The direct result of the intervention of the law is thus that it *divides* the subject and introduces a morbid confusion between life and death. The subject is divided between (conscious) obedience to the law and (unconscious) desire for its transgression generated by the legal prohibition itself. It is not I, the

12. For Badiou, St. Paul's fundamental problem was that of the appropriate discourse: to assert authentic Christian universalism, St. Paul has to break with Greek philosophical sophistry as well as with Jewish prophetic obscurantism, which is still the predominant discursive mode of the Gospels. Here, however, one should perhaps complicate the picture a little: maybe Christ's obscure parables in the Gospels are more subversive than they appear; maybe they are there precisely to perplex and frustrate the disciples who are unable to discern a clear meaning in them; maybe the well-known statement from Matt. 19:12 (NRSV)—"Let anyone accept [or understand, as it is also translated] this who can"—is to be read literally, as a signal that the search for a deeper meaning is misleading; maybe they are to be taken like the parable of the Door of the Law in Kafka's *The Trial*, submitted to an exasperating literal reading by the priest, a reading that yields no deeper meaning. So maybe these parables are not the remainder of the old Jewish prophetic discourse but, rather, its immanent mocking subversion. And, incidentally, isn't it striking that this "Let anyone accept this who can" is pronounced by Christ regarding the problem of castration? Here is the quote in verse 11: "Not everyone can accept [understand] this." What is ultimately ungraspable, beyond comprehension, is the fact of castration in its different modalities.

subject, who transgress the law; it is nonsubjectivized "sin" itself, the sinful impulses in which I do not recognize myself, and which I even hate. Because of this split, my (conscious) self is ultimately experienced as "dead," as deprived of living impetus, while "life," ecstatic affirmation of living energy, can appear only in the guise of "sin," of a transgression that gives rise to a morbid sense of guilt. My actual life-impulse, my desire, appears to me as a foreign automatism that persists in following its path independently of my conscious will and intentions. St. Paul's problem is thus not the standard morbid mortalistic one (how to crush transgressive impulses, how finally to purify myself of sinful urges), but its exact opposite: How can I break out of this vicious cycle of the law and desire, of the prohibition and its transgression, within which I can assert my living passions only in the guise of their opposite, as a morbid death drive? How would it be possible for me to experience my life-impulse not as a foreign automatism, as a blind "compulsion to repeat," making me transgress the law, with the unacknowledged complicity of the law itself, but as a fully subjectivized, positive "Yes!" to my life?

Here St. Paul and Badiou seem fully to endorse Hegel's point that there is evil only for the gaze that perceives something as evil: it is the law itself that not only opens up and sustains the domain of sin, of sinful urges to transgress it, but also finds a perverse and morbid satisfaction in making us feel guilty about it. The ultimate result of the rule of the law thus consists of all the well-known twists and paradoxes of the superego: I can enjoy only if I feel guilty about it, which means that, in a self-reflexive turn, I can take pleasure *in* feeling guilty, I can find enjoyment in punishing myself for sinful thoughts, and so on. So when Badiou speaks of the "morbid fascination of the death drive," and so forth, he is not resorting to general platitudes but referring to a very precise "Pauline" reading of the psychoanalytic notions he uses: the entire complex entanglement of law and desire—not only illicit sinful desires that go against the law but also this morbid intertwining of life and death in which the "dead" letter of the law perverts my enjoyment of life itself, changing it into a fascination with death; this perverted universe in which the ascetic who flagellates himself on behalf of the law enjoys more intensely than the person who takes innocent pleasure in earthly delights—is what St. Paul designates as "the way of the flesh" as opposed to "the way of the spirit." "Flesh" is not flesh as opposed to the law but flesh as an excessive self-torturing, mortifying morbid fascination *begotten by the law*. (See Rom. 5:20 [NRSV]: "Law came in, with the result that the trespass multiplied.")

As Badiou emphasizes, here St. Paul is unexpectedly close to his great detractor Nietzsche, whose problem was also how to break away from the vicious cycle of the self-mortifying morbid denial of life: for him the Christian "way of the spirit" is precisely the magic break, the new beginning that delivers us from this debilitating morbid deadlock and enables us to open ourselves to the eternal life of love without sin (i.e., law and the guilt the law induces). In other words, it is as if St. Paul himself has answered Dostoyevsky's infamous "If there is no God, every-thing is permitted!" in advance—for St. Paul, *precisely since there* is *the God of love, everything* is *permitted to the Christian believer*—that is to say, the law, which regulates and prohibits certain acts, is suspended. For a Christian believer, the fact that he does not do certain things is based not on prohibitions (which then generate the transgressive desire to indulge precisely in these things) but in the positive, affirmative at-titude of love, which renders meaningless the accomplishment of acts that bear witness to the fact that I am not free but still dominated by an external force: " 'All things are lawful for me,' but not all things are beneficial. 'All things are lawful for me,' but I will not be dominated by anything" (1 Cor. 6:12 NRSV). ("All things are lawful for me" is often translated also as "Nothing is prohibited to me"!) This rupture with the universe of the law and its transgression is most clearly articulated in a very provoking "analogy from marriage":

> Do you not know, brothers and sisters—for I am speaking to those who know the law—that the law is binding on a person only during that person's lifetime? Thus a married woman is bound by the law to her husband as long as he lives; but if her husband dies, she is discharged from the law concerning the husband. Accordingly, she will be called an adulteress if she lives with another man while her husband is alive. But if her husband dies, she is free from the law, and if she marries another man, she is not an adulteress.
>
> In the same way, my friends, you have died to the law through the body of Christ, so that you may belong to another, to him who has been raised from the dead in order that we may bear fruit for God. While we were living in the flesh, our sinful passions, aroused by the law, were at work in our members to bear fruit for death. But now we are discharged from the law, dead to that which held us captive. (Rom. 7:1–6 NRSV)

To become a true Christian and embrace love, one should thus "die to the law," to break up the vicious cycle of "sinful passions, aroused by the law." As Lacan would have put it, one has to undergo the second, symbolic death, which involves the suspension of the big Other, the symbolic law that hitherto dominated and regulated our lives. So the crucial point is that we have *two* "divisions of the subject" that should not be confused. On the one hand, we have the division of the subject of the law between the conscious ego, which adheres to the letter of the law, and the decentered desire, which, operating "automatically" against the subject's conscious will, compels him to "do what he hates," to transgress the law and indulge in illicit *jouissance*. On the other hand, we have the more radical division between this entire domain of the law/desire, of the prohibition generating its transgression, and the properly Christian way of love, which marks a new beginning, breaking out of the deadlock of law and its transgression.

3

Paul and Subtraction

CRESTON DAVIS

One can witness a great neurosis in the very act of Slavoj Žižek's engagement with St. Paul. Žižek expresses so much interest in Paul's radical stance that it is much like watching him engage his philosophical "twin," as if he and St. Paul were separated at birth. But what is at stake here exactly? For Žižek the basic point with his engagement with Paul is his understanding of the idea of the law and its precise relationship to love. His provocative engagement is seen in a number of different places among his vast works but is visible most poignantly in his reading of St. Paul's letter to the Christians in Rome (Rom. 7:7–18). It is here where Žižek identifies and characterizes an inherently conflicting logic occurring between, on the one hand, desire irrupting from within the self (sex drive, selfish greed, death wish, etc.) and, on the other hand, the "no" inscribed in the law[1] external from the body. Žižek asserts that "the universe we live in, *our* 'way of all flesh,' is the universe in which sin and law, desire and its prohibition, are inextricably intertwined: it is

1. Of course the notion of the "law" is itself very complex and diffuse, especially when one attends to the history of the term. This chapter examines only one aspect of the notion of "law." Thanks to Randi Rashkover for pointing out to me this extremely important aspect of the complexity of the law.

the very act of prohibition that gives rise to the desire for its transgression, that is, fixes our desire on the prohibited object."[2]

St. Paul highlights this logic when he says that even his own actions are mysterious to himself: "For I do not do what I want, but I do the very thing I hate. Now if I do what I do not want, I agree that the law is good. . . . I can will what is right, but I cannot do it. For I do not do the good I want, but the evil I do not want is what I do" (Rom. 7:15–16, 18–19 NRSV). Paul's sensitivity to his own interior fragmentation is what Lacan identifies as the break from the Mother (that is, a primordial oneness) that introduces into the world an insatiable desire that longs to overcome the lack (created in the very break with the Mother) in an ultimate return to a point where desire is totally neutralized. The very appearance of the law here enacts the point of lack and a logic of fragmentation shot through life. Paul's formulation thus perfectly expresses the deadlock that the law presents to the world in its very existence—at once the conditions for sin (for without the law there is no sin) and yet the precise way to traverse sin. Put differently, the prohibition of the law simultaneously establishes the desire to transgress that prohibition and the *prohibition* as such. And these two couplings actually generate a vicious cycle. This circle of law/prohibition/desire/transgression/law ad infinitum is that very thing that produces a need to be rescued from this very entrapment. As Paul says, he is held captive and asks, "Who will rescue me from this body [circularity] of death?" (Rom. 7:24 NRSV). With all the fanfare of the return to Paul in continental philosophy, it is Žižek above all who most accurately identifies the vicious circulation between desire and death.

Of course, his comrade Alain Badiou's own version, as seen most prominently in his book *Saint Paul: The Foundation of Universalism*, largely influences Žižek's Paul.[3] It is in his assessment of Badiou's version of St. Paul that Žižek best situates the radical stance of Christianity by juxtaposing two basic oppositions: On the one side is the "the positivity of Being, the order of the cosmos regulated by its laws, which is the domain of finitude and mortality (from the standpoint of the cosmos, of the totality of positive Being, we are merely particular beings determined by our specific place in the global order—the law is ultimately another name for the order of cosmic justice, which allocates to each

---

2. See chap. 2, p. 95.

3. Alain Badiou, *Saint Paul: The Foundation of Universalism*, trans. Ray Brassier (Stanford, CA: Stanford University Press, 2003).

of us his or her proper place)." On the other side, Žižek insists that this "is not 'all there is'; there is another dimension, the dimension of true life in love, accessible to all . . . through divine grace."[4] These two sides include the impersonal law of "cosmic Justice" on the one hand, and on the other, love, which is the true universal but only grasped through the reversal of "divine grace."

Having posited these two sides of law vis-à-vis grace, Žižek (both with and without, and both informed by and taking his distance from Badiou) gives the coordinates through which the circularity of "desire and death" that Paul articulates in Romans 7 can be circumvented. But there is a twist: what may appear to be universal—that is, the universality of the law—is in truth turned on its head. The universal is effectively reduced to the mode of particularity, whereas the particular, seen in its exceptionality (which cannot fit into the coordinates of the law/prohibition/transgression matrix) as divine grace, paradoxically becomes the foundation of universality. Grace becomes the universal precisely because its eventual "happening" radically ruptures the accepted and normative truths of how the world "really" works. Here is how Žižek frames grace:

> In a contingent and unpredictable way, a truth-Event can occur that opens up to us the possibility of participating in another life by remaining faithful to the truth-Event. The interesting thing to note is how Badiou here turns around the standard opposition of the law as universal and grace (or charisma) as particular, the idea that we are all subjected to the universal divine law, whereas only some of us are touched by grace and can thus be redeemed: in Badiou's reading of St. Paul, on the contrary, it is law itself that, "universal" as it may appear, is ultimately "particularist" (a legal order always imposes specific duties and rights on us; it is always a law defining a specific community at the expense of excluding the members of other, for example, ethnic communities), while divine grace is truly universal, that is, nonexclusive, addressing all humans independently of their race, sex, social status, and so on.[5]

It is the exceptional event (the truth-Event in Badiouian parlance) that founds the truth—a truth that cannot fit into the *apparent* "universality" of law and so reveals itself as being the "exceptional-truth" that opens the way for the true universalism beyond the law. So the truth-Event breaks out of the circulation of death and entrapment. Moreover, the example of this "truth-Event" for Badiou is the resurrection of Christ,

4. See chap. 2, p. 94.
5. Ibid.

which nicely shows how the logic of the circulation of death (law/sin) is subverted; for the law of a human-centered universe is broken in God becoming human (and in an Athanasian twist, "man becomes God"). Here Badiou via Paul reveals how the Christian Reformed notion of a universe bifurcated between a sphere of "common (universal) grace" into which all creation somehow fits and, within this common grace, a sphere of "specific grace" particular to Christians and to the exclusion of nonbelievers falls into the error of what Bonhoeffer aptly called "cheap grace." For "common grace" is just assumed (like the law)—as if it were already built into the material universe as the order of creation. But does this not already hijack the radical nature of the Incarnation insofar as it already determines the logic of salvation before it happens? Badiou's and Žižek's point here is that Paul effectively reverses the universality of the law, which is shown to be a fake, in favor of the radicality of grace, which is the real universal exception. In so doing, they turn the Christian tradition against itself and thereby recover and reactivate the radicality of the Christ-Event.

Consider, for instance, how it is that the apparent "law" effectively crucifies the Christ. But the reality is that this "law" is revealed as not being alive at all. What at first appeared to be true actually turns into something quite the opposite. In this case, then, what appears to be one way—namely, that the empire of Rome, in carrying out the law and murdering Christ, reveals the true inner essence of the law—proves to be unable to sustain itself; indeed, the law left to itself will eventually self-implode.

One can think of the recent film *I, Robot*, in which the logic of the new generation of robots is so rational and coherent that it finally has to break the foundation of all robotic laws in order to actually fulfill them. Similarly, according to Paul, in Christ's death, death is itself defeated. So Paul makes the connection clear: the law on its own (death) is overcome through this "exceptional" event in Christ. What is thus introduced here is a logic of folly—that the law is ultimately hollow and self-destructive; indeed, Christ's resurrection reveals a deeper, more profound truth: that salvation is wrought not by death but by life, not by the "law" but by its very exception, namely, divine grace. In this way to say that grace is specific to one set (Christian believers) is already to domesticate the chaos of love in the name of a law. This is the precise ingredient of death and violence.

This is the most radical point, which founds Paul's basic stance in the world. "Love" is found not by being a nice, morally upright citizen who pays her taxes and debts on time, nor is it even reserved for a subset of human beings (read: Christians), but is better seen in taking a radical stance for the other that makes sense only according to the Event of Christ's crucifixion on the cross. As Michael Hardt and Antonio Negri write in the conclusion to *Multitude*, "love" is not only a private but also a political term.[6] In this way, love is better understood as taking the ultimate risk as paradox: in death there is life, in life there is death. Love then is that stance that arises in the most unlikely of places, namely, in the very grip of death. But, of course, this basic approach to love cannot be comprehended *directly*, as if its very disclosure violently empties out its core content without reservation: neither propositions (universal axioms and other bare-bone "truths") nor any subgroup of people can capture the truth of love. Love does not, if you will, display its heart on its sleeve; rather, love is like the unconscious, which operates on a deeper, more indirect level that takes time, patience, and a relationship to know it; and yet its appearance is never predictable.

This is precisely the point in Albert Camus' famous novel *The Plague*, in which the city of Oran is confronted by its imminent death. The plague establishes the true conditions of life such that the inhabitants of the city move from indifference prior to the plague toward a deeper appreciation of life by staring death down. And here we arrive at my central thesis, which is that Paul has identified love's very truth by his insight into love's unfolding through a *negative* (or subtractive) logic—a logic totally unavailable and out of reach to those unwilling to risk living into the journey that love calls us to follow, a journey that involves every aspect of our lives, as Paul writes in his letter to the Romans: we are living sacrifices. In this way, reading Paul along the lines of Žižek's "universal exception" provides us with a rich theological synthesis between John Milbank's robust universal (catholic) ontology and the Barthian (fragmented) and incommensurate linguistic structure. It is Žižek's reading of Paul that may provide us with the theological resources to construct a synthetic and dynamic structure that sublates both universalism and fragmentation.

I will unpack this chapter's thesis by first situating Paul's radical notion of love within the context of the ancient philosophical argument concerning the basic structure of the world as either One or Multiple. After setting up this philosophical ontology, I will then turn to Socrates,

---

6. Michael Hardt and Antonio Negri, *Multitude: War and Democracy in the Age of Empire* (New York: Penguin, 2004).

whose very method opens a way into Paul's subtractive (Incarnational) ontology. From here, I conclude with and against Hegel, who, I argue, expresses a logic of Pauline love that finally outflanks ancient Greek philosophy through a radical subtraction that eliminates any attempt to delimit Incarnation within the walls of thought, logic, and traditions founded on unbending truths.

Ancient Greek Ontology: Parmenides' Question and the Law

The question that St. Paul raises when we think through the relationship between ontology and the political pertains first and foremost to the basic status of being qua being. By this question, we directly confront (in a precise antipostmodern key) two basic options posed in a singular question: is this world fundamentally stable or unstable? Put differently—and in the parlance of ancient philosophy—we may ask: is the world ultimately One or is it Multiple? As this essay will show, St. Paul radically opens up and uncovers the most fundamental logic of the world, a logic founded not on a stabilizing principle but rather on its opposite, a destabilizing multiplicity that goes against the law.

But we must first begin with this most sensitive and radical of questions by approaching the philosopher who provides us with invaluable insights and without which understanding of Paul's negative ontology is impossible. We therefore begin with Parmenides. For Parmenides the question of the world's stability or instability turns on the exact reality of the Many:[7] does (or can) the Multiple exist at all? And indefatigably, Parmenides' response is in the negative: the Many cannot exist. This is because for him, the Many is not. But the attachment of the negative with the Many presents a positive and curious insight. If the Many is not, then the opposite of the Many, namely the One, must be. The One is.

The logic from this insight nicely sets up the following hypothetical statement: if the One is not, then perforce, nothing can be. Because something is, then it must follow that the One is. Stated differently, according to Parmenides' view, nothing can only be if the One is not. Parmenides leaves us, therefore, with a surprising and mysterious connection between the Multiple (the Many) and nothingness. What ex-

7. When discussing the most basic structure of the world, the ancient philosophers framed this discussion in terms of an opposition between the One (the world is ultimately Oneness or a more fundamental Whole-thing) and the Many (the world is ultimately not reducible to a Whole but is rather fragmented into different parts that cannot ultimately relate to one another under the banner of One-thing).

actly is this connection? It is the connection between non-Being and the
Multiple as well as the link that connects beingness to the One. Being as
One is, whereas non-Being as the Many is not. But what would happen
to Parmenides' structure of the One as Being if we were to conjoin,
following Badiou's lead, Being and non-Being by stating that there is
both Being and non-Being?

The logic here is that because the Many is conjoined with the One,
it must force the One out of existence. (Or at least the One is forced
out of existence according to the logic of Parmenides.) So we can formulate the following statement: "Being and non-Being" is not being
(i.e., nothing). So this then means that the Nothing (or the Void) can
only ever exist under two formal conditions:

> If the Many exists, and
> If the One and the Many exist conjointly,
> The Void (in its broadest sense) does not exist if and only if the One
> exists by itself.

How do we know that either the One alone exists or else something
other than the One exists? If the latter, then nothing exists. How do we
decide between Parmenides and Badiou? And how might we even attempt to approach this? I want to suggest, along with my friend Tzuchien
Tho, to whom I am indebted here throughout this discussion, that we
can best approach this question with the concept of "consistency" or
"determination." That is to say, we must first and foremost be able to
distinguish something from some-other-thing—a "this" from a "that."
But notice that what undergirds the operation of determination is a
notion of something being unique; that is, something must persist in
its identity over time as One-thing. After all, one thing is different from
another thing, leading Parmenides to assert, "Look around you, are there
any exceptions to this rule?" Well, there do not seem to be any identifi-
able exceptions at all. So the logic of determination (or consistency)
must be embedded within a more primordial and universal Oneness.
And because there are no exceptions to this rule of determination, then,
as Tzuchien Tho says, "the fundamental intelligibility of being is tied
to the intelligibility of oneness."[8] Therefore, Parmenides concludes,
Oneness is the ground for consistency. This further entails that Being
is forced into the composition of Oneness, otherwise Being is forever

8. Email, February 28, 2008.

rendered unknowable, unintelligible, and ultimately incoherent. Another conclusion we can draw here is that if Being is unintelligible, then it is not being—that is, it is nothing. But once again we come back around to the hypothetical statement: If the One is not, then nothing is. And if the Nothing is, then there is nothing *but* the Multiple. If all there is to Being is the Multiple, then we are left only with chaos or disorganized multiplicity.

It is this precise line of thinking that brings us closer to St. Paul's basic destabilizing, indeed apocalyptic, stance on reality. To be sure, St. Paul does not subscribe to the Parmenidean view of the world as reducible to the One (for this would be the same logic of reducing all things to the authority of the law alone), but neither does he go completely "dark," falling, as it were, off the cliffs of reason and into the mouth of the Void. Paul finds himself in a moment in which he neither accepts the law as final nor can he ignore it by simply dismissing it. Paul's position here is not totally dark, as if his thinking arrives from out of chaos, and neither is it arrogant in that he rests all things on the law. Something else opens up for Paul, some other logic that is "foolishness" when seen from Greek foundational logics and fails to conform to the status quo. Paul has located some other "unforeseen" form of truth that resists both a reduction to the One and a fragmentation of the Multiple (left to itself). And this truth is "scandalous" to those in power (or to those who interpret the world in terms of power or the law). Paul claims (in Jesus Christ) a different logic that does not fit into the normal predetermined coordinates that determine the truth of the world before it happens. We must be precise here. Paul does not perceive the scandal of the cross (the creator Christ dying at the hands of the created) in light of the law. (The law cannot shed its light on such incoherence.) Nor does he see the crucifixion as a total moment of chaos. Rather he sees it by its own light—the light of the irrational paradox that cross(es) over and yet holds the two oppositions of law and chaos together.

This cross(ing) logic that Paul announces works subversively. That is to say, it works under the cover of its veiled truth, which discloses itself on its own terms—the terms of a universal beyond the status quo. In this way, the truth of Paul's "cross(ings)" appears under a truth condition determined not by an a priori foundationalism of power or philosophy but by infinite love. For Paul, therefore, the meaning of the crucifixion is fundamentally disruptive without being totally chaotic.

There are several figures in the history of philosophy that embody Paul's logic. I want to flesh this out in one respect by the example of Socrates, who articulates truth-claims not in the possessive, arrogant sense but in the negative, humble sense of letting the truth emerge by paradox—by crossing between the One and the Many.

Socrates and Subtraction: The Way of the Cross

Before we relate this Parmenidean ontology of the One as Being to St. Paul's unstable ontology, I want to first relate this to the Socratic structure of wisdom. In so doing, we will see a movement of the Void (or the negative) understood differently than is often conveyed, especially in recent theology. In Plato's account of Socrates' Athenian trial, in 399 BCE, there is a basic contention established between the fundamental opposition of the law (of the polis) and divine wisdom. While Athens is under a great exertion of pressure from the militant state of Sparta (ultimately falling to it in 404), the desire to neutralize all threats to the law and security of the polis is correspondingly heightened. In the wake of this immanent social anxiety, Socrates is brought to trial by Meletus, Anytus, and Lycon and charged with several offenses, from atheism to corrupting the youth and even sophistry. Of course the charge of atheism is not only the disbelief in God or gods but is rather more interesting than the modern or even Victorian reified form of atheism. Socrates is accused of not believing in the Athenian gods *of the state* (which is the basic charge lodged at the early Christians in the first few centuries under Roman rule). The upshot is that the Senate interprets Socrates' "atheism" as seditious and thus pits him against the very foundations of the state. Atheism is the principle charge lodged against Socrates precisely because not believing in and thus not worshiping the deities of the state was to not believe in the very existence of the state itself. Belief was construed as a prerequisite to the rights of citizenship, as the civil religion of the state was seen as the necessary foundation for social and political cohesion. Religious practice, the law, and the political were inextricably bound up together in such a way that modern dualism between the public and the private (the material and the spiritual) was utterly unthinkable in Athens.

The second basic charge against Socrates is that he is systematically corrupting the youth. Socrates' dialectical method by which he would question his interlocutor's position in hopes of showing the inherent weaknesses of maintaining such a stance (and, perhaps in the end giving it up) is well known. The method—later to be called the Socratic method—is equally perceived as inherently destabilizing and ultimately subversive. The image here cannot be passed over: Imagine the gospel of Socrates spreading like wildfire across Athens in younger Socratic disciples. These "corrupt" youth would quickly start to gain a certain power beyond the normative political structures and parties in the city. Socrates' prosecutors were right to recognize how this growing and even formidable threat would need to be confronted, as the alternative would effectively and in due course dissolve the very cohesion by which the city is organized.

The third charge leveled against Socrates is that of sophistry. Here the worry is that Socrates is ultimately a windbag, full of nothing but bullshit, whose procedure is that of overcoming a solid argument simply by appealing to little more than rhetoric and not the force of thought. And we observe the assumption of such a charge, namely, the opposition set up between substance (logic/law) and rhetoric (the negative/questioner). But such an opposition, as we will see below, is problematic.

Three different charges, but what lies at the heart of each is the fear of subversion: fear of the subversion of the city's relation between itself and the gods (and so its ontology), fear of the gospel of questioning (the fear of a more fundamental and universal logic), and finally fear of substance-less argumentation (that is, empty rhetoric). Although all three charges are different, at a deeper level they all merge together on a more reactionary level—a level founded on fear. It is a fear that the law of the polis will be compromised, a compromise embodied in the very person of Socrates, who represents the most threatening entity to the polis. This basic hypothesis becomes clear when one observes the specific charges leveled at Socrates in the trial. From this point of view, the charges even appear hastily cobbled together and thus display a fundamental anxiety residing within each of them. This anxiety is another name for the law.

But this is precisely where the sheer brilliance of the Socratic method is observable and in two ways: first, Socrates' very method results in confronting the law (the state—or the state of the situation), for the law itself trembles in the wake of the Socratic method. Moreover, this method can thus be seen as unearthing a rudimentary truth about the law. Despite the seeming omnipotence of the law, Socrates reveals the rudimentary truth that the law is actually secondary. The law is not finally ontological but merely appears as such. This means that it always attempts to naturalize itself as ontological but is wholly incapable of accomplishing this task. This is why the law remains situated at the level of an apparatus of action that masks both inequality and injustice, which in Marxist parlance is precisely the notion of "ideology." By contrast, Socrates' questioning penetrates beyond the veneer of the law (polis, Athens, and so on) by assuming the quest(ion) is never satisfied with answers that mask untruths; indeed, all thinking committed to truth necessarily penetrates beyond all barriers, material and spiritual. Thus the quest of *questi*oning is nothing short of an infinite procedure. Based on this we can formulate a tentative axiom: the procedure of quest(ing) poses a truthful threat to the law and by extension the ideological apparatuses that reside in it. Thus Socrates' infinite method for apprehending truth is the second feature that illuminates the general assault against power devoid of truth (i.e., political power represented in the trial by senators Meletus, Anytus, and Lycon). For the law is precisely that which covers over the instantiation and reproduction of power emptied of its content of truth.

To repeat, there are two seminal features we identify in Socrates' method: first, the law trembles when confronted with serious questioning, and second, that questioning itself is an infinite procedure. The quest for truth (which is the true and original task assigned to philosophy) is an infinite process because it never rests by hiding behind the unbending foundation of unquestioning "truth" claims that steal away the name of truth for the name of politics. Questing is therefore an infinite procedure because as long as a further question can be raised there is no final answer that can foreclose that procedure.

So, in the first place, this feature is disruptive. This method is disruptive because it revolts against the law's presentation of itself as final and beyond questioning. But there is a second feature that alights inextricably with the deterritorializing force that the question in itself poses—namely, the qualitative aspect of the infinite procedure of apprehending truth. This quality is subtractive and negative. It is subtractive because its quality is predicated on a prior claim to which it responds. Subtraction is the logic of Socrates' questioning in the exact sense that questioning confronts positive assertions whose assumption is always possessive in form. Claims inherently put stakes in the world, carving out what is possessed from what is not. Socrates' procedure of questioning is subtractive and infinite; that is, it is infinitely subtractive, and being formed as such, it is no surprise that it poses an immediate and intractable threat not only to the law but also to every and all possessive claims to truth—including, incidentally, the fundamental premise upon which capitalism is predicated, namely, private property.

The moment of subtraction happens at the precise point when Socrates is distanced from the pre-Socratic philosophers,[9] precisely because he posits a subtractive ontology of questioning and avoids coming down with a vulgar positive and possessive ontology of either, for example, Parmenides' One or Heraclitus's flux (Many). Additionally, this subtractive logic marks a decisive turn in the history of philosophy, a current of which Paul is a part a few centuries later in the wake of the onslaught of God's breaking into the world as Jesus Christ.

We established that for Parmenides being must either be One or it is nothing. But there is something (and not nothing), so it follows for Parmenides that being is One. Moreover, this notion of Being as One simply cannot contain any difference (that is, the destabilizing multiple truth-claims) similar to the law, which must annihilate all competition against itself, and this exactly because the law determines what is socially permissible based solely on what is not permissible. Again, this is Žižek's point when he maintains that the law hides an innate destabilization, which is precisely that which establishes the law in the first place.

For an example of this one need only think about the 2002 Steven Spielberg film *Minority Report* (based on Philip K. Dick's short story by the same name) in which a Washington DC police operation can perceive future murders through three "precogs" (semiconscious human beings with precognitive powers), who deliver a report minutes or hours before the crime is to happen. Based solely on this precog report, the Precrime Unit officers are authorized to arrest the person who has not yet committed the future crime in question and perhaps never would have. Moreover, at times the three precogs cannot agree, and the report that conforms least with the other two (the minority report) is discarded. But the very existence of a minority report reveals that the future is not determinate and in fact does possess other options and outcomes. But what is of the greatest secrecy is that the creator of Precrime, Lamar Burgess, has committed a murder himself and so committed the fatal error that ends up permeating the logic of the "law" until its truth finally comes to the surface. In the end, the minority report from the strongest precog, "Agatha," catches Burgess in the act, and he is brought to justice. The moral here cannot be missed and bears on the double bind of the law/prohibition: the very existence of Precrime is analogous

9. *The Apology.*

to the existence of the liberal nation-state, because the law that allows it to run smoothly presupposes a necessary hidden violence on which the law itself must rest in order to be. John Milbank makes the same point, showing in his pathbreaking book *Theology and Social Theory* that the entire notion of a secular political law and state requires the unwarranted sacrifice of innocent blood. In short, the law is the big cover-up that presents the world as stable but all the while hides from view the truth of its own violence. It is precisely this hidden truth of the law that Paul uncovers in the shadow of the death of Christ.

But one fundamental aspect of Paul is his thoroughgoing disdain for any category that persists in the name of a fake truth. For example, if one's identity persists in being reducible to surface characteristics (as important as they may be) such as gender, race, class, nation, and so on, then it is literally captured not by the deeper truth of the world's *actual* difference but rather by its fake appearance in the name of "difference." This is precisely what makes Paul a militant for the universal-exception and that which reverses truth in the name of the Father for truth in the name of a world radically thrown off balance. In this regard we can see in Paul a surplus logic that transcends the current coordinates of the world. The world is more than what it appears to be—for it is reducible neither to pure Oneness nor to the Many. More radically still, for Paul all things are more than what they "are": Being is more than its reduction to itself such that there is a kind of surplus to existing beings. Said differently, all things ultimately give way to a more fundamental truth, and for Paul that truth is the shattering truth of Incarnation—God became human.

It is precisely this radical intervention by God (the transcendent One), who breaks into the material, immanent domain of Being, that shatters both the law of transcendence and the logic of immanence at once. For if the logic of transcendence operates on the level of infinity, eternity, and the unchanging, and if the logic of immanence works on the order of limitation, the bounded, and flux, then when God breaks into the created order something is introduced into the matrix of Being, after which nothing is ever the same again. This new logic of Incarnation is something that neither transcendence nor immanence (in themselves) can reconcile while remaining true to their respective logics. What Paul grasps here is the radicality of this new Incarnational logic in all its awesome fallout.

The logic of Incarnation is an irreducible logic of the neither/nor. It is neither transcendence (closed off from everything external to itself—that is, the law) nor immanence (closed off from all things beyond itself). As

Stanislas Breton nicely puts it, "It is the Cross that unites those whom an apparent wisdom divides, as if there were an ever-concealed affinity between the Nothing and the One."[10] In other words, it is a logic that poses itself in opposition to the either/or—either "this" or "that"—and this breaks with what we mentioned above in regards to the Parmenidean law of consistency, that is, the law of the One. The world must be either "this" thing or "that" thing. The world is supposed to follow the rules of intelligibility. But here, Paul breaks with the Parmenidean One and founds a new logic of the neither/nor—a logic of a new universal, the universal-exception. The standard idea of a universal is that which holds true at all times and in all circumstances. For example, "All bachelors are unmarried men." But Paul's new universal breaks out of a universal founded on formal logical foundations; indeed, this new universal (that is, neither transcendence nor immanence) throws off the standard appeals that protect and preserve such categories and enters the realm of absolute risk, which wholly abandons the security of the law. As Paul expresses in his meditation on love in 1 Corinthians 13 (NRSV):

> If I speak in the tongues of mortals and of angels, but do not have love, I am a noisy gong or a clanging cymbal. And if I have prophetic powers, and understand all mysteries and all knowledge, and if I have all faith, so as to remove mountains, but do not have love, I am nothing. If I give away all my possessions, and if I hand over my body so that I may boast [or "to be burned"], but do not have love, I gain nothing. . . .
>
> Love never ends. But as for prophecies, they will come to an end; as for tongues, they will cease; as for knowledge, it will come to an end. For we know only in part, and we prophesy only in part; but when the complete comes, the partial will come to an end. . . . For now we see in a mirror, dimly, but then we will see face to face. Now I know only in part; then I will know fully, even as I have been fully known. And now faith, hope, and love abide, these three; and the greatest of these is love.

The movement here is extreme and holds nothing back; indeed, it is nothing short of a leap into the absurd, because nothing preserves the subject who risks love. There is no insurance or security for risking love as it leaves the safety net of the banks and bureaucracy behind. There is not even an insurance policy in case love simply does not work out.

When we fold this radical idea back to the truth of the One and its opposite, pure flux, it becomes clear that love is irreducible to either

10. Stanislas Breton, *The Word and the Cross*, trans. Jacquelyn Porter (New York: Fordham University Press, 2002), 3.

transcendence (for love is a risk founded above all in relation to someone else) or immanence (for it does not rely on a positive source of power for it to be). What we thus have here is a universal truth insofar as love is infinite and beyond the power of logic to guarantee the process of inference and connection. Here love calls us to abandon all structures that return glory back upon anything at all. What then is love but nothing short of forgoing the ethical doctrine of consequentialism (among other things), which states that one must always measure the consequences of an action and make a decision based on the preferred outcome among rivaling possibilities? Love for Paul then is the infinite in-breaking as the world's very appearance as such and reveals that no "security structures" (from the military to the police to the banks and their auditors and even to insurance companies) are ultimately effective in preventing the truth of subversion from taking hold in the world—that truth is the truth of Incarnation, the ultimate subversive act.

For the Love of Hegel

Like Paul, Hegel is obsessed with the logic of love. In his early work (before his system closes in upon itself) Hegel attempts to define love in a fragment written a year or so before his *The Spirit of Christianity and Its Fare*. Here Hegel struggles with the idea of fragmentation and competitive opposition founded between humans, within the human himself, between humanity and nature, and finally between humanity and God. Like Paul, Hegel's view of love ultimately seeks an ontological principle in and through which harmony and peace emerge as the mode of the world's truth not reducible to either the Whole (the One) or the Many. In other words, Hegel seeks to overcome the view that the world is premised on a false division in which hatred and opposition found the logic of the world. Of course, on the surface, division and hatred seem omnipresent and even expected—not unlike this joke, which taps into the truth of this perspective: A bachelor finally finds the woman of his dreams and asks her to marry him. He tells his mother he wants her to meet his fiancée, but he wants to make a bit of a game out of it. He says he will bring the girl over with two other women and see if his mother can guess which is the one he wants to marry. His mother agrees to the game. That night he shows up at his mother's house with three beautiful young ladies. They all sit down on the couch, and everyone has a wonderful evening talking and getting to know one another. At the end of the evening, the young man asks his mother, "Okay, Mom, which one is the woman I want to marry?" Without any hesitation at all, his mother replies, "The one in the middle." The young man is astounded. "How in the world did you figure it out?" "Easy," she says. "I detest her." The core of the joke gets at the very kernel of the truth of the world premised on opposition and division. If a good friend of yours is excited about your meeting her longtime friend, you instantly think the axiom: a friend's friend is necessarily an enemy, whereas an enemy's foe is a friend. This line of reasoning follows from one of the basic premises that grounds Carl Schmitt's conception of the political, namely, the friend-enemy distinction, which is the first and original step that structures the entire domain of political life. Schmitt defined the foe/enemy as someone who is "in a specially intense way, existentially some*thing* different and alien, so that in the extreme case conflicts with him are possible."[11]

Against the appearance of violence and hatred, Hegel penetrates deep into the world in an attempt to circumvent a logic predicated on opposition and loss (lack), which presuppose that subjects are reduced to mere objects, a presupposition so dire and depressing that finally the subject "cannot bear to think himself in this nullity. [For he] exists only as something opposed [to the object]."[12] This stance turns the subject into an inert object, which is as good as dead. (This is the basic insight that inspires Marx's notion of the commodity-fetish.) By contrast Hegel states that "true union, or love proper, exists only between living beings who are alike in power and thus in one another's eyes living beings."[13] In the end, "this genuine love excludes all oppositions." And this for Hegel overcomes the law as premised on opposition founded on "the understanding (whose relations always leave the manifold of related terms in a knot and whose unity is always a unity of opposites qua opposites) [and] reason (because reason sharply opposes its determining power to what is determined). [By contrast] love neither restricts nor is restricted; it is not finite at all."[14] Love is the irreducible infinite appearing in the world *as* the world.

The upshot reveals that Hegel's solution, which overcomes the problem of violence by transcending ontological opposition (in a movement

11. Carl Schmitt, *The Concept of the Political*, trans. George Schwab (Chicago: University of Chicago Press, 1996), 27.

12. G. W. F. Hegel, "Love Fragment," in *Early Theological Writings*, trans. T. M. Knox (Philadelphia: University of Pennsylvania Press, 1975), 304.

13. Ibid.

14. Ibid.; translation altered slightly.

of living relation between subjects), is that love is the very process of jettisoning a secure place of power, calculation, and comfort for the sake of something external, something new and living. But do we not here discover a basic opposition founded in the locus of Hegel's ontology? On the one hand, there is love consisting of a living, dynamic relationship, and, on the other hand, there is the brutality of fear imbued by commodification, objectification, and finally death. But this dualism, when read through Paul, gives way to the revelation of the breaking of the fake universal of competition, whose reality is shown to be meaningless because such a truth presupposes the primacy of the law that, once again, hides the inner violent truth of the One.

In sum, love is made love by risking the very possibility of subjectivity in the face of commodified objectivity inherent in the very core of the brutalizing matrix that has matured into the logic of late capitalism. Attempting to break out of the deadening nonexistence of objectivity (and commodification) was one of the basic problems that animated Karl Marx and Friedrich Engels's Communist project in the mid-nineteenth century, a project that has been inadvertently passed on to the Christian church in the twenty-first century. Love risks something absolutely new and unknowable. It is the opening of the infinite in terms of a superfinite being, but no longer wholly transcendent. In short, it is an emptying out of transcendence enclosed in on itself. Love is, to use another one of Paul's central concepts, kenosis.

Kenosis: A Cosmic Fallout Shelter

Kenosis is a seminal idea located in the heart of Paul's radical philosophy. The central passage of this idea is found in Paul's Letter to the Philippians. He writes: "Do nothing from selfish ambition or conceit, but in humility regard others as better than yourselves. Let each of you look not to your own interests, but to the interests of others. Let the same mind be in you that was in Christ Jesus" (Phil. 2:3–5 NRSV). And then Paul breaks into a hymn:

> who, though he was in the form of God,
>   did not regard equality with God
>   as something to be exploited,
> but emptied himself,
>   taking the form of a slave,
>   being born in human likeness
> And being found in human form,

> He humbled himself
> And became obedient to the point of
>   death—
> even death on a cross. (Phil. 2:6–8 NRSV)

In Hegel's terms (as interpreted by Žižek), the God of absolute transcendence (God the Father in the Trinity) decides on the bases of love to empty himself into the world (in his son, Christ) without any reserve whatsoever. God thus commits an absolute risk—a certain suicide, if you will, because he abandons the very thing that keeps him from the material world (and so he remains stuck in his bubble of the total protection of transcendence). But the other side of this risk is decisive. By emptying himself of all content—of his total self-contained transcendence—God abandons all contingent plans to back up his existence. In this decision to risk everything for the sake of the world, the almighty God suddenly becomes as vulnerable as a fragile newborn baby, which in due course will be crucified on a Roman cross. Following Žižek's analysis further, for love to work on this cosmic level, God gives up the preservation of God's own life in order to save the life of the world. In this fashion, then, the very appearance of God in the world is itself the appearing of this risk as such—the risk that goes all the way to the absolute limit: a humiliating death on the cross of empire.[15] This is why Christ's death as the complete exposure of total risk and love is so difficult to comprehend in all its brutal perversity—it is literally too much to bear. But in the process of this absolute self-emptying, God leaves his own fate entirely in human hands. God's survival is thus wholly dependent on the memory of the church and its actions, and the church's language and action make sense only in light of this cosmic perversion. Humanity must now live into its truth. Humanity has now become God.

Žižek's stance here is no different from traditional nineteenth-century humanism. This is why Žižek follows Hegel's lead, for in the latter part of his *Phenomenology of Spirit* Hegel reverses the roles of consciousness (finitude) and the Absolute. Alenka Zupančič nicely summarizes the role that this finite/Absolute reversal plays for Hegel: "If, prior to this section, the principal role belonged to consciousness which, in the spirit of the world, had to come to its own Absolute, the main role now goes to the Absolute, which has to achieve its self-consciousness."[16] What this means

15. This is my take on Žižek's and Hegel's view of the Father's risking of his own transcendence.

16. Alenka Zupančič, *The Odd One In: On Comedy* (Cambridge, MA: MIT Press, 2008), 14.

is that God as the Absolute transcendent being must come to terms with the meaning of self-emptying (kenosis)—that is, the self-consciousness of itself as fully contingent. The question "is no longer simply that of how consciousness conceives of or sees the Absolute, but also of how the Absolute sees itself."[17] God himself must come to terms with the radicality of such an act of love, and here Zupančič tells a joke that takes place within the context of an Enlightenment society of revolutionary terror: "A man is put in prison because he believes in God. By various means, but above all by means of an enlightened explanation, he is brought to the knowledge that God does not exist. When he is freed, the man comes running back and explains how scared he is of being punished by God. Of course he knows God does not exist, but does God know it, too?"[18]

God's total vulnerability comes to terms with itself in the precise act of death: Jesus Christ dies on the cross for the sake of the world. And now the world must come to terms with the very meaning of this act. This is how Zupančič (and Žižek) reads Hegel. But to what extent does this understanding of the meaning of the crucifixion conform to Paul's new logic of Incarnation, a logic in which, as we have seen, there is neither transcendence nor immanence, but the beyond that incarnates itself through itself paradoxically beyond the in-itself? By contrast, with Hegel, at least as Zupančič and Žižek read him, the logic of Absolute immanence wins the day. This contrast should allow us to approach Paul's logic again, focusing specifically on the question of what exactly a neither/nor (or subtractive) logic looks like.

In addressing this question, we must first discuss what Paul identifies as the "universal." For Paul the inner core of the universal is unknown even to itself. It is a universal not in the totalizing sense that already hijacks all things within its own totalizing becoming. It is a universal totally devoid of the security of transcendence (in-itself) and immanence (in-and-for-itself). The point here is that the perverse Incarnational logic must risk giving up the security that guarantees its own egocentric truth in order to continue its movement toward emancipation and salvation from death. More precisely, Paul's Incarnational universalism happens at the intersection where the cosmic Void (the Nothing) and the One of transcendence meet face-to-face in the form of a crossing of the Void into Being itself: "For the message about the cross is foolishness to those who are perishing, but to us who are being saved it is the

17. Ibid., 14.
18. Ibid., 15–16.

power of God. For it is written, 'I will destroy the wisdom of the wise, and the discernment of the discerning I will thwart'" (1 Cor. 1:18–19 NRSV). Here therefore is the crux of Paul's new universalism: "God chose what is foolish in the world to shame the wise; God chose what is weak in the world to shame the strong; God chose what is low and despised in the world, *things that are not, to reduce to nothing things that are*, so that no one might boast in the presence of God" (1 Cor. 1:27–29 NRSV, italics mine).

It is this universal that is difficult if not impossible for power to identify and target; this because its power is harnessed within its kernel of unknowing. And yet paradoxically it can be known, but in a humble, dispossessive *way*—it is not as if what Paul points to is totally unknowable and beyond the reach of comprehension. But this knowing or comprehension must be thought of as "holding a precious gift" (like a baby), in opposition to what is supposed in analytic philosophy, that to know something is to possess it—to carve out one's own egocentric intellectual "private property." In this sense, Paul's idea of the cross is a cosmic type of intellectual communism (communionism), in that ownership (method) no longer has a claim, but the truth of the world after the cross becomes a dispossessing gift of wonderment and awe. Indeed, method becomes something like a vanishing cause, appearing as if to make something temporarily visible but then ineluctably fading into thin air, as if it never happened.

Truth arrives as a cosmic destabilization in the form of the cross and is revealed in the movement of self-emptying (a subtractive movement), as God in Christ took the form of a slave being obedient to the point of death by following the outpouring trajectory of God, who, on the one hand, set aside transcendence but, on the other hand, did so without being subsequently swallowed up in pure immanence, as Zupančič (via Hegel) reads it. To make the latter mistake is to fail to see the crucial nuance of an emergent and subtractive ontology. The logic of pure immanence renders the cosmos in simply either/or terms: either it is everything or it is nothing—either the Absolute or death. But is not the radical truth of Incarnation, as Paul saw it, much more interesting in that it fails to be arrested by another a priori logic of either theology's "transcendence" or a totally banal materialist's "immanence"? Abstract concepts like transcendence and immanence, far from clarifying the logic of truth, actually occlude its materialization.

There is a children's story by Eugene Trivizas titled *The Three Little Wolves and the Big Bad Pig*, in which the traditional folktale *The Three*

Little Pigs is turned on its head. In Trivizas's revision, the Big Bad Pig is the antagonist who seeks to devour the three little wolves. The three little wolves, like the three little pigs in the traditional folktale, seek protection first in a wooden house, but the pig blows it away. Next, they move to a house made of concrete. But this too is blown away. Finally, and this is where Trivizas's story really takes a different turn, when the wolves are totally out of options they end up weaving their house out of beautiful flowers, which effectively neutralize the evil and destructive power of the pig, for the house cannot be blown away. The moral here is as simple as it is romantic: precisely by living in a house that is hopelessly fragile, the house paradoxically becomes a great and formidable dwelling that resists evil. In other words, the real truthful security actually happens in a reverse logic (or what I am here arguing for, namely, an Incarnational logic) from the normative operating one. Security happens not in building walls or dumping an irrational amount of money into the military industrial complex but rather in the beauty delivered from the grip of nihilism (which is to say, the greed that runs a capitalist system into its own demise).

Conclusion

Paul's basic truth-claim that we have identified and traced out here appears indirectly—its truth turns on its subtraction, its tarrying with the negative. In this sense, Paul's claim that truth abides in the negation (and subversion) of a positive and arrogant corpus of knowledge-claims hijacked by apparatuses of power is thereby repulsive to the basic premises that found Western philosophy. This is the case not only because Western philosophy (as founded by Socrates and as intensified by the likes of Descartes and Kant) is premised on the law of illusion—a fundamental misperception of reality seen only in terms of possession whereby knowledge equals power and vice versa. This too is why Michel Foucault's entire corpus is captured by an ontology of violence, precisely because power is equated with knowledge, and knowledge with power. Paul's claim radically departs from both Greek and modern philosophy because its power and strength happens in the very act of the impossible—the truth appears in the world not by owning it but by its very disownership and dispossession—a communism. By not owning or mastering it, one can be (dis)possessed by it. It is the truth of death on the far side of its own logic. Death's grip on reality suddenly slips.

It is this paradox of Incarnation that births the truth with whom one does not need a master but a friend—a truth whose dwelling place is hidden from the view of philosophy dislodged from the dogma of both transcendence and immanence.

This is the very truth of the idea whose very inner content is devoid of itself—its truth is empty of itself and so gives birth in ways immeasurable and infinitely beyond the possible.

PART 2

On the Liturgy

4

Liturgy and the Senses

CATHERINE PICKSTOCK

A Christian understanding of liturgy confounds many of our common understandings of the nature of worship. Liturgy is not simply an outward and symbolic honoring of a God whom we know already through internal experience or conceptual reflection. Rather, it is the most important initial way in which we come to know God and the path to which we must constantly return—in excess of the relative poverty of our private emotional experiences and the equal poverty of abstract speculative theology. This is because human beings are mixed creatures—part beast and part angel, as Pascal expressed it. This apparently grotesque hybridity is our miniature dignity. Unlike angels, we combine in our persons every level of the created order from the inorganic, through the organic, through the animally psychic to the angelically intellectual.

It is true that God must communicate to us through our bodies and senses as a tilting of his sublime thought toward our mode of understanding. But this does not denote condescension and economic adaptation. Human beings have a privileged access to the mute language of physical reality. The latter is an essential part of God's creation for a biblical outlook, part of the plenitude of the divine self-expression. Even if it is less than angelic rational being, it must be, as part of this plenitude, an essential part, and so reveal something of God hidden even from the angels themselves, just as the angels (according to the New Testament) could not comprehend the mystery of the Incarna-

tion. The dumb simplicity and lack of reflexivity in physical things, or
the spontaneity of animals, show to us aspects of the divine simplicity
and spontaneity itself, which cannot be evident to the somewhat reflec-
tive, discursive, and abstracting operation of limited human or angelic
minds. This is why sacramental signs have for us a *heuristic* function;
they are not just illustrative or metaphorical. They prompt us to new
thought and guide us into deeper modes of meditation because they
contain a surplus that thought can never fully fathom.

Liturgy is not simply a public duty relating to collective concerns
(often today almost excessively expressed in the political focus of pe-
titionary prayers) that stand in contrast to inner spiritual formation.
Rather, it is itself the primary way in which the Christian, throughout
her life from baptism to extreme unction, is gradually inducted into
the mystery of revelation and transformed by it.

Liturgical Mystery

"Mystery" for St. Paul names the primal secret shown to us through
Christ's life and the liturgical participation in that secret: "the wisdom
shown in mystery that was once hidden," as one might translate the
phrase in 1 Corinthians 2:7. (See also Matt. 13:11; 1 Cor. 15:51; Col.
1:27). "Mystery" is a Greek term whose context was the mystery religions,
especially those of Eleusis, which reenacted the descent of Persephone
into the underworld and her partial rescue. While such rites had initially
been seen as local fertility cults, when they were later observed by perplexed foreigners they often became fused with a more metaphysical element and were thought to offer participants an induction into immortal
life for their souls. The word *mysterion* referred to the rite itself that
revealed and yet preserved a secret. One can say that Paul's use of the term
for the revelation in Christ as perpetuated by the church implies that he
regarded the historical drama of Christ's life (which indeed began with
his obscurely liturgical baptism by John in the Jordan) as itself a liturgy,
the perfect worship of the Father, which could be performed by the Son
alone (a theme that became dear to French mystics of the seventeenth
century, beginning with Pierre Bérulle). However, Paul implicitly saw
the liturgy of the church as a genuine making present again, and even a
continuation of, the original salvific drama.

And so we are redeemed and can be redeemed only through participation in the liturgical process; this is at once a speaking, acting,

sensorial, and contemplative process, as the twentieth-century German liturgist Dom Odo Casel insisted.[1] The Christian mystery, like the pagan

1. See Odo Casel, *The Mystery of Christian Worship*, trans. Burkhard Neunhauser, OSB (London: Darton, Longman & Todd, 1963). Louis Bouyer was originally critical of Casel's "mystery" thesis but later came substantially to accept it. However, he continued to be critical of Casel's cautious suggestion that early Christianity either adopted in part or was able later to communicate itself in the language of the pagan mystery religions and echoes of its practices. However, even Bouyer was forced to concede that one cannot rule this out, and that the word *mysterion* in Greek would have had this association. Moreover, his arguments against Casel appear to have been partially mistaken. He insisted that "mystery" in the mystery religions referred only to the rite, whereas in St. Paul it refers to the apocalyptic secret that the rite discloses and that concerns the entire history of the relation of God to the world. However, Andrew Louth's radicalization of Bouyer's reflections on "mysticism" suggests that in order to insist with Bouyer on the rooting of mysticism in both the liturgical mystery and the "mystical" sense of scripture, one should insist that "mystical" refer not directly to a spiritual level but to the ritual or textual level that both guards and partially purveys a hidden secret; see 1 Cor. 2:7, where Paul speaks of "a wisdom in mystery" that "we speak of." All the evidence would suggest (though Louth does not say this) that this is true also of the word *mysterion* in the case of the pagan mystery religions—the rites of Eleusis, Dionysus, and Orpheus—and it is clear that they were concerned with an entering of the divine into the life of the world that allowed initiates in turn to rise to immortal life, even though they lacked a historical dimension. Bouyer suggested that Plato saw the "secret" of the mystery religions as a mere metaphor for the true secrets disclosed by philosophical dialectic. But many scholars would now agree that Plato sees his philosophical secrets as akin to those of the mystery religions and regarded dialectic more in terms of a propaedeutic to an entering into religious experience of the kind that these cults encouraged. Furthermore, there seems to have been a long history, since Pythagoras, of interaction between the mystery cults and philosophy—an interaction that "theurgic Neoplatonism" in late antiquity revived but did not invent, contrary to what Bouyer implies. Bouyer is correct to modify Casel by pointing out how Paul's sense of mystery is suffused with an idea of the disclosing of the secrets of divine wisdom in a realized apocalypse. However, it is plausible to surmise a merging of such Jewish discourse with a pagan element, because it is true that the notion of a "dying and rising god" is not a Jewish thematic. When Paul speaks of dying with Christ in baptism in order to be raised with him, or of putting on the garment of Christ, his language does indeed sound closer to that of the mystery cults than to that of Hebrew tradition. Moreover, a precursor to baptism in the Hebrew Bible can be found only in the purifications undergone by priests before entering the sanctuary, whereas in the mystery cults immersion in water was often part of the proceedings for all initiates. Significantly, Christ himself had already undergone baptism by John the Baptist, and in very ancient iconic depictions of this event—for example in Ravenna—it is shown to have resulted in the defeat of the "god" or the demonic spirit of the Jordan River: perhaps this fuses a pagan notion of overcoming chthonic gods with a Hebrew one of defeating the primordially "chaotic" dimension of water and the sea. What motivated twentieth-century theologians almost universally to reject any association with pagan mysteries was that this was proposed by opponents of Christianity such as James Frazer and was then adopted by German liberal theologians trying to show either that the sacramental dimension of Christianity was a false pagan contamination or that Christianity could be syncretistically linked to universal human religious impulses. However, the highly orthodox Catholic monk Odo Casel realized that a certain New Testament fulfillment of certain pagan ritual intuitions (as celebrated by Cicero, for example) is entirely compatible with the universalism of the Christian religion. "Jewish" does not simply equate to "revealed," and "Hellenistic"

mysteries, concerns an induction into things shown, said, and done (the latter being the *dromena* of the pagan cults). Otherwise, Christ would be only a human example and not the God-man who infused into us a new sharing in the divine life by conjoining his own body with the body of the church. However, the Christian mystery, unlike pagan mysteries, is an initiation offered to all—to slaves and metics as well as to freemen, women, and children. It brings together initiation with universal citizenship and an entering of all into a school of wisdom, synthesizing mystical, political, and philosophical elements that classical antiquity had tended to keep apart.[2]

Nor is liturgy to be seen purely as a "spiritual exercise" of an Ignatian sort, however valid that may be in its own place. It is not merely intended to transform the consciousness of the worshiper by a vivid appeal to his imagination, even if this is indeed one of its aspects. Rather, as the early twentieth-century German Catholic philosopher and priest Romano Guardini emphasized, liturgy is a kind of play, something carried through like a game for its own sake and not for the sake of anything else.[3] Indeed, the only real reason for performing a liturgy is that there might be more liturgies and that we might eventually offer ourselves in the eschatological liturgy.[4] That ultimate worship, like all preceding worship, enacts and celebrates the outgoing of all things from God and the return of all things to God, including the rejection of God by created things through the perverse will of human beings and fallen angels, and the divine overcoming of this rejection through the "mystery" of the divine descent and human elevation.

does not simply equate to "secular." Today, indeed, we understand that the world in which Jesus was born was a Jewish-Greek-Roman world in which there was a combining of these diverse cultures. The fact that Justin Martyr, for example, polemically accused the Greek mystery religions of false interpretations of the biblical messianic prophecies suggests strongly that Christians of this period were highly aware of the links between Christianity and the mystery cults. Casel notes that Mediterranean cultures previously, or even still in post-Christian times, suffused by these mysteries, have proven more consistently hospitable to Catholic Christianity than either Jewish or Germanic cultures. See Louis Bouyer, *Life and Liturgy* (London: Sheed & Ward, 1978), 86–115; Andrew Louth, "Afterword: Mysticism: Name and Thing," in *The Origins of the Christian Mystical Tradition*, 2nd ed. (Oxford: Oxford University Press, 2007); Edward A. Beach, "The Eleusian Mysteries," in The École Inititative, http://users.erols.com/nbeach/eleusis.html.

2. Bruno Blumenfeld, *The Political Paul: Justice, Democracy, and Kingship in a Hellenistic Framework* (Sheffield: Sheffield Academic Press, 2001).

3. Romano Guardini, *The Spirit of the Liturgy*, trans. Ada Lane (New York: Sheed & Ward, 1934), 176–84.

4. Catherine Pickstock, *After Writing: On the Liturgical Consummation of Philosophy* (Oxford: Blackwell, 1998), 176–92.

Liturgy is a play more serious than any seriousness. It incorporates the drama of cosmic redemption in the fashion just mentioned: a drama of descent and elevation, because to be fallen means to be without the capacity of rising again on one's own account. Once Adam had asserted himself against God and so ceased to offer all back to God in worship, it was not possible for him to correct himself by recovering a true concept of the divine. This true concept was available only through the right orientation of the human person—spirit, soul, and body—in worship, for reasons that we have seen. To restore human worship of God, God must himself descend in person to offer again through the human being such true human worship.

This kenotic movement, which is central to Christian liturgy, is repeated within the ordering of the individual human economy itself. Even though the body and the senses can constantly teach the mind something that the mind does not know, requiring the mind's humility if it is to be properly proud, it is nonetheless the case that the mind should govern the body on account of its greater capacity to abstract, judge, and comprehend, just as for St. Paul the man should rule the woman in marriage, even though she has an indispensable contribution to make (beyond that of childbirth, unlike Augustine's perhaps more reductive reading). But when Adam and Eve yielded to temptation, they allowed their greedy and power-seeking passions to overrule their intellects, just as, for the church fathers, a man had followed too closely the advice of a woman! In this way, the natural government of the mind over the passions, the senses and the body, was overthrown. However, Augustine, other church fathers, and Aquinas all taught that this natural order is to be restored through a further humiliation of the mind. The body, the senses, and the passions, like our mother Eve, are relatively innocent; they have simply been given undue weight. The mind, like Adam, is guilty of a far more positive perversity. So the senses must now be deployed, liturgically, to reinstruct the mind.

And it is hinted that, because the means deployed was in the first instance the incarnation of the Logos, and this involved, beyond any mere instrumentality, the eternal elevation of Christ's human nature, including his body, to unity with the Godhead, all human sensation is likewise eternally raised higher than its originally created dignity.[5] As the

5. John Milbank and Catherine Pickstock, *Truth in Aquinas* (London: Routledge, 2001), 88–111.

Eastern Orthodox tradition has emphasized, matter—and particularly the human body—is now more porous to the passage of the divine light. The play of the liturgy is therefore a play of the newly transformed and heightened senses, beckoning the intellect to follow them back into the true divine ludic economy.

Since the passions and the sensations have now become ontologically heightened, the tradition also intermittently recognized a subtle transformation in the ontological order of gender relations: a man, Christ, stands still highest among humanity, yet only as more than human, as divine reason incarnate. But within the ranks of human beings, a woman now stands in the highest place: Mary the mother of God. Since the supposedly weaker sex first fell subject to temptation, it is the weaker sex that must reverse this temptation and be raised to the status of first among mortals, more elevated even than the cherubim. As certain medieval writers suggested, while it was Eve who seized the fruit of the knowledge of good and evil from the tree, it is Mary who through a passionate yielding to the Holy Spirit now bears in her womb the living fruit of the Word of God itself, and this is later transformed into the fruit of the Eucharist, which all may eat for their salvation.[6] The liturgical action is not only primarily a sensory affair; it is also a movement of active receptivity on the part of the church, which is identified with Mary as the bride as well as mother of Christ. As passionate bride she is conjoined to the bridegroom of true reason in order once more to engender the bridegroom as human Son in the new form of a sacramental food that is nourishing to our entire person—body, senses, imagination, and intellect.

Finally, liturgy is neither passive contemplation nor merely a human work of art. Rather, it exceeds this contrast. The liturgy is indeed first given to us because the life of Christ is, itself, as we have seen, the first liturgy and continuing inner reality of our own liturgies. This is just the way in which the full grace of Christ comes to us—liturgically, in baptism, the Eucharist, and the other sacraments. But because it comes to us liturgically it is not something in which we must simply passively believe and so be "justified," as for the Protestant misreading of St. Paul.[7] Because grace is liturgical, the transmission of a mystery through a sharing in that mystery, the reception of grace has from

6. See Ann W. Astell, *Eating Beauty: The Eucharist and the Spiritual Arts of the Middle Ages* (Ithaca, NY: Cornell University Press, 2006), 27–61.

7. Casel, *Mystery of Christian Worship*, 9–49.

the outset also a practical dimension. For us to receive the action of the liturgy, we must also perform it, and in this respect it is indeed a "human work of art." The Opus Dei of the liturgy, as it was known to the Benedictine order, could not be "work" at all unless it were also a human work.

However, as Guardini suggested, liturgy exceeds the pathos of human life and the pathos of human art.[8] The former is all too real, not just falling short of hopes and expectations but also often lacking in authentic aspiration. Art, on the other hand, offers an idealization of life, a continuous consolation without which life would be rendered unbearably naked and forsaken. The images of art offer us visions of the good, new possibilities of human self-realization that lie, as it were, just out of sight. These images also redeem and conserve the fleeting passage of the images offered us by nature herself. In this way they half abolish death and can even image death itself as suggesting an eternal life beyond life as we know it: much of the grandest human art is funereal art.[9] Nevertheless, between art and life we continue to live in a duality of life without meaning that is doomed to death, and meaning that is yoked to a virtual life and a kind of spectral eternity. Guardini suggested that liturgy overcomes this duality because here the contrast between "real" history and artistic representation is foregone as long as one suspends disbelief in such a possibility or rather suspends belief in a fallen, secular reality. Within liturgical time and space, we borrow those liturgical roles that we put on more intensely than we inhabit our everyday characters. Just as liturgical symbols and objects are hyperreal, more real than everyday instrumental things or words, so the worshipers become themselves as being "works of art." In this way, we can see how liturgy fulfills the purposes of art as imaging according to the modern Russian filmmaker and photographer Andrei Tarkovsky.[10] The image should displace the original because the original thereby becomes more itself, if what a created thing and especially the human creature is, is after all "image," the image of God. So when in the course of liturgy we are transformed into a wholly signifying—because worshiping—body, we are at that moment closest to our fulfillment as human beings.

8. Guardini, *Spirit of the Liturgy*.

9. See Andrej Tarkovskij [Andrei Tarkovsky], *Luce istantanea: Fotografie* (Milan: Ultreya, 2002).

10. Ibid.

The "Spiritual Senses" in Liturgy

In these four aspects we find a context for thinking about liturgy and the senses: (1) sacraments are heuristic and not metaphoric; (2) the physical and sensorial liturgical enactment is itself the work of saving mystery; (3) liturgy involves a redemptive heightening of the senses into the playing of the divine game; and (4) liturgy exceeds the contrast of art and life, transforming the human body into transparent image. All these aspects must be borne simultaneously in mind in any further reflection.

"Sensation," in a liturgical context, has both a passive and an active dimension, in accordance with the principle that the liturgy is a divine-human work because it is a christological work. In liturgy the participants undergo sensory experiences, but they—collectively—produce this sensory experience, along with the natural materials they deploy. In a liturgy the spectators are also the actors, or the other way around, while also the roles of acting and spectating keep exchanging one with another. Only in part since the Baroque period and only emphatically in the nineteenth century did Catholic worship degenerate into a one-way spectacle. Even though, in the Latin Middle Ages, there was, as in the East, a sharp division between chancel and nave, at least in the earlier phases of this epoch the laity (admittedly mostly the male laity, except in the preconquest British churches)[11] would on some occasions sit in the choir, while the bishop or priest would come down into the nave to sit on a subthrone reserved for him.[12]

First, let us consider the sensing, spectatorial aspect, remembering that this cannot readily be divided from the sensation-forming, acting aspect. Sensory experience in liturgy is not a kind of "prompt" or "cue" for the intellect to speak the real lines of the drama in its interior chamber. It is not an instrumental pedagogy of the mind. Indeed, insofar as the sensory and aesthetic experience of the Mass is a mode of instruction adapted to our humanity, as the Latin Middle Ages (including Thomas Aquinas) emphasized, it is seen as inciting our spiritual desire to penetrate further into the secret and worship ever more ardently.[13] Were the smell of incense or the sight of the procession or the savor of the elements mere triggers for the recollection of concepts, they would do

---

11. In Durham Cathedral one can still see the thick black line placed in front of the baptistery beyond which women were not allowed to pass even further up into the nave, following the custom of the Norman conquerors that was alien to Anglo-Saxon England.

12. See Louis Bouyer, *Architecture et liturgie* (Paris: Éditions du Cerf, 1991), 63–75.

13. See Milbank and Pickstock, *Truth in Aquinas*.

their work once and for all. But the fact that they must constantly be repeated and returned to suggests that they are vehicles for the moving of our spiritual desire, which can never entirely be disincarnate and so separate from these physical lures.

This point can appear to be contradicted by the long Christian tradition of "the spiritual senses." It was linked with meditation on Solomon's Song of Songs, an erotic poem about the love between an unidentified man and an unidentified woman, which the church has read allegorically to refer both to the love between God and the soul and between Christ and his bride, the church. Since this poem involves an active catalog of bodily parts and sensations, a luxuriant *allegoresis* sought to find both spiritual and ecclesial equivalents for every one of these physical aspects. It spoke, for example, following certain beginnings with St. Paul, of "the eyes of faith," of the neck as representing steadfastness, of hair that cannot suffer even when cut as representing spiritual endurance, of the ears as actively obedient to God's Word, of the lips as pouring forth the honey of divine praise, of the feet as the heart's following in the footsteps of previous saints and hastening to welcome Christ the bridegroom.[14]

It might seem that this amounts to the operation of a rather mechanical sort of metaphor: the senses as they function within the liturgy are natural symbols for an inner attentiveness and responsiveness to divine meaning. However, we need to recall the point that the sacraments are heuristic rather than metaphorical and add that we can think of all the gestures and actions of liturgy as sacramental in character. If then sensations are essential lures for our true thinking, and all the more so in the order of redemption after the fall, can it be simply that the "spiritual" sensations are all that really matter?

Jean-Louis Chrétien has shown in his book about the tradition of commentary on the Canticles (the Song of Songs) why this is not the case. First, the idea of the "spiritual senses," or the notion that there are psychic equivalents for physical sensations and even parts of the body, is a tradition traceable to the church father Origen, as thinkers such as Karl Rahner and Hans Urs von Balthasar have already pointed out. It is a tradition rooted in the Bible rather than in Greek thought, since the Bible speaks of "the heart" of a human being in a way that is both physical and spiritual, and includes both thinking and willing as well as suggesting a kind of concentration of the whole human per-

---

14. See Jean-Louis Chrétien, *Symbolique du corps: La tradition chrétienne du Cantiques des Cantiques* (Paris: Presses Universitaires de France, 2005).

sonality. This sense is preserved today in the liturgical *sursum cordis*: "lift up your hearts." It is, however, the Christian reading of Canticles as referring to our love for Christ, who is God *incarnate*, that seems to have suggested a kind of "physicalization" and "diversification" of the biblical "heart," which, in Origen, becomes more commonly thought of in terms of the soul, or *anima*, though Augustine often reverts to heart, or *cordis*. One should not read this, Chrétien argues, as simply many analogues for the essential unity of the heart or soul: only in God is it the case that the diversity of the spiritual senses is mysteriously "one" in pure simplicity. Rather, there is a real diversity in the human soul, on account of its close link with the body of which it is the form, in Greek philosophical terms. The soul "hears," for example, in its imaginative recollection or in its mental attention to God because it is primarily conjoined to the hearing function of the physical body.[15]

However, Chrétien implies something more radical. The point just made can be reversed. It is not that, in a secondary move, "sensation" is metaphorically transferred from body to soul; rather, it is the case that "sensing" has a dual aspect, outer and inner, from the very outset, in accordance with the double biblical meaning of the term "heart." When we see something in the first place, we see it only because we simultaneously imagine and grasp it to some degree with our minds. Unless we see something with "the eye of the mind" from the outset, we will not see anything with our physical eye at all. The same is true for all our sensations, and it is for this reason that (as Chrétien mentions) Martin Heidegger suggested that we have ears because we can hear just as much or even more than it is the case that we hear because we have ears. Likewise, Jean-Paul Sartre suggested that we have sexual organs because we are sexual creatures rather than the other way around.[16]

A related and equally crucial point is that if we see from the outset also with the inner eye, then from the outset we relate one mode of sensation to another. Clearly our seeing dark trees against the far background of the setting sun is deeply affected by our awareness that we can touch the one and not the other. And were it not for our sense of hearing, we would never be able to see the organ in a church as an organ, a musical instrument, at all. The mysterious mental operation of synesthesia (often heightened in creative personalities such as Charles Baudelaire and Olivier Messiaen) lurks from the outset whenever just one of our physical sensations is at

15. Ibid., 15–44.
16. Ibid., 35.

work. The church fathers sometimes spoke in synesthetic terms when they suggested that our eyes should listen, our ears see, or our lips attend like ears to the Word of God through a spiritual kiss, suggesting that in our inner sense contemplation is also active obedience and vice versa, while all our speaking to and of God must remain an active attention to his presence. But, once again, this kind of language does not so simply remove us from our literal bodies as one might think; instead, an inner and a synesthetic response invades the very surface of our sensitive skin in the course of our original sensitive responses.

What this implies for liturgical practice is that in worship we are always making a response of our incarnate souls—a response of the heart—to the incarnate God. This response is immediately inscribed in our bodies and requires no interpretation—just as, to use Chrétien's example, a stiff-necked person will often be literally just that. Many different psychic postures are immediately given in the stance of the human neck, as we all know. In liturgical terms this means that worshipers are invited to adopt diverse postures appropriate to the various phases of worship and the various stances that we should take before God. Sometimes we should stand before him, alert and ready as his militant troops, as Guardini suggests.[17] Sometimes we should kneel before him, adopting a posture that, according to some writers in the Christian tradition, rehearses both corporeally and psychically the fetal position of a baby in the womb. Here we express our birth from mother church as well as our utter dependence on God. The drawing closer together of the knees and the cheeks suggests for some sources a concentration around the eyes, the source of tears, which should be constantly shed by the Christian soul, both for sorrow and for joy. This suffering includes a constant spiritual shedding of blood. According to a sort of "synorganic" logic, psychic blood is clear blood with the luminosity of tears that are transparent to the divine light.[18] At other times, in processions, the soul and the body should be in movement toward God, toward other members of the congregation, or outward toward the world.

As for the feet, so for the hands. Sometimes they are tightly clasped together as though we were guarding our own psychic or bodily integrity. At other times, they are placed palm to palm in a more serene self-meeting through self-touching that allows the beginning of our

17. Romano Guardini, *Preparing Yourself for Mass* (Westminster, MD: Newman, 1993), 21–23.

18. Chrétien, *Symbolique du corps*, 42–43.

psychic reflexivity. Equally, however, as every child used to be taught, this gesture expresses our microcosmic identity with the church and its attentive pointing toward God. Hands may also be raised in supplication or openly uplifted by the priest in a gesture of triumphant saturation by the divine. Finally, the priestly hand is often raised in blessing, which is a kind of necessary acknowledgment of what is there and what has been done, which is a conferring of "grace" and which allows what is there fully to be at all, echoing the divine benediction—"and God saw that it was good"—in his very act of creation.[19]

St. Paul implies that every single part of the body is of spiritual significance, since each has its equivalent as a role within the collective body of Christ within the church. This, he says, applies even to our *pudenda*, to which the Canticles do not directly refer (1 Cor. 12:2–26). Here also, according to Paul, the Christian kenotic logic of sensation is to be observed: the most "shameful" part of either the individual or the social body is now elevated to play a significant role, since we treat our *pudenda* with the greatest of all honor by modestly concealing them. But here Paul's daring has scarcely been followed through by later commentators who, concerning the "most secret" and so "most mysterious" parts of our body, have tended to remain silent, even though they will have been aware that their role is implied by the entire nuptial imagery to which they are making appeal. This Pauline thematic allows us to say that a certain aspect of the eucharistic rite is only fulfilled in the sacrament of marriage by its ritual and actual consummation.

If, as we have seen, bodily postures are also inward, then conversely, inner sensation has an outward aspect. Because sensation has an inward aspect from the outset, it becomes possible for this inward aspect to be deepened, and so for the sight of material things to turn into the sight of spiritual things. However, the very possibility of this deepening is paradoxically connected with the excess of material things over rational thought. The mind can exceed abstract reflection in the direction of "mystical" encounter (the inward absorption of the liturgical mysteries, which was always one of their crucial aspects) only through the constantly renewed prompting of corporeal sensing of the sacramental realities. The "distance" of material things from us is a vehicle for conveying the infinite "distance" of God from us. And indeed, because of the Incarnation, in the eucharistic liturgy these two distances become one and the same.

19. Romano Guardini, *Sacred Signs*, trans. Grace Banham (St. Louis: Pio Decimo, 1956), 15–18, 81–84.

This is the valid sense in which the Eucharist can become an object of contemplation that extends beyond the eucharistic service itself. Here one has to be judicious. There is certainly a danger that the reserved sacrament or the elements carried in a Corpus Christi procession will become a mere spectacle linked with the loss of a real sense that they become the body and blood of Christ only in the context of bringing about the church as the true living body of Christ.[20] And certainly this danger was historically realized. Yet the encouragement of Corpus Christi devotion that one finds in Thomas Aquinas involved no substantial step toward such degeneracy. He did not conceive of transubstantiation as a miracle merely to be gazed at but rather completed the Dominican reaction against the Cathar heresy, which regarded matter as evil, by insisting on the physical manifestation of God within current time and space and our need to dwell upon this wonder.

In a similar fashion, the use of complex music can and has encouraged the reduction of the eucharistic service to the level of a concert for mere listeners. And yet we can recognize, far more than traditional theology was prepared to, that a complexity of musical response—which perhaps reached its acme in Bach's B Minor Mass—does not betray the message of the words it accompanies so much as it accentuates the hearing of the Word in such a way that it acquires a physical richness commensurate with the other sensory and performed elements of the Mass. The accentuated "flow" that music provides serves to convey more powerfully the truth that the Mass is the repetition and making present of the fundamental story of the world as such.

If the Eucharist renders the distance of matter from us also the distance of God from us, then when we partake of the eucharistic elements, God comes to be as close to us as food and drink entering our stomach. Hegel suggested that human religion began when people stopped seeing nature as simply something to be eaten and started to contemplate it instead. But this would be to suggest, as it were, that sacramentality began with the "reservation" of nature. It is rather the case, following modern anthropological research, that specifically human eating has always had a ritual dimension. Religion began with a sacred doing, not a sacred looking, even though the latter was involved as an aspect of the former. And ritual eating has always been at the heart of most religion, conjoined with sacrificial practices. Eucharistic worship sustains this human universality,

20. Henri de Lubac, *Corpus Mysticum: The Eucharist and the Church in the Middle Ages*, trans. Gemma Simmonds, CJ, et al. (London: SCM, 2006).

but with the radical stress that the supreme creator God has himself been sacrificed for us and offers himself to us more than we offer ourselves to him, since he sustains us through a spiritual feeding.[21]

In the eucharistic rite, moreover, we find a strange combining of spectacle with feasting. Not merely is the sacred food accompanied by ritual; it is itself the supreme ritual object and the very thing that is most displayed, in the elevation by the priest. Albert the Great spoke of the supreme beauty of the eucharistic host in terms that once more combine inner and outward aspects. The elements, like the crocus flower, exhibit *claritas*, *subtilitas*, and *agilitas*, since they show the splendor of the fullness of grace, penetrate to the height of deity, and flow with the fragrant odor of the virtues.[22] There may seem to be something shocking in the idea that we then proceed to "eat beauty," but as Ann Astell has shown, this idea was thematized in the Middle Ages. Whereas under ordinary circumstances to eat beauty would be to destroy it, here we are partially assumed by the very beauty we consume, and so our own being is transfigured and shines with a new inward and outer light. By a further process of synesthesia, we are called on in the Mass to "taste and see," not first to see and then to taste, but through tasting literally to see further.[23]

And yet the Middle Ages did not neglect the ugliness of the crucified Christ or the sorrows of Mary, which had distorted the appearance of a woman whose beauty was held to exceed even that of Helen of Troy. The Christ of the Eucharist is the Christ of the passion, a grotesquely wounded divine-human form. However, by grace even this grotesqueness is transfigured into beauty, just as the destruction visited upon Christ on the cross is transformed into a positive voluntary self-destruction of the body of Christ through our eating, which permits him to nourish the church as his body.[24] Hegel saw in the passion of Christ the source of "romantic" art, an art that combines the symbolism of the monstrous found in most pagan art with the beauty of divinized human form found in Greek art. But for Hegel this spelled the "end" of art and its displacement into philosophy and politics, since the sacred was here shown in the ordinary, the ugly, the discarded, all the sufferings of the human subject through which it develops—and which exceed—the idea of beauty. But from a Christian viewpoint, the perspective of art is infinitely opened

21. Astell, *Eating Beauty*, 227–53.
22. Ibid., 54–61.
23. Ibid., 1–26.
24. Ibid., 99–135, 227–53.

up and cannot be superseded. In the light of the cross, the ugly is not discarded but integrated into the divine beauty itself. God is not identified with the abandoned ordinary by which we come to an abstract self-realization; instead, all our specific human narratives of suffering become suffused with a significance that allows them in their specificity to mediate the divine. So instead of Christ abandoning his broken body for internal consolation, he appears as the resurrected Christ whose wounds are now glorious. And instead of Christian people abandoning the bread and wine as only that, in order to fulfill human unity in the political state, they must again and again find the source of this unity in the transubstantiated physical elements themselves.

This is the Christian truth of paradox rather than the truth of dialectic; the latter never exceeds a merely negative relation between opposites.[25] For a paradoxical perspective, God is also man—not God as mere manhood, but both God and man at the same time. By analogy, body and blood are also bread and wine, and our inner senses remain conjoined with our outer ones. It is this very outerness that allows our interior being to rise to new heights.

The sensory aspect of the liturgy is, however, not merely something passively received by the individual worshiper; it is also actively and collectively produced. All together we pray, sing, process, look forward, exchange the *pax* through mutual touch. The resultant sensory experience can to some degree be received by an individual worshiper, but it exists more fundamentally for an angelic and a divine gaze.

A Unity of Souls and Community

The collective body of the congregation is nonetheless made up of individual bodies. It is the individual body that stands as the gatekeeper between the two different allegorical senses for the bodies of the lovers in Canticles. The parts of these bodies and their sensations have spiritual aspects as "the spiritual senses." Thereby, as we have seen, Christianity diversified the unity of the soul. And yet bodies and their sensations, following St. Paul, represent offices in the church, since the latter, more emphatically than the soul, is taken to be the "bride" of the Canticles. And so Christianity unified the human social community in a very specific manner.

25. This paragraph might be read as a critique of Slavoj Žižek, *The Parallax View* (Cambridge, MA: MIT Press, 2006), 68–123.

The relationship between the inner soul and the collective body as mediated by the individual body is crucial to a deepened grasp of the liturgical action that dramatizes nothing other than the relationship between Christ and his bride. In doing so, it draws like Christianity itself upon a certain fluidity within Canticles, a book Chrétien suggests the church effectively raised to the status of a kind of "Bible within the Bible," a hermeneutic key to the relationship between the two Testaments.[26] It was a key despite or because of its own obscurity and need for interpretation. Chrétien observes that we do not know who its protagonists are at a literal level, and their status as lover and beloved is not exhausted by any conceptual equivalence. They are God and Israel, Christ and the church, Christ and the soul, but also human marriage partners (given the Pauline notion that these signify Christ and the church) as the supreme model of interhuman love, and so by extension they also represent any human loving relationship. We can see a pattern here: a sensory image elevates us but does so because and not despite the fact that it is a sensory image. It can further elevate us only if it is constantly returned to, just as we can grow in love for God only if we are constantly reconfronted with the challenge of our human neighbor.

In the liturgy, all these loving relationships are at stake. Yet the individual, sensing, physical body is their pivot. Just how are we to understand its mediating role? One can start with the earlier observation that while Christianity diversifies the soul, it also grants organic unity to the human collectivity. Instead of the polis being compared with the hierarchy of the soul, as for Plato, St. Paul compares the church polity to the cooperation of the various functions of the human body. However, this is no more a metaphor than was the case with the relationship of the physical with the spiritual senses. If anything, as Chrétien points out, metaphoricity runs from the collective to the individual body. This is because St. Paul speaks of eye and hand, head and feet, announcing their need for each other like holders of different offices within the church (1 Cor. 12:21). Yet this is to compare eye and hand, which in reality are mute, with individual Christians, who are not, rather than the other way around.[27] One might argue that there is an equal metaphoric transference of the unity of the body to the unity of the Christian people. However, the "bodiliness" of a social body is not a fiction; it is literally the case that human beings physically and culturally depend upon one another.

---

26. Chrétien, *Symbolique du corps*, 291–95.
27. Ibid., 45–72.

To revert momentarily to the case of the spiritual senses, it might appear that "diversity" is metaphorically transferred from the body to the soul. Surely the body has hands and feet and can run and smell and eat, whereas the soul cannot. However, we have already seen that without the soul there is no sensing at all, and that ears require the capacity to hear as well as vice versa. It follows that "diversity" is introduced by the soul into the body as much as the other way around. Considered simply on its own, the body is an undifferentiated mass or a flow within a wider flow—it is a "body without organs" (to use the phrase of Deleuze and Guattari) and possesses only an arbitrary, ascribed unity. For the heart is only heart as our heart, as sustaining the life of ourselves as subjects, and the same goes for livers, kidneys, hands, and feet. The physical body is only one insofar as the soul unifies it and our minds and wills command it.

The parts of the soul-body remain as parts, however, and might be regarded as merely apparent diversifications on the surface of something more fundamentally one. It is rather through the comparison of the eye and hand and other bodily parts to members of the church that this possibility is interpretatively avoided, and so the body, and then in consequence the soul, are dramatically diversified. Only the collective body of the church possesses decisively distinct parts, since these are independent people with independent wills, even if they are diversified according to specifically defined offices—priesthood, prophecy, the diaconate, and so on—rather than according to their biological individuality. For this reason it is only the church, unified through the Holy Spirit, that possesses a fully organic or bodily unity, namely, a unification of genuinely independent parts that nonetheless exceed their sum.

This reflection confirms the priority that traditional theologians have always given to the church reference over the soul reference with respect to the import of the bride. Our bodies and souls are to be conformed to the church more than the other way around. This is why there can be no Christian nonliturgical spirituality, for the rich potential of diversity specific to the Christian soul is only opened up through participation in collective worship, just as true unity of individual character is only given as a unique mirroring of the collective character of the church. When we lose ourselves in the liturgical process, then we find ourselves, whereas when we cleave to a supposedly natural unity of our souls and bodies we will find that this hysterically dissolves.

At the same time, the individual is not absorbed into the congregation as though this were a modern mass or "crowd," which represents an anticongregation.[28] Individual rumination within and upon the liturgy is crucial, and this is shown especially with respect to the traditional Canticles imagery of the teeth. Collectively speaking, the teeth guard the church, but they also allow entrance of the divine word and a "mastication" of this word by church doctors in order that they then further utter through their mouths truths appropriate to time, place, and audience. But this digestive process can be fully consummated only within the individual person, the organic unity of soul and body.[29]

There is, therefore, a liturgical tension between the priority of a congregational construction of sensation, on the one hand, and a private sensory meditation, on the other. This tension is benign and positive and in a sense never resolved. All the same, one might suggest that three rites in particular tend to hold this tension in balance. The first is the rite of marriage, in which bridegroom and bride are directly personified, so returning both the collective and the psychic allegory to their literal base. Here the inward and the outer sensory responses are at one, since the private is immediately the communal when two bodies become one. In more general congregational terms, as exhibited in the exchange of the *pax* from hand to hand, one could say that it is *relationality* that provides the real synthesis. The sensory "spectacle" of bride and bridegroom then shows to the whole church this at once literal and allegorical synthesis of the psychic with the collective.

In the Eastern churches, the marriage partners are crowned, since they have been restored to the unfallen condition of Adam and Eve, the lone monarchs of creation. However, the rite of the anointing of monarchs itself, which survives within the Anglican rite and is still technically crucial for the very constitution of Anglicanism, as it once was for the Byzantine church in practice and still is in theory, suggests a certain synthesis, gently hinted at by Chrétien at the end of his book.[30] Here one sees that the unity of the Christian body depends both on the sense of a continuous "invisible" collective body, associated with the eternal church in heaven, and on the actual personal authority of one man, a role by no means abandoned by republics that still have presidents and so forth. This dual requirement was theologically thematized in the Middle Ages as the theme of the "king's two bodies," his literal one and his "fictional" undying one, which came to be associated with

---

28. Elias Canetti, *Crowds and Power*, trans. Carol Stewart (New York: Farrar, Straus & Giroux, 1984).

29. Chrétien, *Symbolique du corps*, 73–88.

30. Ibid., 294–95.

the "mystical body" of the church, once this term had migrated from meaning the body of the eucharistic elements to meaning the body of the church itself.[31] But here we can note something quite striking: the "inward" spiritual aspect of the body now belongs to the *collective* body and the outward physical aspect to the *individual* body of the king.

This reversal is linked to the notion that the monarch reflects Christ as king, which is his more ultimate eschatological role, since the mediation of priesthood will at the end of time have ceased. Christ as head of the body is essential to its constitution, and yet he is complete and integral in himself, even if this integrity paradoxically resides in his very ecstatic self-giving to the body of the church. The same modification of the usual picture occurs, in the third place, with respect to his eternal priesthood. Christ as the one high priest is conjoined to the church and yet in excess of it. As represented by the bishop or priest in the rite of ordination, Christ in his concrete person constitutes the church in its (here relatively ethereal) collectivity. But because of this reversal the synthesis achieved by coronation and ordination is not as complete as that achieved in marriage, for in the latter case concreteness and mystical symbolism stand equally on either side of the relationship.

From the examples of coronation and ordination, we are reminded nevertheless that the church is not only an organism but a hierarchic organism. Since hierarchy is always after Dionysius a matter of instruction and elevation of person by person, not of fixed positions, we can see how hierarchy itself tends in general to fuse the individual with the collective.

The hierarchical offices of the church are provided liturgically and are reproduced through liturgical performance, which is always sensible in character. They concern the relative verbal activity of the priesthood and the relative verbal passivity of the laity. On the other hand, they also concern the relatively contemplative vocation of the clergy and the relatively active vocation of laypeople in the outside world. We are always talking therefore of a mixture of seeing and hearing, or of looking at and enacting the Word. Since, however, the two are inseparable, the danger of exegesis has always been, as Chrétien points out, to see every office of the church as ideally and exemplarily fulfilled by its supreme leaders, like St. Paul himself. And this seems somewhat to

31. Chrétien suggests that his book is a "preface" to the work of the German Jewish scholar Ernst H. Kantorowicz, *The King's Two Bodies* (Princeton, NJ: Princeton University Press, 1997).

destroy the requirement of a necessary diversity. And yet it also stresses the nonmechanical fluidity of roles, like the synesthetic fluidity of the spiritual and bodily senses. The liturgical context does not celebrate a fixity of bodily parts and sensations but rather appeals to the unknown, dynamic, and almost interchangeable character of our bodily and sensory powers. But how then is this fluidity compatible with a real diversity? Chrétien suggests that the Venerable Bede supplied an implicit answer: because any role within the church is a charismatic one, it always repeats differently the "same" christological shape, whether at the level of general differentiation of offices or the way in which these are individually fulfilled (which requires a certain fluidity between these "official" distinctions).[32]

Conclusion

In liturgy, as I have tried to show, we never leave our senses behind, and we must work together to produce a collective "sensation" that fuses life with art. But with respect to questions of government and human relationship, we have started to see how liturgy opens beyond what happens inside church buildings. In excess of church worship as such, the redemption of the world means nothing other than the increasing absorption of all human and cosmic life within liturgical celebration. This is what monks once and still try to do, but today (as literary visionaries like Balzac and Dostoyevsky realized) we require a more radical extension of this process by the laity itself. Individually and collectively we need to conjoin the Christian mystery with those natural sequences that were the origin of the pagan mysteries: to remember at each twilight that this moment, in the light of the resurrection, is the dawn of the next day and so to treat each night not only as the herald of our death but also as the expectation of heaven. On the feast of St. John the Baptist, who was beheaded for announcing Christ, we need to recall that this is also midsummer day, the start of the decline of the light, and the time of year at which Tammuz-Adonis was thought to have descended into the underworld, mourned by his bride, Inanna, during the ensuing "dog days" of intolerable heat and unnatural luxuriance that he was thought to fertilize. Supremely, at the feast of Easter, we need to recall that this is also the festival of natural rebirth upon which our very lives as human beings depend, but which

32. Chrétien, *Symbolique du corps*, 65–68.

modern worship of mere power has thrown into jeopardy.[33] As G. K. Chesterton suggested, Christianity requires us to be more and not less pagan, in a way that is quite impossible for atheists, with respect to the positive, life-affirming aspects of paganism. In exactly the same way, Christianity requires us to be more and not less attentive to our bodily senses, in order both to fulfill their infinite capacities and yet to rise beyond even their astonishing compass.

---

33. For this reason, Romano Guardini was perhaps the first to announce a recognizably "postmodern" cultural moment. See *The End of the Modern World*, trans. J. Theman and H. Burke (London: Sheed & Ward, 1956).

5

Subtractive Liturgy

CRESTON DAVIS

The Plurality of Being and Mind

In this chapter I would like to take the conclusion I arrived at in chapter 3 and attempt to square it with the Christian liturgy. My precise point in chapter 3 was that the constitution of the world's most basic reality takes place not through a positive and possessive ownership of truth (such as propositional truth) but rather through a negative (subtractive) movement. Thus truth appears not as a dominant institutional apparatus but rather in a moment of radical dispossession:[1] as Paul says, a self-emptying movement that lays claim to truths organized "in the between-ness" of the world's appearing. This subtractive ontology enables the world to relate to itself but not through a mode of mediation that traverses self-mediation (Hegel's notion of the in-itself), nor through a mode of total fragmentation, but rather through a negative movement that, in William Desmond's terms, "always keeps in mind the excess of being's plenitude that is never exhaustively mediated by

1. This phrasing is indebted to Stanislas Breton, *The Word and the Cross*, trans. Jacquelyn Porter (New York: Fordham University Press, 2002).

us."[2] Mediation of the world happens, but its "happening" takes place through our mindfulness and activity, and yet—and this is the crucial part—mediation *is never exhausted* by our mindfulness or activity within the negative unfolding process of the world. Thus the act of thinking does not sublate Being through its very mode of thinking. Mind, in other words, does not determine Being's process or phenomenological show in and of itself as mind. The basically Cartesian picture of how thinking operates is a good example of a positive and rather unfortunate ontology. The possessive movement of thought does not determine how things "appear" or materialize because, as Desmond rightly argues, Being's plenitude always traverses mind (within which the mind is as it participates in Being's subtractive unfolding). Being's excess gives itself over for thought but does so without leaving the power of thinking in the dust of the nihil. Thinking only ever exists insofar as it empties itself out of Being's happening. In other words, thinking happens, and its happening is real and in a way determinative, but its determination does not tyrannically shape the world's truth to itself as the only and unchallenging power that exists (as with Kant). This is precisely why thinking is subtractive from Being and yet is also not pitted against Being. There is something of a brokenness to Being's structural unfolding, and yet that too remains a negative determinacy that penetrates through Being's brokenness; indeed, Being's brokenness can be said to be the very condition of truth.

So we can establish that existence is other to the mindfulness of Being (forming something broken from Being), and yet mindfulness nevertheless remains determinative and meaningful as the very condition of brokenness. There is an otherness to the mind thinking, and yet this otherness to the mind is also integrally connected but not in a possessive way—potency (as this "forcing of the positive") would soon enough overtake and outstrip the broken "gap" between Being and our thinking Being from within (and in subtractive difference from) it. This weaving of otherness to thought's differentiational thinking and to its togetherness that unites thinking and Being beyond pure identity is ontologically ambiguous. And insofar as this subtractive mode is ambiguous and nuanced it seems to fly in the face of modernity's desire to nail everything down into its predetermined, scientifically assigned compartment in which there can be no surprises; there are only blind

---

2. William Desmond, *Being and the Between* (Albany: State University of New York Press, 1995), 177.

and mechanical reproductions of itself as automata. Ontology as the study of Being qua Being has too often yielded to this unambiguous scientism, and instead of abiding within the flow of the world's relational nuance and irruptive ambiguities that continue to call us (and the whole world) continually into question, it opts out too quickly for a sterile logic of reification and the banal.

Modern ontological structures such as dualism, the equivocal, and the univocal are all examples of arresting ontology by a prior logic of the unsurprising and the predictable. By contrast, the subtractive-Incarnational mode calls one to the edge of their seat but without throwing all to the whims of chaos and the Void of unpredictability. It is this nuance of Being that is always concretely in the middle of beings and that merges with the poetical; it is an honest way of attempting to account for the world's truth without prematurely committing to a logic that arrests the truth of the world prior to the world's unfolding of itself.

The turn away from the mechanical ontologies (univocity, equivocity, and dualism) results in responding to the logic of the world's unfolding openness in a manner that is both poetical and nuanced. The world's logic is poetical in that there is a real sense of playfulness in Being's disclosure and enclosure of itself. There is a certain openness to the formation and makeup of the political subject, which springs from a subtractive-Incarnational space of liminality. It is nuanced because its disclosure and enclosure (or what Desmond refers to as the "determinate" and the "indeterminate"[3]) is not simply a mechanical reproduction of itself but instead requires much more of an organic model that overcomes the temptation to merely re-present the world's unfolding through a possessive "capitalistic" modality that for all its force simply fails to capture the truth of the world's nuance, owing to its pathos and its limiting view of the world. In his discussion of the relationship between determination and indeterminacy, Desmond employs the word "play" as a means of metaphorically grasping this relationship.

> We discover a relativity between beings, one being contributing to the determination of another, another being bringing about the opening of yet another being, in the continuing of a dynamic process of becoming. So not only do beings in their *singular play* resist exhaustion in terms of determination and self-determination; beings in their *communal interplay* escape beyond singular dialectical determination. The community of beings in interplay is not a dialectical self-mediating

3. Ibid., 178–82.

whole; it reveals a metaxological intermediation between beings who are open wholes unto themselves, without being completely determined in themselves. Their relativity to others and of others to them shows multiple mediations that cannot be finalized, for the ontological freshness still flares there too.[4]

This "play" of the community of being in the between is poetical and open. The mind moves out beyond itself like a dance that sets the mind at rest all while being in motion.[5] Josef Pieper nicely identifies this engaged and yet relaxed intellectual tension and grasping in his example of what happens when the eyes gaze upon a rose. He asks, "What do we do when that happens?" And his response is like Desmond's notion of "playfulness." Pieper's response: "Our mind does something, to be sure, in the mere fact of taking in the object, grasping its color, its shape, and so on. We have to be awake and active. But all the same, it is a 'relaxed' *looking*, so long as we are merely looking at it and not observing or studying it, counting or measuring its various features."[6] We thus combine Desmond's poetical playfulness of beings related to other beings with Pieper's idea of a relaxed looking or "intellectual vision," and we derive from these the idea of the *communal relation of beings* that transcends Ernst Jünger's charge that relation is finally a pure "act of aggression."[7] Instead of perceiving beings as relating via a fundamental competition or "act of aggression," we perceive the communion of being as harmony that enacts the "dance" of relation as the interrelation or even a poiesis or a living poem.

The happening of the between as a negative dispossessive forcing—if it is truly in the poetical *between* and is a world that is not idealized away into either the Void or a projection of an immaterialized-material "world"—must unfold materially. For if the between were to happen in the world in a nonmaterial modality, it would be happening only abstractly and therefore would not have circumvented the intractable mechanical structure of the Cartesian *cogito*.

4. Ibid., 182, italics in original. For this notion of poetical playfulness of the plurality of beings in their relation to other beings, see William Desmond, *Perplexity and Ultimacy: Metaphysical Thoughts from the Middle* (Albany: State University of New York Press, 1995), esp. chap. 1, "Being Between: By Way of Introduction"; and William Desmond, *Beyond Hegel and Dialectic: Speculation, Cult, and Comedy* (Albany: State University of New York Press, 1992).

5. The mind in motion, or animation, was first argued in a sustained way by Aristotle in *De anima*.

6. Josef Pieper, *Leisure, the Basis of Culture*, trans. Gerald Malsbary (South Bend, IN: St. Augustine's Press, 1998), 9, italics mine.

7. Ernst Jünger, *Blätter und Steine* (Hamburg: Hanseatische Verlagsanstalt, 1934), 202, quoted in Pieper, *Leisure*, 9.

Incarnational materiality must be the sine qua non of our ontological notion of the subtractive ontology. Without the material (as more than merely the reduction to itself), all simply remains in the ether of speculation. Yet the material cannot be captured or determined by Descartes' metaphysical dualism, in which matter and spirit are forever disrelated.

In furthering our discussion about materializing Being's community of beings we must first delineate what we mean by materiality. Prima facie, there are two different notions of materiality. There is first a banal and reductive materiality. This view of materiality is inherited from dualism and cannot within itself escape from it. John Milbank defines this view of materiality as "atomistic, mechanical, passive and inert, and tends to explain away meaningful action and volition as illusion."[8] The second and more productive way of thinking about materiality is a nonreductive version of matter, which Milbank tells us, is the site of "a spontaneous and unpredictable energy."[9] This spontaneous and always surprising energy corresponds to a specific but crucial aspect of Desmond's metaxological ontology, in which there is an irreducible and always renewing and renewable surplus or plurivocity of Being's happening. Being's happening is plural and always arrives in refreshing newness—as recently birthed from the eternal Void. Something beyond, some form of otherness is—and its very singularity exists somehow together with Being's consciousness of itself as mindfulness. Indeed, it is precisely this surplus and ex-static plenitude in Being's happening that allows mind to escapes from the tautological circuit of pure self-consciousness. We can relate this to my chapter on Paul (chap. 3), in which this "ex-static plenitude of Being's happening" is finally and fully expressed in the Incarnation, which prevents the reduction of all to the One and the Multiple to pure fragmentation and flux. This surplus energy as material, in other words, is the only event that happens within Being's happening, which finally becomes the true alternative from Being's suffocating asthma of capitulating to the view that all is finally consciousness becoming conscious of itself as self-consciousness. This surely is the trap that gives rise to an ontology (the framing of the world) that prematurely commits itself to a quasi transcendence within the horizon of immanence.

8. Creston Davis, John Milbank, and Slavoj Žižek, eds., *Theology and the Political: The New Debate* (Durham, NC: Duke University Press, 2005), 393.
9. Ibid.

The modernist view—a view that takes materiality as the "all in all"—
marks the death of Being, relegating it to the dungeon of anthropocentri-
cism sundered from transcendence. Being essentially dies because there
is nothing outside the pure representation of Being's self-consciousness
of itself as conscious. Pure consciousness of itself as conscious is already
a configuration of death, and this because thought is never able to tran-
scend itself, and in this precise regard Hegel is right when he remarks that
the arrival of historic consciousness is the mark of the end of history.[10]
In contrast to this view of history's death, the totality of all past events
that culminates in a determination of all future possibilities (i.e., the
impossibility of any future at all), we must not simply posit an alternative
subtractive ontology that may be equally guilty of idealism, but we must
do so in concrete and materializing ways: without the materialization of
the infinite appearing of truth from the Void, there is simply nothing.
Toward this end, we must think the relation between Being's surplus with
(and perhaps against) a nonreducible materialism that is spontaneous
and life giving. This relation between materialism and Being's surplus
springing out of the Void will be attended to in the next section, but for
now I want to think through the logic of Being's surplus in relation to
perceiving the truth of Being from this vantage point.

Yet it would not be altogether correct to think of Being's surplus as
simply a convenient alternative to the self-enclosure of Being's logic.
To think of the surplus of Being as merely a way out of Being's self-
representation would be to reduce its existence to a mere function premised only on the primary existence of Being's terminal but inevitable
self-enclosure. Rather, I propose that we think of this unpredictable
and yet spontaneous and overdetermined energy as the kernel of life's
arrival, "the life of life," as Alexander Schmemann once put it. In the
beginning of his extraordinary study *For the Life of the World*, Schmemann raises the question that is the wellspring of the world: "What is
the life of life itself?"[11] His question is not conditioned upon either the
primacy of nihilism, as Jean-Paul Sartre's point of departure clearly

10. History here thus becomes the condition of possibility, that is to say, the Kantian transcendental category, which folds back into a dualist metaphysical structure. In this regard, Hegel's
"history" as the telos of "thought thinking itself" (i.e., Descartes' basic formula of "I think,
therefore I am," which founds modern philosophy) already begins to prefigure Heidegger's notion of "death" as the telos that determines authenticity. See Martin Heidegger, *Being and Time*
(New York: Harper & Row, 1972).

11. Alexander Schmemann, *For the Life of the World: Sacraments and Orthodoxy* (Crest-
wood, NY: St. Vladimir's Seminary Press, 1963), 13.

was,[12] nor is his question only about trying to find the reified "escape hatch"[13] in Sartre's nihilistic structure, seen most poignantly in Sartre's drama *No Exit*, the traces of which echo loudly in Alain Badiou's *Being and Event* (but are somewhat mitigated in *Logics of Worlds*).[14]

Significantly, Schmemann's question cast in a positive mode helps us to experience a more honest approach to the birth of Being's surplus: "What is the life of life itself?" Later on in his text Schmemann deepens the scope of his question, saying that this very possibility of the world's otherness of life as life "is not an escape from the world, rather it is the arrival at a vantage point from which we can see more deeply into the reality of the world."[15] This is all to say that we must resist thinking of this spontaneous surplus of Being's otherness to mindfulness as a simple convenience that finally escapes from life's meaningless return to itself in absolute nondifferentiated repetition. This would be tantamount to thinking within the domain of dualism: on the one side would be "surplus," a total otherness that never touches the world, and on the other side would be nothing but nihilism.

The basic question that we confront here is how to climb to the "vantage point from which we can see more deeply into the reality of the world." We have already linked up the specific aspect of St. Paul's subtractive-Incarnational ontology with this precise point—namely, a vantage point from which the reality of the world can be seen even "in a glass darkly." That is to say, the birth of the world's reality happens in the happening of the arrival of the world's plenitude that overflows Being as other to beings. It is this spontaneous irruption of the world's ex-staticality that becomes and "is" (in its flowing "appearancial" sense) the world's vantage point of truth. The vantage point is thus never actually a "point" in the sense of a static and immovable geometric entity identified between two or more axes on a plane. Rather, the vantage point is itself on the move, but its process must not be confused with Hegel's ontological Becoming, in which the Becoming of the world is always a

---

12. Jean-Paul Sartre, *Being and Nothingness: A Phenomenological Essay on Ontology*, trans. Hazel E. Barnes (New York: Washington Square Press, 1956).

13. I say "reified 'escape hatch'" because the very notion of an "escape hatch" that exists within Being's self-enclosed nihilism already capitulates too much to nihilism. I suppose that the world is nihilistic, and the only way out is to invent a threshold through which true freedom can be achieved. An example of this would be the 1997 film *Cube* (DVD, directed by Vincenzo Natali [Lions Gate, 1999]).

14. See Creston Davis, "Badiou's Twin Problem" (paper presented at the annual meeting of the Society for Phenomenology and Existential Philosophy, Pittsburgh, 2008).

15. Schmemann, *For the Life of the World*, 27.

more fundamental *self*-Becoming. For we want to go beyond Hegel's point here by submitting the thesis that the Becoming of the world is something even alterior to the a priori "self" in "self-Becoming." In other words, something other than just the return to the "self" is unfolding, and this is crucial to grasp in order to take seriously the very notion of Becoming-as-subtraction as a kind of abiding with that which cannot be seen. The Becoming is thus something other than otherness defined by the dualism of the same/other, and this is the radical point that Hegel presents to us in a way that gets to the heart of Paul's antiphilosophy.

In this regard the "vantage point of reality" as I am arguing is always in movement beyond and other to its self-movement (in the negative sense), and this is because it is itself predicated upon a more fundamental movement of Being already *beyond* and yet miraculously together with mindfulness. To argue that we actually reach the unshakable heights of a static reality would commit us to one unforgivable error: this move to connect the world's reality (as pure and transparent) with the surplus of the world's Being in its ex-staticality would too quickly and too neatly domesticate reality's "truth," which would in this case be predetermined by the world's surplus. In other words, the "world's Incarnational surplus" is itself captured by the concept of the "world's surplus" as such, and therefore is not properly an unpredictable "surplus" as much as it is a predictable "surplus," which is not surplus at all but a curtain behind which one can pull the strings of the ontotheological puppet. For surplus to be true otherness to Being's disclosure to mind, by its nature, it cannot be captured in this way; indeed, it cannot be captured in any way at all, as it comes at us like a wave on a sea, lifting us up and dragging us down in its wake.

Desmond has already given a *way* to prevent us from making this fatal error, and this way is the metaxological—the happening of Being within the middle of beings. In the *middle, the surplus of being* arrives from without and is the precondition of itself as the middle of Being's happening. That is to say, we must be faithful to that which we can only be faithful to—and that is the happening of Being in all the anxiety that emerges out of our radical contingency and temporality. Thus the broken middle cannot, if you will, overtake the surplus, plenitude of its very arrival; it must rather await and yet still be an intimate part of the show of Being's happening. Thus the very logic of the subtraction prevents us from making this link between "reality's truth" and the "surplus of Being." We as codeterminers of Being's truth cannot forge this link between reality's truth and the birth of Being's pure surplus.

This is also true because Being's pure "surplus" in the paradox of the Void is determined by its integral constancy in the face of change. In this case the "subtractive surplus" would be that which brings "newness" to the world. However, surplus's newness can only be received within the matrix of the world's middle—that is, in its Incarnate brokenness. Thus there is something "new" as the surplus, and yet there too is something "old" in the arrival of the "new" within the middle (which gives us the self-transcending ground from which reception of this is capable of being received). And yet there is something "old" and seemingly unchanging in the middle of Being, and thus this middle is itself radically "new" too. In other words, "the middle" is dynamic precisely because it refuses to determine "truth" before it happens—and yet does not *not* determine it either.

The surplus of the world's irruptive and unpredictable energy must remain in tension with, on the one hand, our thinking of it and, on the other, its otherness beyond thought that is its birth in the death of Logos (the world's broken and dispossessing first principle). But then we must turn our attention to what this "tension" in which thought and the surplus of Being are related is—how it persists over time, traversing the flux of change and yet remaining coherent enough, we assume, to maintain a minimal level of "tension." To understand this "existential tension," we must start by laying out what we have grasped thus far.

In this section we have canvassed how the relation between mindfulness and Being's plenitude (or surplus) is much more nuanced and plural than other ontologies that simply collapse thought and Being into a monolithic univocity. This plural relationship between mind and Being, we saw, is related in a communal, interrelated, and even poetical way. We also briefly introduced into our discussion the seminal notion of materiality, which, as we observed, could take on either a univocal logic or a plural logic of Being's plenitude and surplus. Finally, we finished this section by trying to relate Being's surplus to a vantage point of "reality," which was ultimately an impossible task: a totalizing foundation of reality is simply impossible to erect if one desires to be faithful to Being's community of plurality.

The Risk of Being in Community

We have identified and characterized the relation between mind and Being, but in what does this "tension" between them consist? We know that Being is always on the move, and we know this because there is always something more to mind thinking itself, and this is what we have identified as Being's "surplus." Moreover, this "surplus" that arrives like a gift does so in a manner that cannot be accounted for by reducing its origin to either transcendence alone or to pure univocal immanence, but rather arrives as surplus in a middle brokenness that alights within the tension of Being's unfolding and our mindfulness of it. Being therefore unfolds in at least two senses: first, there is something more to thought thinking itself (contra Descartes), that is, surplus; and second, the mind thinks by traversing this very surplus in relation to itself as mind. It is within these two senses—of Being's surplus and of the surplus of thought thinking itself in relation to itself (as thought)—that this "tension" indwells. In this respect this notion of the indwelling tension of Being and mind is another way to understand what we name as an ontological community. I say "community" because of the interconnectedness of the poetical "play" of beings that happens in the incomplete betweenness of Being. This "community" of Being and mind is the locus that births singularity (or Oneness), and yet there coexists with Oneness difference or subtractive multiplicity within itself.[16] The community of this synthesis is one united plane on which Being and mind relate without canceling themselves out in a dialectical overcoming, and yet the community is composed of difference. There are many minds, and there are many different *differences* of the world's display of itself in various modes. In Aristotle's words, "Being is said in many senses."[17]

This idea of community—the community of Being and mind that richly gives unity and difference—can never, by its nature, be a self-determining community. This community does *not* determine Being— it cannot because it is not Being in-itself (which is impossible), but it nevertheless unfolds within Being's dynamic unfolding. That is, the community of Being rests upon a dynamism and flux that inherently resists an ontological closure of "truth" captured and domesticated. Moreover, this community cannot determine mind either. Thought thinks relation and difference beyond community, and yet community persists as that which reunites thought to itself differently and Being's arrival in surplus beyond thought *and* in mind thinking the surplus in

16. We will see later in this chapter exactly how relation between Oneness and difference works within the ontological community.

17. *Metaphysics* 4.

relation to itself. Without community, Being and thought would unite, and we would return again to either a monism or a dualism; and the Incarnational tension would give way to ontotheology. Ontological community thus gives us an abiding structure that is always changing (and incomplete) and yet remaining true to itself as community.

Community gives us the gift of conceptualizing ontological relation between relation (difference) and nonrelation (identity) without reverting to one side or the other. In this manner we can clearly see that this sketch of the ontological community is wholly different from Fichte's means of overcoming dualism by positing the unified structure of the ego-principle. Fichte, as glossed by Lukács, "formulates the philosophical starting-point," that is "the subject of knowledge, the ego-principle . . . [which] can be taken as a starting-point. . . . [This] conception of the subject . . . can be thought of as the creator of the totality."[18] The subject for Lukács is able to ascend to the zenith where "the subject and object coincide, where they are identical."[19] The problem, as we have seen, is that this reduction to a unified ego-principle is twofold. First, the unity ascribed to the ego is a unity solely dependent on the horizon of the subject (the "subject's intuition," as Fichte put it). Thus there may be unity (which prima facie overcomes the intractable problems of dualism), but this *unity* is a *self-determining unity* locked into the delimited and intuitive "space" of the subject qua subject. The second problem flows from this: once a unity is configured in terms of the subject, then the problem becomes getting from the subjective "ground" of ego to an intersubjective "ground" beyond ego in community. Fichte, as Lukács tried to show, attempted to traverse the subjective ground into the common (in which egos can coexist in some harmonious manner) via consciousness that springs from the aesthetic delivered from the Kantian sublime. (This is where Heidegger acquires his view of art as the "world's openness to the voice of Being" in his question of the origin of the work of art).[20] Yet again the movement from the subjective ground of ego to a transcendental "consciousness" no matter what the mode (aesthetic, sublime, or otherwise) fails to solve the problem of the logic of self-determination. That is, a ground of Being simply

18. György Lukács, "Reification and the Consciousness of the Proletariat," in *History and Class Consciousness: Studies in Marxist Dialectics*, trans. Rodney Livingstone (Cambridge, MA: MIT Press, 1971), 122–23.

19. Ibid., 123.

20. Martin Heidegger, *Poetry, Language, Thought*, trans. Albert Hofstadter (New York: Harper & Row, 1975), 17–20, 32–65, 71–75.

returns to itself as absolute and unbending. And this is why, in the final analysis, Heidegger must posit a reified view of "death" as that toward which all Being propels itself. "Death" is thus already self-determined prior to its happening in the world.[21] Consciousness thus becomes the ego-principle extrapolated, and this was ironically the thrust of Feuerbach's critique of religion, which in the end saw religion as a projection of one's ego that is imagined to exist in objective reality, which in turn becomes that into which all difference is diluted and to which it must conform in order to be. This realm of "projective-objective ego" becomes a heaven oppositionally related to earthy existence. From this point of view of the structure of historic consciousness, Lukács thinks that we arrive already at the concept of activity that indwells within the unified ego-principle. But once again, "activity" only unfolds according to the logics of self-determination. Again we find ourselves back in the prison of Parmenides' Oneness.

Where does this idealized version ultimately lead us? In the end there is no ontological community at all but merely a field of individuated egos that finally must require an artificial means of attribution founded by the liberal doctrine, which rested on the defining distinction between the state and the civil sphere of society.[22] Within civil society, "members are governed neither by political power nor by other members; each of them is the source of his actions" (i.e., *causa sui*), whereas the liberal state "by representing and serving the individuals' instinct for self-preservation . . . promulgates laws that guarantee to each person security and free pursuit of happiness as he conceives of it."[23]

21. Insofar as death is that toward which all Being moves, such that death is already "known" in a sense prior to its existential happening (i.e., a transcendental a priori), then death is idealized into existence. For a different view of "death" that does not rely on idealism, see the forthcoming work of Conor Cunningham, *The End of Death*.

22. This is Thomas Hobbes's view of civil society in *Leviathan*. See also G. W. F. Hegel, *Philosophy of Right*, trans. T. M. Knox (Oxford: Oxford University Press, 1952).

23. Pierre Manent, *An Intellectual History of Liberalism*, trans. Rebecca Balinski (Princeton, NJ: Princeton University Press, 1995), 66; see also 78. Thus there is an irony that emerges in our study, namely, the very attempt to ontologically ground the world's relation into a unified structure (i.e., ego-principle). This very move already precipitates the same move that founds liberal democracy, the very structure that is reinforced and promulgated by bourgeois capitalism. Lukács was certainly critical about how the laws of the state were over time bent so as to underwrite the capitalist, but what he failed to see was that the move to found a unified structure of reality within the ego was simultaneously the move that justifies the liberal state. For Lukács's critique of law, see "Reification," 103–10, esp. 108. See also Hegel's notion of the state in his *Philosophy of Right*. See also Eric Weil, *Hegel and the State*, trans. Mark A. Cohen (Baltimore: Johns Hopkins University Press, 1998).

The ontological community that I am bringing to light from the metaxological does not overcome the problem of dualism by positing a unified, predifferentiated, and self-mediating ego-principle, as Fichte argues. Thus this ontology does not implicitly or otherwise endorse an ontological structure of pure subjectivity in a way that requires positing the birth of liberal doctrine premised on the separation of the state from civil society. (An inquiry into the precise relationship between an ontological community of the sort I am espousing here and political authority falls outside this study's purview.)

This view of the ontological community is much more organic in nature. Its mode of mediation arrives not through a self-determinative structure of community in-itself (as an end in-itself) but is always mediating itself through its own arrival within the milieu of Being's unfolding otherness and Void beyond and yet united to mind. Dualism, in other words, does not dictate the terms of overcoming dualism via a self-returning method, such as Descartes'. Dualism is overcome by the broken community of the world, by opening up oneself to the porous nature of the world's unified/flow beyond self-mediation. The very method on which dualism is formulated, a decisive and pathological drive to knowledge beyond any form of doubt, supplies the poisonous ingredients by which it will eventually die. Lukács, following Hegel and Marx, attempts to overcome this problematic structure of dualism without questioning the problematic nature of the structure itself, and indeed goes on to employ a method that is derived from the same metaphysical presuppositions on which dualism rests. In the final analysis, we must ask: is there really a basic difference between Descartes' *cogito* and Fichte's ego-principle?

Ontological community is constructed by an anxious pathology driven to formulate an unshakable ground on which one can resist the unpredictable irruptions that inevitably alight in the world. In this sense, the persistence of ontological community across time is not guaranteed—indeed, the logic of its abiding in the broken middle within beings is disruptive, as it is always in flux, overturning, turning anew time and time again. There is an unavoidable risk inherently built into the rubric of the world's mediation of itself in community. Yet this risk does not justify pointless despair in the face of the total nothingness; risk here is not chance as in an arbitrary or capricious universe controlled by a pantheon of interrelated and competitive fates, jealous gods, and other minor deities.

In this section we have seen that our ontological community is defined by risk. In the first place, it must always risk itself; it must risk its own security at every turn. In this precise sense it must be seen in opposition to Bush's administration in the wake of 9/11, which ignored the risks of democracy and otherness. In the second place, risk comes with the benefit of true plurality—a true belief in the coexistence of difference on the plane of existence. The enemy of risk is thus the movement that attempts to determine how difference works in relation to a predetermined plane of possibility (i.e., the owners of the modes of production hijack true plurality in the name of selfish greed and security). This was the birth of the liberal state. As we move on to further develop our thesis, we must therefore keep in mind not only the truth of plurality in the Being of the broken between, but we must also remain faithful to risking our attempt to turn Being into our own image. Having argued for these two truths thus far in this chapter, I want to devote the next section to comparing our ontological view, through which the world's mediation mediates itself, with philosophy's first hypotheses. In this way we can start to bring together our argument as we move closer to the conclusion.

On Materializing the "Ontological Community"

Let us review the argument up to this point. In this argument, I have tried to characterize a cosmic balance of the world's mediation in which creation participates without hijacking or overtaking the world's mediation in self-mediating terms (i.e., a vulgar humanism—or to put it more brutally, Marx's notion of *species being*). Indeed, as I have argued elsewhere, the birth of philosophy is founded in its characterization of a cosmic balance known as first principles.[24] By contrast, modern philosophy has failed to attend to the crucial conditions of mediation, opting instead for taking the easy way out via a metaphysical dualism seen supremely in Descartes and later in Kant. The philosophers Hegel, Marx, and Lukács attempted to overcome this dualism, but doing so came at the great cost of positing a mediational drive in which the human became the determiner of all reality through itself as human. Confronted with the ontological problems borne in this logic, we observed St. Paul's subtractive insight (following Socrates and Hegel) of the brokenness of Being, which reveals that the truth of the law (of the state, religion, etc.) can inhibit the truth of the world as love from its self-actuality in death as such. Following this Pauline instinct, I have attempted to construct an

24. See Creston Davis, "The Practice of Being: Liturgy as Concrete Philosophy" (PhD diss., University of Virginia, 2006).

ontological axiom that does not rely on a dualism or a monism. Hence,
this chapter is an attempt to build on St. Paul's subtractive ontology
identified earlier by embodying subtraction as the broken community
realized within a liturgical action. Although the ontological community
is able to found a tentative (im)balance that is itself always in the act of
returning to itself nonidentically, the basic problematic of materialism
still remains. At this stage of the argument we are in danger of being
guilty of all the problems that we have attempted to engage. Unless we
are able to show that the subtractive-Incarnational ontology has within
its own structure a true materialism, then our argument will finally
fall short, amounting only to senseless talk. At this stage we now must
inquire into the possibility of the ontological community expressing
itself in the world as material.

The Liturgical Event

By the "liturgical event" I mean a material event taking place in the
world that, like Michelangelo's depiction of God and Adam, contains
within its eventual horizon the relation between transcendence and
immanence not reducible to either side of these two terms. More than
this, not only is there a central focus of the liturgical event founded in
the relation between the infinite and the finite, but the *relation* itself
cannot be constituted in terms of either dualism or monism; it transcends a logic that attempts to define this relation in terms other than
those that emerge from this self-transcending relation; indeed, this self-
transcending relation of the liturgical event is a logic through which
all relation of the world is activated. This founding relation lying at
the heart of the liturgical event, according to the Christian tradition,
actually becomes the mode by which the finite and the infinite coalesce
and so embodies and discloses the Incarnational-Event that cannot be
captured by either Greek philosophy alone or the law as ideological.
At this stage this relation would only seem able to take hold in one of
three different forms. The relation between the infinite and the finite
is defined in terms of one side of the equation or the other. So the first
form would be that the infinite side determines the relation in terms of
the infinite. The second option would be to define this relation in terms
of finitude. Pausing here for a moment, we notice that both of these
forms by which relation is determined (by either finitude or infinitude)
neatly follow along the lines of a self-mediating logic. For if the infinite

overtakes the relation between finitude and infinitude, then finitude cannot possibly be more than mere illusion. Conversely, if this relation is determined by the logic of finitude, then not only is the infinite an illusion but the meaning of finitude itself can only ever be a self-defining logic, unfolding in terms of itself, which, as I have argued in this chapter, is impossible. Thus the only option for us is the third option, in which neither the infinite nor the finite alone determines the nature of the relation between the infinite and the finite. Rather it is the *relation* itself that determines the logic of the liturgical eventual horizon in which the infinite and the finite coalesce. This relation, as argued in the section above, is the community between transcendence and immanence, which gives birth to the liturgical horizon of Being as poetry.

The liturgical event is defined by the milieu that intrinsically transcends the static categories of the infinite and the finite. Or to put it slightly differently, the liturgical event is the milieu in which the meaning of the infinite and the finite arrives through itself as self-transcending *relation* beyond "self-relation." This is not to say that the infinite (as infinite) is defined by something "less" than infinity, and thus to steal away the very meaning of the infinite. On the contrary, the core relation of the liturgical event is itself the very arrival of the infinite in/as finite materiality. The two logics merge into a noncollapsible and nondialectical logic that reveals the true relation of all things beyond self-relation and absolute nonrelation. This event takes on the logic of what we have characterized in this chapter as the "subtractive happening," which takes place within the liturgical celebration materialized as the cosmic relation between self-relation and absolute nonrelation.

The event happens when the infinite (One) is fused with the finite (Multiple), limited reality through an exteriorization of the One that exists, in a manner, beyond the One and yet remains intimately within the One. The One as God in three persons—Father, Son, and Holy Spirit—comprises the cosmic community and thus becomes the unfolding and super self-transcending ground on which all reality is communal within this relation. Further, the Triune community of love, excess, and death, in effect, overflows as the "work" of the Logos (Son), which creates the material world and consequently is reconciled back into relation (beyond creation qua creation) with the Father through the Holy Spirit. Thus, John Milbank and Catherine Pickstock argue that such a Triune community of love and glory "should draw near to humanity in the most radical and unexpected fashion, because God as infinite and replete cannot possibly be rivaled, and therefore can give himself entirely—even his own divine nature to human nature."[25]

It is this "radical" act of God's drawing near to humanity that is witnessed to and performed as a material, concrete, and active liturgical movement that takes hold within (and not opposed to) the world—indeed, it completes the world as created gift. The word "liturgy" means "service," which describes the movement of God's excessive outpouring in love and glory "beyond" God's Triune life and into all levels of Being.

Furthermore, this movement or process can be seen as joining up all disparate and unrelated forms of beings in the world, and yet the conjoining (or reconciling) effect of this kenosis and return does not dilute all difference of beings into a singular mode of Being as univocal. God remains different from the world and yet immanently relatable to the world in the very Being of God. The reaching out of God as Logos therefore effectively relates all to everything else on a complex level of relation, and yet through this relation all difference retains both their requisite uniqueness and difference in mutually reinforcing ways. The logic of relation is thus fulfilled for what it truly is: a relation of all and every existent entity that yet, within this relation, maintains a true and uncollapsible difference. There is difference and there is sameness. Difference relates to sameness through God's relation within the life of the Trinity, the life of which spills out beyond itself and becomes the ground of relation of the world to itself as world.

The cosmic relation founded in the very being of God (within the Triune life) externalized from God (in the world via the work of the Logos) and reconciled back to God (via the work of the Holy Spirit) fulfills the destiny of philosophy's quest for the truth of the world's mediation of itself. Only instead of this relation repeating itself identically, as with the law of the state or of (post-Socratic and Platonic) Greek philosophy, this relation returns to itself nonidentically—precisely through the brokenness of Christ's death (i.e., Paul's subtraction), and so is self-transcending, but in a manner not reducible to violence. Moreover, this configuration is not some idealized speculation wholly removed from concrete reality. In fact this cosmic relation of all things to everything else that still retains within it a sustainable difference is materialized in the very expression of the world's mediation of itself within a performed liturgy.

25. John Milbank and Catherine Pickstock, *Truth in Aquinas* (London: Routledge, 2001), 62.

The liturgy thus advances the aesthetic form beyond the limiting mediums of the subjective sublime, or even art forms such as painting and sculpture. For these mediums that try to capture the dynamic interaction of the infinite and the finite are somewhat helpful but in themselves simply too limiting. They are restrictive insofar as they fail to "host" the space in which we (as human beings, along with other lesser forms of beings, such as animals, plants, and even stones, and higher forms of beings, such as God, archangels, angels, and the heavenly hosts)[26] can actually perform within the dynamic interaction/relation of the world with itself in God's appearing at the center of the liturgy as the Word (Logos) celebrated in the Eucharist, which is activated and inspired by the Holy Spirit's procession from the Father to the Son and back again to the Father.[27]

The bread and the wine (which make up the "host") are brought to the liturgy from the harvest of the fields—the *surplus* bounty of the earth. These fruits of the earth become, according to Rite 2, an offering of "our [human] sacrifice of praise and thanksgiving to you, O Lord of all; presenting to you, from your creation, this bread and this wine."[28] But before the bread and the wine can even become "ready" to be such an offering, it must be taken into consideration just how contingent this "sacrificial" economy really is. In the first place, the harvest of the field is never guaranteed; everything is utterly dependent on a range of relations—the relation between the earth and the sun (which is galactic) as well as the relation between the sky and the earth that happens through the fruits of the sky in precipitation: rain, snow, sleet, and wind. Further, there is the relation of the earth to itself in the soil that hosts the vegetative seed and establishes a permeable relationship whereby the minerals and nutrients give the seed health and nourishment. All these relations must be relatable for the fruits of the earth to grow and mature. Then there is the relation between human beings and the earth

26. "Therefore we praise you, joining our voices with Angels and Archangels and with all the company of heaven, who for ever sing this hymn to proclaim the glory of your Name" (Holy Eucharist Rite 2, *Book of Common Prayer*, 362). For the participation of animals in the liturgy, see the "Blessing of the Animals." As for plants and even stones, these natures also participate in the liturgy: the stone is the altar on which the consecration of the host, that is, the great sacrifice, is witnessed and performed by the priest, and plants are used in the making of the bread and wine.

27. The priest asks the Father to send forth the Holy Spirit: "We pray you, gracious God, to send your Holy Spirit upon these gifts that they may be the Sacrament of the Body of Christ and his Blood of the new Covenant" (Holy Eucharist Rite 2, *Book of Common Prayer*, 369).

28. Ibid.

relative to all phases of the seed's life: preparing the seed, plowing the earth, weeding, waiting, and finally, harvesting.

The sacrificial economy is far from over after the grain and grapes are protected from the harms of an unbalanced relationship to the natural elements (i.e., too much sun, too much rain, etc.). To prepare for the eucharistic liturgy, the wheat must be ground to flour, the yeast must be measured, and yet another complex relational ensemble must be carefully traversed. The grapes too must be smashed and delicately mixed with yeast and sugars and stored in barrels and undergo great expanses of time. The bread rises and the grapes ferment, and after all this process nothing is guaranteed, for all may turn too flat and too sour and thus become unworthy of "relating" to human beings. Because there are no guarantees in the outcome of the making of bread and wine, there is something quite magical about the entire process from seed to the finished products of bread and wine. From this perspective, human interventions in this process of relation and transmutation, although crucial, are in some ways disproportionately small.

Being aware that the fruits of the earth are reliant on all these fitting and meet relationships (from the cosmic to the mundane and even to the magical) reveals that the liturgy (as the world's relation to itself and beyond) is not defined in terms of space or time: the liturgy is not a place but the relation of all relation beyond self-relation. Thus one does not so much bring "our sacrifice of praise and thanksgiving" to the liturgy as one participates in the liturgy as it is always already unfolding through the world beyond one's own doing. And yet the liturgy of the world mysteriously accommodates (or hosts) our human intervention/subjectivity into its own positive and exceeding logic in such a way as to be enhanced by all participatory and meet action within itself. In this way, it becomes exceedingly clear that the eucharistic elements of bread and wine are not in fact a result of mere human sacrifice but are more rightly perceived as a result of a cosmic excess and birth of something beyond itself.

But once again, as we have already observed in this chapter, this surplus or excess of Being does not overtake and sublate *the way in which* the surplus relates to the mundane and quotidian rhythms of Being; indeed, the surplus and the mundane all fold into Being's unfolding without either side overtaking the other. That is to say, even in the world's bountiful "surplus" of bread and wine, they are paradoxically *more* than surplus insofar as they are inextricably bound up within all cosmic relation to itself as self-transcending. That is why the centrality of eucharistic sacrifice in the liturgy cannot possibly be understood outside the context of the entire cosmic procession of the liturgy.

From this cosmic perception can we not say that the eucharistic liturgy is itself related to the cosmic excessive relation to itself as self-transcending? The eucharistic liturgy is related as a product of the cosmic liturgy and yet is also the very enactment of the destiny of all cosmic relation *in its performative unfolding*. That destiny is, in short, the very joy of the world. That is why, in the movement up to the climax of the cosmic liturgy in the Eucharist, no one can hold back the world's celebration, or the maintaining of an excessive feasting[29] and a conjoining of all the different voices into a singular song:

> Holy, Holy, Holy Lord, God of power and might,
> Heaven and earth are full of your glory.
>> Hosanna in the highest.
> Blessed is he who comes in the name of the Lord.
>> Hosanna in the highest.

The liturgy links up all cosmic antinomies: heaven and earth are no longer sundered but are joined (noncompetitively) in the fullness of glory—the joy of the world. Nothing can block this cosmic embrace of glory's enfolding logic of all difference back into the singular One but without diluting these differences. In the glow of glory, difference, in a sense, transcends itself into a *different* difference that is neither absolute Oneness nor defined by difference in and of itself.

This "joy" is not something that we simply observe from the safe distance of our indifference but is that in which we can participate; and in this, a participatory voice is given to us as we join together and sing with all the company of heaven, angels and archangels, friend and foe. Liturgy is not so much that which we come to, as if the liturgy and the world were set over against each other in some kind of vulgar dichotomy. To the contrary, the liturgy enraptures us, taking us up into its own logic, and thus this movement is more like a journey whose very destiny is the journey itself, or as Catherine Pickstock asserts: "Liturgy is therefore not a constative representation now and then of what is praise-worthy, but constitutes a whole way of life."[30]

---

29. At the moment of announcing that "Christ our Passover is sacrificed for us," the response is "Therefore let us keep the feast. [Alleluia.]" (Holy Eucharistic Rite 2, *Book of Common Prayer*, 364).

30. Catherine Pickstock, *After Writing: On the Liturgical Consummation of Philosophy* (Oxford: Blackwell, 1998), 39.

At points, Alexander Schmemann is very close to seeing the eucharistic liturgy as the world's exceeding joy. But at other moments, Schmemann falls back into an all-too-convenient dualism in which "the liturgy . . . [becomes] a real separation from the world."[31] Instead of setting up this separation from the world, I argue that the eucharistic liturgy is the fullest active and participatory expression of the world's true relation beyond a static and fixed space. Thus, to force such a separation would be to sever the lines of relation and difference that unfold in the world, and if this liturgical fullness in glory is never fixed, then it can never be possessed as one's own and thus used as a means to further a mundane telos. Glory unfolds beyond any capture, and yet it accompanies us right into the kernel core of its very essence. And it is precisely this glory that transcends philosophy (as the violent drive to domesticate truths into static propositions, logics, and foundations) that links to Paul's notion of the cross. For the cross is that which crosses out any claim to truth through an artificial means (the law, state power, philosophy, etc.). So in the moment of subtraction—the negative movement that reconciles the differences of the world in a manner that traverses ownership (or entrapment)—there is glory. But this glory as the zenith of the liturgical movement of relation (beyond pure relation and nonrelation) is never guaranteed. That is to say, the liturgy cannot serve for us as a foundation that will always come out right—on the contrary, the liturgy is that leap of faith that calls us to risk everything for the sake of truth.

Where Schmemann is more correct is in his emphasis on the liturgy unfolding, as Pickstock has said, like a journey. "The liturgy of the Eucharist," he says, "is best understood as a journey or procession."[32] But this "journey" motif unfortunately slips back into another dualism. He continues, "This journey begins when Christians leave their homes and beds. They leave, indeed, their life in this present and concrete world, . . . whether they have to drive fifteen miles or walk a few blocks."[33] And then, finally, Schmemann hints at the liturgy as the sine qua non of all reality. For this "journey" becomes "a sacrament[al] act [and] is already taking place, an act which is the very condition of everything else that is to happen."[34] Thus Schmemann is somewhat unclear about the relation

31. Alexander Schmemann, *Sacraments and Orthodoxy* (New York: Herder & Herder, 1965), 31.
32. Ibid., 29.
33. Ibid., 30.
34. Ibid.

between the liturgy and the world. In one moment, they are founded on a fundamental dichotomy, and in the next moment, the liturgy becomes "the very condition of everything else that is to happen." But I would argue that this "condition" is not a transcendental "condition," which again would posit a dualism, but is the never restful truth of the world's relationality beyond difference and sameness. This condition is the condition of Paul's "cross" that will surely call one to give up everything for the sake of glory. For the procession of the liturgy undoes the proposition of philosophy, but there is no insurance backed by financial corporations—there is, however, life in the negative sense of faith.

This ontological process turns on its head a self-mediating ontology grounded in the reductive mode of human "productibility" à la Marx/Lukács, or on Hegel's "Absolute Spirit."[35] Against these self-mediating ontological modes of Being, Rowan Williams reveals an alternative mode of Being founded within the unfolding milieu of the ontological community:

> [According to this view] we are free to consider the eucharist as a gift whose sole motive and purpose is gratitude—a gift which therefore shares the character of the Son's eternal praise of the Father in being an act of gratuitous love, and so may be called an offering of the Son to the Father. We give what we have been given—the flesh and blood of Jesus which opens to us the vision of eternal praise and glorification. To see the eucharist in such terms prevents us from falling into the obvious and dangerous traps of treating our prayer and praise and thanksgiving as primarily functional, designed to obtain something, or at least to fulfil an obligation whose non-fulfilment would cause God to withdraw his grace; and of separating our worship from the life of God.[36]

The liturgy is the material participation in the active ontological movement[37] of the world's mediation of itself through which the world returns

35. As John Milbank points out, siding with Baudrillard and Lyotard, Marx's notion of human "productivity" becomes "a kind of ahistorical social transcendental." Against this reductive view of human value, Milbank goes on to argue that " 'productivism' is rather the sheerly contingent invention (unknown to most of humanity) of a purely secular and immanent goal which at once parcellises matter into the atomically concrete and at the same time evaporates it into thin air" (John Milbank and Slavoj Žižek, "Geopolitical Theology: Economy, Religion, and Empire after 9/11," unpublished manuscript, 22 [available as a working paper at http://theologyphilosophycentre.co.uk/online-papers]).

36. Rowan Williams, Eucharistic Sacrifice—The Roots of a Metaphor (Bramcote Notts, UK: Grove Books, 1982), 12.

37. In The Shape of the Liturgy, Dom Gregory Dix argues that the liturgy is an action (see chap. 1, "The Liturgy and the Eucharistic Action" [Glasgow: Glasgow University Press, 1945], 1–12).

nonidentically to itself in the everlasting glow of God's glory. It is the material participation because, in the heart of the liturgy, the invisible God made manifest in the Logos takes on the material form of bread and wine (and beyond) that are consumed and therefore conjoins the world to that which is beyond the world without either reifying the Logos or dismissing the truth of the world's materiality. God in Christ via the Holy Spirit is thus materialized in the very bodies of the liturgical participants (as the whole world), which open out the material passage into the divine life of the Trinity.

6

A Meditation on Michelangelo's
Christ on the Cross

SLAVOJ ŽIŽEK

What occupies me in this chapter is the meaning of the death of Christ, the question of *what* really dies on the cross, and how to read this event. So I begin with the question of the precise meaning of the death of Christ on the cross and further ask, what is it that dies on the cross? Is it not the case that, for most of us anyway, trying to understand this issue leaves us boggled and confused?

My claim is that, in a sense, our imagination of the picture of Christ dying on the cross assumes a world in which God is up there somewhere, while we are here on Earth. And then God sends a messenger—a Son— down to us. But basically the whole thing fails. The failure is proved by what happens in the narrative itself: the Son returns up to heaven so God might be able to try it again. I think the moment we even start to think along these lines, we raise the entire problem of sin as a debt requiring repayment (the doctrine of atonement). This view of the crucifixion in terms of financial dealings—that Christ died to pay for our sins—raises a basic question for us. The question here is: to *whom*? To whom did God pay this debt? In the first centuries of Christianity the doctrine of the atonement was debated, and many different positions were taken. One of the Gnostic positions, which looks reasonable in

My thanks to Scott Chisholm for preparing a transcription of my lecture on December 4, 2007, at the Cornell Fine Arts Museum of Rollins College, where these ideas were first presented. This lecture was published in a slightly altered form in 2008 in *specs Journal* (http://www.specsjournal.org/).

purely rational terms, states that the debt was paid to the devil, who is the lord of earthly life, of fallen life. The idea is that God made a deal with the devil: "I want humanity back. I'll pay you the highest price: My very own son." But the problem here is extremely serious. For example, I have asked traditional theologians a very simple question: "Why did God have to die on the cross?" They say: "To pay for our sins." Then I ask: "To whom? Was there another guy with whom God had to make a deal?" Then they rejoin: "No, Christ died out of a sense of justice." Then I say: "Wait a minute, the moment you say this, you're back in the pagan universe, where gods are just higher-level beings much like us, and there is a kind of cosmic justice controlling them as well. And what you have effectively done is construct a universe in which God, in all his power and glory, is subordinate to the impersonal laws of abstract justice." The upshot is that even God cannot violate the impermeable laws of cosmic justice. But the way I see it, the whole point of Christian ethics—the very core of it—is that yes, this can be done: God *can* abrogate the laws of cosmic justice. The whole point of the gospel's good news is the subordination of this cosmic law of impersonal justice. In other words, with the traditional view of the meaning of Christ dying on the cross, the entire point of the irruptive logic of the gospel would be domesticated under the banner of a pagan notion of "justice."

This is why I'm skeptical of attempts to unify all religions in the name of "oneness." I think that all other religions, with the exception of Judaism, and up to a point, Islam, still rely on the ethics of cosmic justice, in the sense that the good life means fitting into the harmony of the universe. Evil is when a part of the whole excessively attaches importance to itself, and justice means banishing the excessive part so that cosmic balance is reestablished. The most elementary form of this ethics is found in Confucius. When asked, what is a good life? Confucius says that it's found in a proper, well-organized state: through the rectification of names, when a father is truly a father, when a king is truly a king, and a woman truly a woman. In other words, we participate in the harmony of the universe when each of us fulfills, respects, and fully identifies with our particular role.

The ethics of cosmic justice is—if I may be obscenely blunt—in a sense, protofascist. The definition of fascism is an obsession with organic unity. This is why fascists hate liberalism. What fascists hate about liberalism is the idea—the fundamental idea of political liberalism—that you, as an individual, independently of who you are—black, white, man, woman—have a right to direct contact with the universal. This idea, apart perhaps from Buddhism, appears primarily in Christianity, which holds, "I'm not only what I am—man, woman, and so on—but what makes me great, or even immortal, is that I cannot be reduced to what I am in my particular existence."

I will argue for this thesis by using Michelangelo's drawing *Christ on the Cross*. The first thing that may be noticed about this drawing is that it's unfinished, and the very reason why it's unfinished is interesting. We know that Michelangelo gave it to his close friend Vittoria Colonna—a passionate, intimate friend, not sexually but intellectually. Colonna was a wealthy woman, a patron of great artists of the time, and in her own way she was an inspiring person. Then something mysterious happened. Michelangelo, immediately after giving Lady Vittoria *Christ on the Cross*, wrote her an urgent message asking—demanding—to be given back the work, since there was something terribly wrong with it. She, in a hypocritical way, pretended to have lost it—"Oh, I must look for it"—but then admitted in a letter that she was aroused by it and asked him why he needed to have it returned. She stared at the drawing—even resorting to using a magnifying glass, looking at it from every angle imaginable, and putting it beside a mirror—intrigued, hoping to find what might be wrong with it, as if the drawing contained some forbidden detail Michelangelo was afraid would be discovered. And if we look at it now, we can clearly see a few interesting details.

The drawing renders the critical moment of Christ's doubt and despair, the famous "My God, My God, why have you forsaken me?" (Matt. 27:46; cf. Ps. 22:1 NRSV). As far as I know, for the first time in the history of painting, an artist attempted to capture Christ's abandonment by God the Father. This moment was not one of pure ecstatic rapture but, on the contrary, was a moment of despair. With this in mind we may ask: why are Christ's eyes more or less turned upward? His face expresses not devoted acceptance of suffering but simply total raw suffering combined with *what*? Here, if we examine the drawing carefully, we can't help but notice a series of unsettling details that indicate an underlying attitude of angry rebellion—of *defiance*—and not of devoted acceptance. First, the two legs are not symmetrical. One leg is raised, and here an amateur was already breaking the rules of how this event is to be depicted, as if Christ is caught in the middle of an attempt to rise up. Christ is attempting to liberate himself. But the truly shocking detail is the right hand. This is what perplexed Lady Vittoria. The finger is raised in a gesture that was commonly understood at that time. The gesture is identified in Quintilian's *Rhetorics* (*Institutio Oratoria*), the standard manual of the era, and a work that was known to Michelangelo. According to Quintilian's work, this gesture functions as a sign of rebellious challenge. It signifies, "No, I don't give way. I persist in my rebellion." So again, Christ's "My God, My God, why have you forsaken me?" is not a resigned or even a passive, why? that gently questions the Father. It is rather an aggressive and accusatory *Why?!*

More precisely, there is in the drawing an implicit tension in the expression of Christ's face. On the one hand, there is despair and suffering. But on the other hand, we can't avoid reading the aggressive rebellion in his face, the defiant rebellious attitude signaled by his right hand, as if the hand articulates the attitude the face doesn't dare to fully express. I would like to develop this idea of the hand, the fist, as an autonomous object of rebellion, a rebellion that asserts one's freedom. We can relate this to classical fairy tales, mythology, and popular culture. For example, take the film *Fight Club*, with Brad Pitt and Edward Norton—a very disturbing film, which is problematic for some. The most fascinating, painful scene is when Ed Norton's character confronts his boss. Recall that instead of hitting the boss, he starts hitting himself. And consider how this scene is shot: The act is not one of a unified subject. When he's confronting his boss, his fist starts to act as an object with its own will. He tries to control it, but it rebels against his own body. The significance and rebelliousness of the fist might also be seen in other contexts. According to one anecdote, Martin Heidegger—a philosopher for whom I have great appreciation—was visited by another philosopher in Rome when Heidegger was in his pro-Nazi period. The visiting philosopher asks Heidegger: "How can you be for Hitler? He's such a vulgar guy. Listen to his speeches!" Heidegger replies: "No, no, forget about the speeches. Look at his fist, at his hand, while he's talking. That is the mystery. There's something about the movement of the hand: It expresses *more.*" And turning to German mythology, there is a wonderful story, one of the fairy tales by the Brothers Grimm, called "The Egotistical Child." In this story, a child is so evil that God punishes and kills him. But then, in a scene reminiscent of a Stephen King novel, his fist begins protruding up from the grave. They repeatedly add dirt to the grave, but the boy's fist still protrudes. His mother then comes with some tools and starts hitting the fist, until finally the boy accepts his own death.

This attitude of irrationality—not in the sense of madness but irrationality in the sense of an inability to justify matters in terms of a rational utilitarian calculation—is crucial. We find it, for example, in

Antigone. The story is well known, but what may have been overlooked is that if we read *Antigone* with fresh eyes, we should think, "Yes, I am for Antigone. . . . But *why* am I for Antigone?" I will not repeat the story here, but when we read it again, we might see that our reason for supporting her is not so self-evident. What Creon tells Antigone, when he prohibits the funeral of her brother Polynices, is quite rational. From the standpoint of a rationally functioning state power, whose primary concern is to maintain public order, Creon is absolutely right. Creon explains: "Listen, we just had a civil war. If I allow the public burial of Polynices, with all the proper funeral rights, then civil war will erupt again. The whole city would be ruined." And typically Antigone doesn't deny this reasoning but simply insists on carrying out the funeral. My point here is not to condemn her but to emphasize that every rebellious movement has to begin with such incessant insistence.

Let's look to a figure that we might see as an American Antigone: Rosa Parks, the hero in the fight against racism, a black woman on a bus who didn't want to stand up to let a white man sit down in her seat. I can imagine the rational response, thinking: "Yes, African-Americans are suffering, my God. But why do you insist so forcefully here? Resist in a more organized way. You will just cause further trouble." But isn't this very rational attitude precisely an illusion? At some point action must be taken, even from a purely utilitarian standpoint. The act of defiance might appear excessive, even when engaging with something that is in itself trivial, because it insists, "No. I will go to the end here." E. L. Doctorow's *Ragtime* is another story of fighting racism in the United States. A film based on Doctorow's novel, made by Miloš Forman, tells a similar story. A white tramp shits on the seat of a car belonging to a successful black middle-class man. A policeman arrives, and while he is not racist himself, he just wants to maintain order. The policeman says: "I know this white guy is trash. I know he's a problem. But please, let's not make a bigger problem here." But the black man insists, and practically causes a civil war in the city. This is the attitude I am referring to.

This brings me back to Michelangelo's drawing. Can we not ask: Doesn't Christ, even if only for a moment, succumb to the temptation of egotistic rebellion? Who is who in this scene that somehow articulates the formula of Goethe that no one but God himself can stand against God? How can this attitude be read? I think some very interesting theoretical and practical conclusions can be drawn from it, beginning with a wonderful slip that Hegel makes when talking about the difference between Western Christianity and Eastern Orthodox Christianity.

It is clearly a mistake because, from reading Hegel's other texts, we can establish that he knew the mistake he was making. Theologically, one of the great divisions between the two churches pertains to the question of the origin of the Holy Spirit. For Western Christianity, the Holy Spirit originates from God the Father and the Son together. For Eastern Orthodox Christianity, this was thought to limit the authority of God the Father too much, so the Holy Spirit originates only from God the Father. Hegel states, however, that in Orthodox Christianity the Holy Spirit originates from both Christ and Father, but in Western Christianity the Holy Spirit originates only from Christ, only from the Son—a very curious mistake. I think we may read this as an honest Freudian slip. I think Hegel was right in a way. Why?

Let me present a few quotes from G. K. Chesterton, whom I consider to be one of the best Catholic theologians from Britain. This is how he defines what he calls the central mystery of Christianity—and the link between what he saw as the mystery of Christianity and Michelangelo's drawing will be immediately clear:

> When the world shook and the sun was wiped out of heaven, it was not at the crucifixion but at the cry from the cross ("My God, My God, why have you forsaken me?"), the cry which confessed that God was forsaken of God. And now let the revolutionists choose a creed from all the creeds and a god from all the gods of the world, carefully weighing all the gods of inevitable recurrence and unalterable power. They will not find another god who has himself been in revolt, nay, (the matter grows too difficult for human speech) but let the atheists themselves choose a god. They will find only one divinity who ever uttered their isolation; only one religion in which God seemed for an instant to be an atheist.[1]

That is Chesterton's key point, which is not to say that he was not a deeply respected Catholic. I think he took the implications of this point to the end, a point that I'll return to below.

Recently at a debate in Vienna, I asked a few bishops a very simple question. They were perplexed and didn't give me a clear answer. I asked, "When Christ says 'My God, My God, why have you forsaken me?' is he bluffing or not?" If he is in fact bluffing—and by bluffing I mean that he is simply saying this aloud but secretly knows that he is God—then the crucifixion is not serious. It is just a spectacle staged for humans. But if we take Christ's statement seriously, then the implication is extremely radical. We must not forget that in Christian theology, Jesus Christ is

1. G. K. Chesterton, *Orthodoxy* (San Francisco: Ignatius, 1995), 145.

not thought of in the same way as messiahs in other religions. Christ is not a *representative* of God; he *is* God. This means that God is radically split. A part of God doesn't know what God is doing. There is a kind of inconsistency in divinity itself, which is I think the crucial insight of Christianity. This is why I ask: how can we rejoin God? In other religions God is a simple transcendence: We are here in our sinful, terrestrial life, but if we purify ourselves, it's possible for us to get closer to and be rejoined with God. In Christianity, when it's said that the only way to God is through Christ, I think what's implied is precisely this Christ at the moment of doubt on the cross. This is why for Christianity you can, paradoxically, reach God only through this moment of doubt. As Chesterton put it, God himself becomes, for a moment, an atheist. The idea is as follows: We experience the utmost despair and alienation. We are here, God is there. We are totally abandoned by God. How then in authentic Christianity do we reach God? Not by somehow magically overcoming this gap but just by means of a shattering insight at the very point when we are abandoned by God. There we occupy the position of Christ. What was thought of only as alienation from God is the position of Christ himself: God abandoned by God.

That is why, for Chesterton, Christianity is terribly revolutionary: "That a good man may have his back to the wall is no more than we knew already: but that God could have his back to the wall is a boast for all insurgents forever. Christianity is the only religion on earth that has felt that omnipotence made God incomplete. Christianity alone has held that God, to be wholly God, must have been a rebel as well as a king."[2] We could go on tracing out the implications of this in political theology. The film *V for Vendetta* with Natalie Portman may be considered here— although in the end it wasn't radical enough. What I thought would happen in that film simply did not; evidently, the filmmakers were too afraid and didn't want to take it to the end. In the film, Britain is reconstituted as a totalitarian country with a dictator who is only seen through television screens, and a famous masked rebel fights against him. A series of signs hints at the link between the two. If the film had been courageous enough, in the end, when the rebel dies and his mask is removed, we would have seen that the rebel is none other than the dictator, fighting himself. But unfortunately, the film was not radical enough.

Now Chesterton is fully aware that here we are approaching a matter dark and awful, one that is difficult to discuss, a matter that the great-

2. Ibid.

est saints and thinkers justly fear to approach. In the terrific tale of the passion is a distinct emotional suggestion in some unthinkable way not only of agony but also of doubt. Returning to Christ's "My God, My God, why have you forsaken me?" Christ himself commits what is for Christians the ultimate sin: wavering in one's faith. So again, while in other religions, there are people who do not believe in God, it is only in Christianity that God does not believe in himself. And here Chesterton reports an insightful anecdote from a visit to Jerusalem in the early twentieth century. He tried to ask an Arab boy who spoke a bit of English: "Where is the garden?" The boy asked if he meant the place where God himself prayed. Chesterton claims that this is unique: in other religions you pray to God, but only in Christianity does God pray to himself.[3]

Job and Inexplicability

The image of a suffering Christ who does not believe in himself brings us back to the Old Testament, to the book of Job, which is praised by Chesterton as the most interesting of ancient books. But then Chesterton adds that it is also the most interesting of modern books. Now in what, according to Chesterton, does the modernity of the book of Job consist? I recommend returning to this text and reading it again carefully. I find the book of Job, if read closely, to be the first example of what we today call the critique of ideology. Why? To begin with it is really a shattering piece, not because of the obscenities that we all know—God and the devil having a nice after-dinner conversation, with drinks, and God exclaiming, "Oh, I have a sucker who believes in me. No way can you corrupt him. Forget about that." And I wholly buy into the story that the narrative is probably the remainder of some previous pagan mythology. But there is another absolutely crucial thing that happens in the text. We know the story: things go really badly for Job. He loses—and I always liked this obscenity in the Bible—his children, goats, chickens. Basically things look really bad for Job, but then what happens? Three theological friends come, and each of them tries to convince Job of something. Here we must be very precise: they try to convince him that if things are bad for him, he must have earned it somehow. The reasoning of the first theological friend is that if you suffer, even if you don't know what for, you must have done something to deserve it. The second and third give more articulate, refined arguments. For example, one of them replies with something along the lines of, "Maybe God is testing Job." What the three of them share is the idea that Job's suffering and misfortunes have a deeper meaning. That is their basic message: it isn't just a trauma without meaning; there's a deeper significance to the event. If we read Job's answers closely, we don't see him insist that he's innocent—he doesn't play the part of the pure, beautiful soul who says, "I didn't do anything. . . . Why this?" Rather we see him insist, "No matter what I did, I don't accept that this terrible event has some deeper meaning." And then comes the big surprise, when God appears at the end and says that everything the three theological idiots said was wrong, and every word that Job said was true. God directly takes the side of Job. And what is God's answer? Again, it is usually misread as implying a simple divine absolute otherness: "Who are you even to talk to me? Who are you, miserable idiot? I created this and that, and you must just accept my radical transcendence. Don't even think—how dare you to think!—that you can even begin to understand me." This is the usual reading of the book of Job: "Trust in God, but accept the divine absolute transcendence." In other words, the final reply of God is usually read as implying that there is a deeper meaning but that there's no way we will get it: "Just trust that I know. It's not yours to know."

I claim that this is exactly what we shouldn't do. If the book is read more closely, I think we will arrive at the conclusion of Chesterton. What is his conclusion here? Chesterton states that "the mechanical optimist endeavors to justify the universe avowedly upon the ground that it is a rational and consecutive pattern."[4] The rationalist points out that the fine thing about the world is that it can all be explained. But this is the one point that God's reply explicitly opposes—if I may put it so—to the point of violence. God says, in effect, that if there is one fine thing about the world, as far as people are concerned, it is that it cannot be explained. He insists on the inexplicableness of everything. In the book of Job, the Father—out of whose womb came the ice— goes further and insists on the positive and palpable unreasonableness of the cosmos. Also in the book of Job (38:26) God states: "Hast thou sent the rain upon the desert where no man is, and upon the wilderness wherein there is no man."[5] Again, to startle humans, God becomes, for

4. G. K. Chesterton, "The Book of Job: An Introduction by G. K. Chesterton," *Putnam's Monthly* 2 (April–September 1907).
    5. Ibid.

an instant, a blasphemer. One might almost say that God becomes, for an instant, an atheist. He unrolls before Job a long panorama of created things: the horse, the eagle, the raven, the wildebeest, the peacock, the ostrich, and the crocodile. He so describes one that it sounds like a monster walking on the sand; the whole is a sort of solemn rhapsody of the sense of wonder. The Maker of all things is astonished at the things he has himself made. Again, here the point is not that God knows the deeper meaning, but it is as if God himself is overwhelmed at the excess of his creation. As Chesterton puts it in wonderful terms, Job addresses God with a question mark, but God does not provide an answer; he merely, as it were, repeats the question, as if you asked me: "Why is this happening?" and I say: "Yes, that's it." It is almost a semantic misunderstanding: You ask me a question of contempt—"Why is this?!"—and I take it as a yes or no question, and say, "Yes, so it is." Which brings us back to the problem of the crucifixion.

I believe that the book of Job has to be read as prefiguring the death of Christ. What God denies at the end of the book of Job is the idea that somewhere there is what in Lacanian psychoanalytic theory would be called the big Other, a kind of guarantee of global meaning that could be a solace for us: "Things might be terrible and confusing, but at least God knows that all of this has some deeper meaning." I claim that this is an unsatisfactory reading. And I have many theological friends who agree with me that this God, this big Other—this guarantee of global meaning on whom we can rely—is precisely what dies on the cross. As Hegel puts it, what dies on the cross is not an earthly representative of God; what dies on the cross is the very God of the beyond—which returns us to Hegel's slip. This is why, as Hegel points out, what we have after crucifixion, the resurrected God, is neither God the Father nor God the Son—it is the Holy Spirit. The Holy Spirit is the love between believers; it is the spirit of the community of believers, according to the famous words of Christ: "For where two or three have gathered together in My name, I am there in their midst" (Matt. 18:20 NASB). I think this passage should be taken literally.

So what does this mean? Even today, the message is very radical. The temptation to be resisted is the temptation of *meaning* itself. Perhaps the clearest instance—which might be the worst recent example of pseudo-Christianity or pagan thinking—is the infamous reactions of Jerry Falwell and Pat Robertson to the 9/11 bombings. They said this was divine punishment: "God lifted his protection from the United States because of our sinful way of life." (Incidentally, Falwell and Robertson basically said the same thing that the massing fundamentalists have been saying.)

A related metaphor that I have always found offensive is that of evil as a stain on a painting. The idea is one endlessly reproduced by theologians and philosophers who attempt to assert the harmony of the universe— the idea that what appears to us as evil is just like an apparent stain in a picture. If you look at a picture too closely, you see it as a meaningless stain. But if you withdraw to a proper distance, you see that what appeared as a stain actually contributes to global harmony. Similarly, what appears to us as evil is just the result of our constrained perspective; from a proper distance we would see that it contributes to global harmony; evil has a deeper meaning. But this presents a big problem in considering phenomena like gulags, the Holocaust, and all the horrors of the twentieth century. Can we really play this game, for example, with Auschwitz and the other concentration camps? Are we ready to say, "Oh, it appears to us as a stain, but if you have true wisdom, you will see how Auschwitz contributes to the harmony of the world"? I don't know what kind of harmony can be paid with the death of millions in gas chambers.

I claim that Christ died on the cross precisely to reject such attempts at finding a higher purpose or meaning. Rather, the message is: "Your standards matter to me. I throw myself into creation, and abandon my place up there." The conclusions are radical. The ultimate meaning of Christianity for me is a very precise one. It is not: "We should trust God. The big guy's with me, so nothing really bad can happen." That is too easy. The message is not: *we* trust God. The message is rather: God trusts *us*. The gesture of Christ says, "I leave it over to you." Usually we read religion as the way to guarantee meaning: we are concerned with the small details of everyday life and never know what will come of it all, or how things will turn out; we can only make wagers, and we do this maybe to ensure that God will arrange things in our favor. But the meaning of the death of Christ for me is the opposite: God made the wager on us. It is really a crazy wager, where God is saying: "I leave it to you. Holy Ghost, community of believers, you have to do it!"

A Community of Outcasts

Many of my atheist friends say to me: "Yes, so this is atheism: there's no god up there, we create god in our image, and so on." But it is not that: I don't think one can translate theology into secular humanism.

Not because of any secret, obscure reason but because there must be a moment of thinking that it is not we who are acting, but a higher force that is acting through us. This element has to be maintained. Here I cannot resist bringing up a metaphor that may be dangerously obscene for some. When people ask me whether I am an atheist, and what I think the Christian rituals of drinking the blood and eating the flesh of Christ mean, I tell them to read Stephen King and they will get it. In films like *The Terminator* and others like it, and in many horror movies, there is sometimes a scene where the hero is possessed. There is a bad guy who is not really bad but is possessed by an alien. Then the good guys think they've destroyed the possessing alien, but some slimy residue of the alien is left lying around. Then comes the standard shot, where the camera slowly approaches the residue, and what we thought was just a bit of squashed alien starts to move and organize itself. We leave the film with the alien organizing itself. This is the divine element. I think horror movies are the negative theology of today. I don't think we can understand the logic of negative theology without appreciating good horror movies. It is as if the good guys in such horror movies are like Roman soldiers: they thought they had destroyed everything in Christ, but that little bit of alien residue remained and started to organize itself into the community of believers. That is a crucial point. Again, what I'm saying here cannot be reduced to simplistic humanism. I think this is the legacy of Christianity—this legacy of God not as a big Other or guarantee but God as the ultimate ethical agency who puts the burden on us to organize ourselves.

This is also reminiscent of a crucial moment in the history of American trade unions and workers' movements. In the film *Woodstock*, Joan Baez performs a classic American working-class song called "Joe Hill." It is wonderful and naively theological: A worker dreams of Joe Hill, who was a trade union organizer executed in the 1920s, having been wrongly accused of murder. When Joe Hill appears in the dream, the worker says, "But Joe, you're dead. How can you be here?" Joe says, "It takes more than a gun to kill a man." And then the dreamer says, "But *where* are you alive?" Joe says, "Wherever you organize a strike, Joe Hill is there." This is a working-class, trade union version of the process of organization, of what happens whenever two or more organize themselves. According to a wonderful formulation, what has power cannot be killed; it only goes on to organize itself.

This link between Christian community and the Progressive movement is crucial. And here I'm not playing a cheap game of identifying radical political movements as a kind of religious community; what I'm referring to is the idea of a radical community of believers. The ideal is that of neither blind liberal individuals collaborating with one another nor the old organic conservative community. It is a community along the lines of the original Christian community: a community of outcasts. We need this today, this idea of an egalitarian community of believers that is neither the traditional heretical community nor the liberal multiplicity. This is why I and many other leftist philosophers, such as Alain Badiou and others, are so interested in rereading, rehabilitating, and reappropriating the legacy of Paul. It is not just a matter of private religious convictions. I claim that if we lose this key moment—the moment of realizing the Holy Spirit as a community of believers—we will live in a very sad society, where the only choice will be between vulgar egoist liberalism or the fundamentalism that counterattacks it. This is why I—precisely as a radical leftist—think that Christianity is far too precious a thing to leave to conservative fundamentalists. We should fight for it. Our message should not be, "You can have it," but "No, it's ours. You are kidnapping it."

PART 3

On Mediation and Apocalypse

7

Thinking Backward
Predestination and Apocalypse

SLAVOJ ŽIŽEK

We effectively live in an apocalyptic time: today, apocalypse is near at many levels: ecology, informational saturation—things are approaching a zero-point, "the end of time is near." Here is Ed Ayres's description: "We are being confronted by something so completely outside our collective experience that we don't really see it, even when the evidence is overwhelming. For us, that 'something' is a blitz of enormous biological and physical alterations in the world that has been sustaining us."[1] At the geological and biological level, Ayres enumerates four "spikes" (accelerated developments) asymptotically approaching a zero-point at which the quantitative expansion will reach its point of exhaustion and will have to change into a different quality: population growth, consumption of resources, carbon gas emissions, the mass extinction of species. To cope with this threat, our collective ideology is mobilizing mechanisms of dissimulation and self-deception that point toward the direct will to ignorance: "A general pattern of behavior among threatened human societies is to become more blindered, rather than more focused on the crisis, as they fall."[2]

1. Ed Ayres, *God's Last Offer: Negotiating for a Sustainable Future* (New York: Four Walls Eight Windows, 1999), 98.
2. Ibid.

Apocalypse is characterized by a specific mode of time, clearly opposed to the two other predominant modes, the traditional circular time (the time ordered and regulated on cosmic principles, reflecting the order of nature and the heavens—the time form in which microcosm and macrocosm resonate with each other in harmony) and the modern linear time of gradual progress or development. The apocalyptic time is the "time of the end of time," the time of emergency, of the "state of exception" when the end is near and we are getting ready for it.

There are at least three different versions of apocalypticism today: techno-digital posthuman, New Age, and Christian fundamentalist. Although they all share the basic notion that humanity is approaching a zero-point of radical transmutation, their respective ontologies differ radically: the techno-digital apocalypticism (whose main representative is Ray Kurzweil) remains within the confines of scientific naturalism and identifies at the level of the evolution of human species the contours of its transmutation into "posthumans"; the New Age apocalypticism gives to this transmutation a spiritualist twist, interpreting it as the shift from one mode of "cosmic awareness" to another (usually from the modern dualist-mechanistic stance to the stance of holistic immersion); and, finally, Christian fundamentalists read apocalypse in strict biblical terms—that is, they search (and find) in the contemporary world signs that the final battle between Christ and the antichrist is near, that things are approaching a critical turn. Although this last version is considered the most ridiculous but dangerous as to its content, it is the one closest to the "millenarist" radical emancipatory logic.

Techno-Digital Apocalypticism

Let us first take a look at the techno-digital apocalypticism. If there is, even more than Bill Gates, a scientist-capitalist who perfectly exemplifies the third "spirit of capitalism" with its nonhierarchic and antiinstitutional creativity, humanitarian-ethical concerns, and so on, it is Craig Venter, with his idea of DNA-controlled production. Venter's field is synthetic biology, a field that focuses on "life which is forged not by Darwinian evolution but created by human intelligence."[3] Venter's first breakthrough was to develop "shotgun sequencing," a method for analyzing the human genome faster and more cheaply than ever before;

---

3. J. Craig Venter, "A DNA-Driven World" (lecture, BBC One, December 4, 2007, http://www.edge.org/3rd_culture/venter.dimbleby07/venter.dimbleby07_index.html).

he published his own genome, the first time any individual person's DNA had been sequenced. (Incidentally, it revealed that Venter is at risk of Alzheimer's, diabetes, and hereditary eye disease.) Then he announced his next great project: to build an entirely synthetic organism, which could be used to save the world from global warming. In January 2008, he constructed the world's first completely synthetic genome of a living organism: using laboratory chemicals, he recreated an almost exact copy of the genetic material found inside a tiny bacterium. This largest man-made DNA structure is 582,970 base pairs in length; it was pieced together from four smaller (but still massive!) strands of DNA by utilizing the transcription power of yeast, and it is modeled on the genome of a bacterium known as *Mycoplasma genitalium*. (Mycoplasma genitalium is a bacterium common to the human reproductive tract; it was chosen purely because it has a relatively tiny genome.) The lab-made genome has thus far not resulted in a living microbe that functions or replicates, but Venter has said it is just a matter of time before scientists figure out how "to boot it up" by inserting the synthetic DNA into the shell of another bacterium.[4] This success opens the way for creating new types of microorganisms that could be used in numerous ways: as green fuels to replace oil and coal, to digest toxic waste, or to absorb greenhouse gases, and so on. Venter's dream is effectively to create the first "trillion-dollar organisms"—patented bugs that could excrete biofuels, generate clean energy in the form of hydrogen, and even produce tailor-made foods.

> Imagine the end of fossil fuels: a cessation of ecologically devastating drilling operations, deflation of the political and economic power of neoconservative oil barons, and affordable, low-emission transportation, heating, and electricity. The impact of this technology is profound, and it doesn't stop there. By discovering the details of biochemical and metabolic pathways, we can more closely mimic their elegance and efficiency to solve problems that plague industrial civilization. Maybe we'll engineer a primitive, self-sustaining bio-robot that feeds on CO_2 and excretes O_2. Perhaps we could remove mercury from our water supplies. The limitations are not known, but the possibilities are awe-inspiring.[5]

There are, as Venter admits, also more sinister possibilities: it will also be possible to synthesize viruses like Ebola, or to build new pathogens. But

4. J. Craig Venter Institute, "Venter Institute Scientists Create First Synthetic Bacterial Genome," press release, January 24, 2008, http://www.jcvi.org/cms/research/projects/synthetic-bacterial-genome/press-release/.

5. Ian Sample, "Frankenstein's Mycoplasma," *The Guardian*, June 8, 2007.

the problem is deeper, as Hope Shand of the ETC Group, a Canada-based bioethics watchdog, points out: "This is extreme genetic engineering that will bring about substantially different organisms and with those comes a new level of unknowns."[6] The problem is our limited understanding of how DNA works: even if we can put together a sequence of synthetic DNA, we cannot predict how this sequence will actually perform, how its components will interact. Jason Chin, who leads a synthetic biology research group in Cambridge, England, says: "DNA communicates with a cell by prompting it to make proteins, but we have a long way to go in understanding the relationship between a given DNA sequence, the proteins it generates and the final properties of an organism."[7]

These dangers are strengthened by the absence of any public control over what goes on in bioethics. As Jim Thomas, another member of the ETC Group, notes, "While synthetic biology is speeding ahead in the lab and in the marketplace . . . there has been no meaningful or inclusive discussion on how to govern synthetic biology in a safe and just way. In the absence of democratic oversight, profiteering industrialists are tinkering with the building blocks of life for their own private gain."[8] Venter has tried to allay the fears of an emerging *Blade Runner* society: "The movie [*Blade Runner*] has an underlying assumption that I just don't relate to: that people want a slave class. As I imagine the potential of engineering the human genome, I think, wouldn't it be nice if we could have 10 times the cognitive capabilities we do have? But people ask me whether I could engineer a stupid person to work as a servant. I've gotten letters from guys in prison asking me to engineer women they could keep in their cell. I don't see us, as a society, doing that."[9] Venter may not see it, but the requests he is bombarded with certainly prove that there is a social demand for the creation of a serving subclass. Kurzweil has offered a different rebuttal of these fears: "The scenario of humans hunting cyborgs doesn't wash because those entities won't be separate. Today, we treat Parkinson's with a pea-sized brain implant. Increase that device's capability by a billion and decrease its size by a

6. Ian Sample, "Tycoon's Team Finds Fewest Number of Genes Needed for Life," *The Guardian*, June 8, 2007, http://www.guardian.co.uk/science/2007/jun/08/genetics.research.

7. Jonathan Leake, "The Synthetic Genome," *The Sunday Times* (UK), January 27, 2008, http://www.timesonline.co.uk/tol/news/science/article3257051.ece.

8. ETC Group, "Venter Institute Builds Longest Sequence of Synthetic DNA (That Doesn't Work)," news release, January 24, 2008.

9. Ted Greenwald, "Q&A: Ridley Scott Has Finally Created the *Blade Runner* He Always Imagined," *Wired Magazine*, September 26, 2007, http://www.wired.com/entertainment/hollywood/magazine/15-10/ff_bladerunner.

hundred thousand, and you get some idea of what will be feasible in 25 years. It won't be, 'OK, cyborgs on the left, humans on the right.' The two will be all mixed up."[10] While this is in principle true (and one can here vary endlessly the Derridean motif of how our humanity always already was supplemented by artificial protheses), the problem is that, with the decrease by a hundred thousand, the prothesis is no longer experienced as such but becomes invisible, part of our immediate organic self-experience, so that those who technologically control the prothesis control us in the very heart of our self-experience.

The paradox is that, insofar as the re-creation of artificial life is the accomplishment of (one of the strands of) modernity, it is Habermas himself who abstains from accomplishing the project of modernity, that is, who prefers modernity to remain an "unfinished project," setting a limit to the unfolding of its potentials. There are even more radical questions to be raised here, questions that concern the very limit of our desire (and readiness) to know: what will prospective parents do when they are informed that their child will have Alzheimer's genes? The recent new buzzword "previvor" (a person who does not have cancer but possesses a genetic predisposition to develop the disease, a "pre-survivor") renders perfectly the anxiety of advance knowledge.

Chinese scientists at the Beijing Genomics Institute have completed the fourth human genome to be sequenced worldwide; they plan to use their genome database to "solve problems related to Chinese-specific genetic diseases," as well as to improve diagnosis, prediction, and therapy.[11] Such phenomena are just the tip of the iceberg of a process going on in China, a process of which not much is heard in a media preoccupied by the Tibet troubles and the like: the expansion of biogenetic revolution. While in the West we are bothered with endless debates on ethical and legal limits of biogenetic experiments and procedures (yes or no to stem cells, questions about how we should be allowed to use the genome, i.e., only to prevent diseases or also to enhance desired physical and even psychic properties in order to create a newborn that fits our desires, etc.), the Chinese are simply doing it without any restraints, and in a model example of the smooth cooperation between their state agencies (say, their Academy of Sciences) and private capital. In short, both branches of what Kant would have

10. Ibid.
11. Hsien-Hsien Lei, "Beijing Genomics Institute Sequences Fourth Human Genome in the World," Eye on DNA, January 7, 2008, http://eyeondna.com/2008/01/07/beijing-genomics -institute-sequence-fourth-human-genome-in-the-world.

called the "private" use of reason (state and capital) have joined hands at the expense of the absent "public" use of reason (a free intellectual debate in the independent civil society about what is going on, how it all infringes on individuals' status as ethically autonomous agents, and so on, not to mention the possible political misuses). Things are proceeding fast on both fronts, not only toward the dystopian vision of the state controlling and steering the biogenetic mass of its citizens, but also toward fast profit-making: billions of US dollars are invested in labs and clinics (the biggest one in Shanghai) to develop commercial clinics that will target rich Western foreigners who, due to legal prohibitions, will not be able to get this kind of treatment in their own countries. The problem is, of course, that, in such a global situation, legal prohibitions are becoming meaningless: their main effect will be the commercial and scientific advantage of the Chinese facilities—to repeat a cliché, Shanghai has all the chances of becoming a dystopian megalopolis like the anonymous city in *Blade Runner*.

How, then, does the digitalization of our lives affect the hermeneutic horizon of our everyday experience? What looms at the horizon of the "digital revolution" is nothing else than the prospect that human beings will acquire the capacity of what Kant and other German Idealists called *intellektuelle Anschauung* (intellectual intuition), the closure of the gap that separates (passive) intuition and (active) production; that is, the intuition that immediately generates the object it perceives—the capacity hitherto reserved for the infinite divine mind. On the one hand, it will be possible, through neurological implants, to switch from our "common" reality to another, computer-generated reality without all the clumsy machinery of today's virtual reality (the awkward glasses, gloves, etc.), since the signals of the virtual reality will directly reach our brains, bypassing our sensory organs: "Your neural implants will provide the simulated sensory inputs of the virtual environment—and your virtual body—directly in your brain. . . . A typical 'web site' will be a perceived virtual environment, with no external hardware required. You 'go there' by mentally selecting the site and then entering that world."[12] On the other hand, there is the complementary notion of the "real virtual reality": through "nanobots" (billions of self-organizing, intelligent microrobots), it will be possible to re-create the three-dimensional image of different realities "out there" for our "real" senses to see and enter

12. Ray Kurzweil, *The Age of Spiritual Machines* (London: Phoenix, 1999), 182.

(the so-called Utility Fog).[13] Significantly, these two opposite versions of the full virtualization of our experience of reality (direct neuronal implants versus the Utility Fog) mirror the difference of subjective and objective: with the Utility Fog, we still relate to the reality outside ourselves through our sensory experience, while the neuronal implants effectively reduce us to "brains in the vat," cutting us off from any direct perception of reality—in other words, in the first case, we "really" perceive a simulacrum of reality, while in the second case, *perception itself is simulated* through direct neuronal implants. However, in both cases, we reach a kind of omnipotence, being able to change from one to another reality by the mere power of our thoughts—to transform our bodies, the bodies of our partners, and so forth: "With this technology, you will be able to have almost any kind of experience with just about anyone, real or imagined, at any time."[14] The questions to be asked here are: Will this still be experienced as "reality"? Is, for a human being, "reality" not *ontologically* defined through the minimum of *resistance*—real is that which resists, that which is not totally malleable to the caprices of our imagination?

As to the obvious counterargument that everything cannot be virtualized—there still has to be the one "real reality," that of the digital or biogenetic circuitry itself that generates the very multiplicity of virtual universes!—the answer is provided by the prospect of "downloading" the entire human brain (once it is possible to scan it completely) onto an electronic machine more efficient than our awkward brains. At this crucial moment, a human being will change its ontological status "from hardware to software": it will no longer be identified with (stuck to) its material bearer (the brain in the human body). The identity of one's self is a certain neuronal pattern, the network of waves, which, in principle, can be transferred from one to another material support. Of course, there is no "pure mind"; that is, there always has to be some kind of embodiment—however, if our mind is a software pattern, it should be in principle possible for it to shift from one to another material support. (Is this not going on all the time at a different level: is the "stuff" our cells are made of not continuously changing?) The idea is that this cutting off of the umbilical cord that links us to a single body, this shift from having (and being stuck to) a *body* to freely floating between different *embodiments* will mark the true birth of the human being, relegating the

13. Ibid., 183.
14. Ibid., 188.

entire hitherto history of humanity to the status of a confused period of
transition from the animal kingdom to the true kingdom of the mind.

New Age Apocalypticism

Brought to this extreme, the techno-digital apocalypticism assumes the
form of the so-called tech-gnosis and passes over into the New Age
apocalypticism. One of the preferred Janus-faced notions mobilized by
the New Age spiritualists is the quantum physics notion of synchronicity
(the instantaneous link between two events or elements, that is, faster
than the time the light needs to travel between the two): the precise quantum notion of synchronicity (two separated particles are interconnected
so that a spin of one of the two affects the spin of the other faster than
their light connection) is read as a material manifestation/inscription of
a "spiritual" dimension that links events beyond the network of material
causality: "Synchronicities are the jokers in nature's pack of cards for they
refuse to play by the rules and offer a hint that, in our quest for certainty
about the universe, we have ignored some vital clues."[15] Here is the New
Age spiritualist description of the new social order that is expected to
emerge as a secondary effect of the more substantial spiritual shift: "If
we are graduating from nation-states to a noospheric state, we may find
ourselves exploring the kind of nonhierarchical social organization—a
'synchronic order' based on trust and telepathy—that the Hopi and other
aboriginal groups have used for millennia. If a global civilization can
self-organize from our current chaos, it will be founded on a cooperation
rather than winner-takes-all competition, sufficiency rather than surfeit,
communal solidarity rather than individual elitism, reasserting the sacred
nature of all earthly life."[16] Does this description—if we scratch away
its spiritualist coating—not render a kind of Communism? How, then,
are we to get rid of this coating? The best antidote to this spiritualist
temptation is to bear in mind the basic lesson of Darwinism: the utter
contingency of nature. Why are bees dying massively, especially in the
United States, where, according to some sources, the rate of decline has
reached up to 80 percent? One of the hypotheses is that the extensive use
of fertilizers and insecticides has rendered the plants poisonous for the

15. F. David Peat, *Synchronicity: The Bridge between Nature and Mind* (New York: Bantam
Books, 1987), quoted in Daniel Pinchbeck, *2012* (New York: Jeremy P. Tarcher / Penguin, 2007),
395.
16. Pinchbeck, *2012*, 394.

bees—is this not a nice example of how an ecological catastrophe might look: a break in the weakest link of the chain of natural exchanges derails the entire edifice? The problem here is that one cannot be absolutely sure that all we have to do is to return to natural balance—to which balance? What if the bees in the United States and Western Europe were already adapted to a certain degree and mode of industrial pollution? Or take the recently discovered vast frozen peat bog in western Siberia (the size of France and Germany combined): it started to thaw, potentially releasing billions of tons of methane, a greenhouse gas twenty times more potent than carbon dioxide, into the atmosphere. This hypothesis should be read together with the report, from May 2007,[17] that researchers at the Albert Einstein College of Medicine have found evidence that certain fungi have the capacity to use radioactivity as an energy source for making food and spurring their growth. Their interest was aroused five years ago when a robot sent into the still-highly-radioactive Chernobyl reactor had returned with samples of black, melanin-rich fungi that were growing on the ruined reactor's walls. The researchers then set about performing a variety of tests using several different fungi. Two types—one that was induced to make melanin and another that naturally contains it—were exposed to levels of ionizing radiation approximately five hundred times higher than background levels; both of these melanin-containing species grew significantly faster than when exposed to standard background radiation. Investigating further, the researchers measured the electron spin resonance signal after melanin was exposed to ionizing radiation and found that radiation interacts with melanin to alter its electron structure—an essential step for capturing radiation and converting it into a different form of energy to make food. Ideas already circulate for the radiation-munching fungi to be on the menu for future space missions. Since ionizing radiation is prevalent in outer space, astronauts might be able to rely on fungi as an inexhaustible food source on long missions or for colonizing other planets. Instead of succumbing to terror at this prospect, it is in such cases that one should remain open to new possibilities, bearing in mind that "nature" is a contingent multifaceted mechanism in which catastrophes can lead to unexpected positive results, as in Robert Altman's *Short Cuts*, in which a catastrophic car accident brings about an unexpected friendship.

17. Kate Melville, "Chernobyl Fungus Feeds on Radiation," Science a GoGo, May 23, 2007, www.scienceagogo.com/news/20070422222547data_trunc_sys.shtml.

Such an openness for radical contingency is difficult to uphold—
even a rationalist like Habermas was not able to sustain it. His late
interest in religion breaks with the traditional liberal concern for the
humanist, spiritual, and other content hidden in the religious form;
what interests him is this form itself: people who *really* fundamentally
believe and are ready to put their lives at stake for it, displaying the
raw energy of belief and the concomitant unconditional engagement
missing from the anemic-skeptic liberal stance—as if the influx of such
unconditional engagement can revitalize our postpolitical drying-out
of democracy. Habermas reacts here to the same problem as Chantal
Mouffe in her "agonistic pluralism": how to reintroduce passion into
politics? Is he, however, thereby not engaged in a kind of ideological
vampirism, sucking the energy from naive believers without being ready
to abandon his basic secular-liberal stance, so that full religious belief
remains a kind of fascinating and mysterious otherness? As Hegel already showed apropos the dialectic of Enlightenment and faith in his
Phenomenology of Spirit, such an opposition of formal Enlightenment
and fundamental-substantial beliefs is false, an untenable ideologico-
existential position. What should be done is to fully assume the identity
of the two opposed moments, which is precisely what the apocalyptic
"Christian materialism" can do with its unification of the rejection of
divine otherness and unconditional commitment.

How are we to combine such radical openness with the apocalyptic
certainty of the end of time approaching? It is here that one should bear
in mind the properly dialectic reversal of contingency into necessity, that
is, of the retroactive nature of the necessity of the forthcoming catastrophe. This reversal was described by Dupuy: "The catastrophic event is
inscribed into the future as a destiny, for sure, but also as a contingent
accident: it could not have taken place, even if, in *futur anterieur*, it appears as necessary. . . . If an outstanding event takes place, a catastrophe,
for example, it could not not have taken place; nonetheless, insofar as it
did not take place, it is not inevitable. It is thus the event's actualization—
the fact that it takes place—which retroactively creates its necessity."[18]
Dupuy provides the example of the French presidential elections in May
1995; here is the January forecast of the main polling institute: "If, on
next May 8, Ms Balladur will be elected, one can say that the presidential
election was decided before it even took place." If—accidentally—an
event takes place, it creates the preceding chain, which makes it appear

18. Jean-Pierre Dupuy, *Petite metaphysique des tsunami* (Paris: Éditions du Seuil, 2005), 19.

inevitable: *This*, not the commonplaces on how the underlying necessity expresses itself in and through the accidental play of appearances, is *in nuce* the Hegelian dialectics of contingency and necessity. In this sense, although we are determined by destiny, we are nonetheless *free to choose our destiny*. This, according to Dupuy, is also how we should approach the ecological crisis: not to "realistically" appraise the possibilities of the catastrophe but to accept it as destiny in the precise Hegelian sense: like the election of Balladur, "If the catastrophe will happen, one can say that its occurrence was decided before it even took place." Destiny and free action (to block the "if") thus go hand in hand: freedom is at its most radical the freedom to change one's destiny.

So if we are to confront properly the threat of a (cosmic or environmental) catastrophe, we have to introduce a new notion of time. Dupuy calls this time the "time of a project," of a closed circuit between the past and the future: the future is causally produced by our acts in the past, while the way we act is determined by our anticipation of the future and our reaction to this anticipation. This, then, is how Dupuy proposes to confront the catastrophe: we should first perceive it as our fate, as unavoidable, and then, projecting ourself into it, adopting its standpoint, we should retroactively insert into its past (the past of the future) counterfactual possibilities ("If we were to do that and that, the catastrophe we are in now would not have occurred!") on which we then act today.[19] Therein resides Dupuy's paradoxical formula: we have to accept that, at the level of possibilities, our future is doomed; the catastrophe will take place; it is our destiny—and then, on the background of this acceptance, we should mobilize ourselves to perform the act that will change destiny itself and thereby insert a new possibility into the past. For Badiou, the time of the fidelity to an event is the *futur anterieur*: overtaking oneself toward the future, one acts now as if the future one wants to bring about is already here. The same circular strategy of *futur anterieur* is also only truly efficient when we are confronting the prospect of a catastrophe (say, of an ecological disaster): instead of saying "the future is still open, we still have the time to act and prevent the worst," one should accept the catastrophe as inevitable, and then act to retroactively undo what is already "written in the stars" as our destiny.

One should thus say about the ecological catastrophe: *If* it will happen, it will be necessary . . . And is not a supreme case of the reversal of positive into negative destiny the shift from the classical historical

19. Ibid.

materialism into the attitude of Adorno's and Horkheimer's "dialectic of Enlightenment"? While traditional Marxism enjoined us to engage ourselves and act in order to bring about the necessity (of Communism), Adorno and Horkheimer projected themselves into the final catastrophic outcome perceived as fixed (the advent of the "administered society" of total manipulation and end of subjectivity) in order to solicit us to act against this outcome in our present. And, ironically, does the same not hold for the very defeat of Communism in 1990? It is easy, from today's perspective, to mock the "pessimists," from the Right to the Left, from Solzhenitsyn to Castoriadis, who deplored the blindness and compromises of the democratic West, its lack of ethico-political strength and courage in its dealing with the Communist threat, and who predicted that the Cold War was already lost by the West, that the Communist block had already won it, that the collapse of the West was imminent—but it is precisely their attitude that did the most for bringing about the collapse of Communism. In Dupuy's terms, their very "pessimist" prediction at the level of possibilities, of the linear historical evolution, mobilized them to counteract it.

Pascal's Wager

There is thus only one correct answer to the leftist intellectuals who desperately await the arrival of a new revolutionary agent that will perform the long-expected radical social transformation—the old Hopi saying with a wonderful Hegelian dialectical twist from substance to subject: "We are the ones we have been waiting for."[20] Waiting for another to do the job for us is a way of rationalizing our inactivity. However, the trap to be avoided here is the one of perverse self-instrumentalization: "we are the one we are waiting for" does not mean that we have to discover how we are the agent predestined by fate (historical necessity) to do the task; it means, on the contrary, that there is no big Other to rely on. In contrast to classic Marxism, where "history is on our side" (the proletariat fulfills a predestined task of universal emancipation), in today's constellation, the big Other is *against* us: left to itself, the inner thrust of our historical development leads to catastrophe, to apocalypse, so that what can prevent catastrophe is *pure voluntarism*, that is, our free decision to act against the historical necessity. This is why theology is emerging again as a point of reference for radical politics: the paradox is

20. Quoted in Pinchbeck, *2012*, 94.

that it is emerging not in order to supply a divine big Other guaranteeing the final success of our endeavors but, on the contrary, as a token of our radical freedom with no big Other to rely on. It was already Dostoyevsky who was aware of how God gives us freedom and responsibility—he is not a benevolent master steering us to safety but the one who reminds us that we are totally onto ourselves. This paradox is at the very core of the Protestant notion of predestination: predestination does not mean that we are not really free since everything is determined in advance; it involves an even more radical freedom than the ordinary one, the freedom to retroactively determine (change) one's destiny itself.

No wonder Pascal (or, more generally, Jansenism) was the only Catholic thinker who accepted predestination—predestination is a paradoxical supplement to Pascal's notion of wager.[21] The first thing that strikes the eye is that Pascal rejects all attempts to demonstrate the existence of God: he concedes that "we do not know if He is," so he seeks to provide prudential reasons for believing in God: we should wager that God exists because it is the best bet.

> "God is, or He is not." But to which side shall we incline? Reason can decide nothing here. There is an infinite chaos which separated us. A game is being played at the extremity of this infinite distance where heads or tails will turn up. . . .
> . . . Which will you choose then? Let us see. Since you must choose, let us see which interests you least. You have two things to lose, the true and the good; and two things to stake, your reason and your will, your knowledge and your happiness; and your nature has two things to shun, error and misery. Your reason is no more shocked in choosing one rather than the other, since you must of necessity choose. . . . But your happiness? Let us weigh the gain and the loss in wagering that God is.[22]

Pascal appears to be aware of the immediate objection to this argument, for he imagines an opponent replying: "That is very fine. Yes, I must wager, but I may perhaps wager too much." In short, if I put my wager on God, and God does not exist, then I really do lose something—when one wagers for God, one does stake something, which presumably one loses if God does not exist: truth, the respect for one's worldly life, and

21. Alan Hájek, "Pascal's Wager," *The Stanford Encyclopedia of Philosophy (Fall 2008 Edition)*, ed. Edward N. Zalta, http://plato.stanford.edu/archives/fall2008/entries/pascal-wager/. I rely here extensively on this entry.
22. Blaise Pascal, *Pensées*, trans. W. F. Trotter (1660), sec. 3, no. 233, quoted in Hájek, "Pascal's Wager."

so on. (It is strange how utilitarian-pragmatist Pascal's reasoning is.) There is then a series of other objections:

1. Pascal assumes that the same matrix of decision and reward applies to everybody—but what if the rewards are different for different people? Perhaps, for example, there is a predestined infinite reward for the chosen, whatever they do, and finite utility for the rest.

2. The matrix should have more rows: perhaps there is more than one way to wager for God, and the rewards that God bestows vary accordingly. For instance, God might not reward infinitely those who strive to believe in him only for the utilitarian-pragmatic reasons that Pascal gives. One could also imagine distinguishing belief based on faith from belief based on evidential reasons, and posit different rewards in each case.

3. Then there is the obvious many-Gods objection: Pascal had in mind the Catholic God, but other theistic hypotheses are also live options; namely, the "(Catholic) God does not exist" column really subdivides into various other theistic hypotheses (e.g., the Protestant God exists, Allah exists, there is no God). The obverse of this objection is the claim that Pascal's argument proves too much: its logical conclusion is that rationality requires believing in various incompatible theistic hypotheses.

4. Finally, one can argue that morality requires you to wager against God: wagering for God because of the promise of future profits violates the Kantian definition of moral act as an act accomplished for no "pathological" reasons. It was already Voltaire who, along these lines, suggested that Pascal's calculations, and his appeal to self-interest, are unworthy of the gravity of the subject of theistic belief.

Underlying all this is the basic paradox of belief as a matter of decision: as if to believe something or not is a matter of decision and not of an insight. So, if we read Pascal's wager together with his no-less-known topic of customs—

> You would like to attain faith, and do not know the way; you would like to cure yourself of unbelief, and ask the remedy for it. Learn of those who have been bound like you, and who now stake all their possessions. These are people who know the way which you would follow, and who are cured of an ill of which

you would be cured. Follow the way by which they began; by acting as if they believed, taking the holy water, having masses said, etc.[23]

—one can argue that the core of his argument directly concerns not belief but acting: one cannot decide to believe, one can decide only to act *as if* one believes, with the hope that belief will arise by itself. Perhaps this trust—that if you act as if you believe, belief will arise—is the wager.

Perhaps the only way out of these impasses is what, in his unpublished "secret" writings, Denis Diderot elaborated under the title of the "materialist's credo." In "Entretien d'un Philosophe avec la maréchale de ***," he concluded: "Après tout, le plus court est de se conduire comme si le vieillard existait . . . même quand on n'y croit pas." (After all, the most straightforward way is to behave as if the old guy exists . . . even if one doesn't believe it.) This may appear to amount to the same as Pascal's wager apropos the custom: even if you don't believe in it, act as if you believe. However, Diderot's point is exactly opposite: the only way to be truly moral is to act morally without regard to God's existence. In other words, Diderot directly turns around Pascal's wager (the advice to put your bets on the existence of God): "En un mot que la plupart ont tout a perdre et rien a gagner a nier un Dieu renumerateur et vengeur." (In a word, it is that the majority of those who deny a remunerating and revenging God have all to lose and nothing to gain.)[24] In his denial of the remunerating and vengeful God, the atheist loses everything (if he is wrong, he will be damned forever) and gains nothing (if he is right, there is no God, so nothing happens). It is this attitude that expresses true confidence in one's belief and makes one do good deeds without regard to divine reward or punishment.

Authentic belief is to be opposed to the reliance on (or reference to) a(nother) subject supposed to believe: in an authentic act of belief, I myself fully assume my belief and thus have no need of any figure of the Other to guarantee my belief—to paraphrase Lacan, an authentic belief *ne s'authorise que de lui-meme*. In this precise sense, authentic belief not only does not presuppose any big Other (is not a belief in a big Other) but, on the contrary, presupposes the destitution of the big Other, the full acceptance of the inexistence of the big Other.

This is also why a true atheist is at the opposite end of those who want to save religion's spiritual truth against its "external" dogmatic-

23. Pascal, *Pensées*, sec. 3, no. 233, quoted in Hájek, "Pascal's Wager."
24. Denis Diderot, "Observations sur Hemsterhuis," *Oeuvres*, vol. 1 (Paris: Robert Laffont, 1994), 759.

institutional set up. A profoundly religious friend once commented on the subtitle of a book of mine, "The Perverse Core of Christianity": "I fully agree with you here! I believe in God, but I find repulsive and deeply disturbing all the twist of celebrating sacrifice and humiliation, of redemption through suffering, of God organizing his own son's killing by men. Can't we get Christianity without this perverse core?" I couldn't bring myself to answer him: "But the point of my book is exactly the opposite: what I want is all those perverse twists of redemption through suffering, dying of God, and so on, but without God!"

Bee Season (directed by Scott McGehee and David Siegel, based on a novel by Myla Goldberg), one of the better Hollywood melodramas, can be of some help in making clear this crucial point. The film focuses on a modern American family whose picture-perfect surface conceals an underlying world of turmoil. Initially, the Naumanns are presented as a harmonious family living in a great Craftsman house outside Oakland. Saul Naumann is an ardent religious studies professor at Berkeley; though he's a bit of a control freak and an intellectual bully, he is also a warm, loving father and husband, a good cook, and a classical violin player. When he realizes that his eleven-year-old daughter, the almost eerily quiet, self-effacing Eliza, is a spelling champion, he takes an aggressive interest in her future wins and starts to coach her: for him, Eliza's triumph is a sign that she possesses a metaphysical gift he may be lacking. Saul's obsessive interest in Eliza (or really, his own success, by proxy) leads him to take over his daughter's training in the secret science of permutation. His once-favored son, Aaron, a socially awkward adolescent, is left to make his own spiritual discoveries. Saul's wife, Miriam, doesn't notice that her husband is turning her daughter into an ancient mystic or that her son is becoming a Hare Krishna, as she is too busy stealing objects from other people's homes to re-create the flawless world shattered years ago by the death of her parents in a car accident.

It is thus as if Eliza's overhuman perfection in spelling triggers a family explosion, disturbing its surface order, compelling all of them to confront the broken pieces of their life. All this takes place against the theological background of *tikkun olam*, the Jewish notion of healing or repairing of the world. According to Kabbalah, God—pure perfection— in his goodness wanted to share his perfection, so he created a receptacle that would receive his gift; however, unable to endure the divine light, the receptacle shattered into thousands of pieces, and it is our duty and universal responsibility to fix what has been shattered, to attempt to restore what has been damaged. In an all-too-obvious metaphor, this is also what the Naumann family needs: the restoring of unity, order, and harmony. With her family disintegrating before her eyes, it's up to Eliza to put the broken pieces of her family's world back together in an unexpected act of selflessness and love.

This act is the movie's final epiphany: the entire film drives toward Eliza's momentous decision, a choice that enables catharsis for the whole family. So how does Eliza order the family chaos? At the climactic moment of the spelling competition, in front of television cameras, when the right answer would make her national champion, she decides to get a word wrong on purpose. While the father is broken, the other two members of the family are relieved, happily, smiling, and even Eliza herself, till now a kind of catatonic monster, manages a spontaneous mischievous smile—what really happens here? Even such a mainstream figure as Roger Ebert got it right: "Eliza's decision [is] to insist on herself as a being apart from the requirements of theology and authority, a person who insists on exercising her free will. This is a stick in the eye of her father. What Eliza is doing at the end of *Bee Season* is Eliza's will. Does that make her God? No. It makes her Eliza."[25] Her act allows her to break out of the enslavement to her father's desire: no longer her father's instrument, she creates a space for herself and for the family to restore its free balance. It is thus the mistake itself, the crack of disharmony, that interrupts the perfect series of her correct answers, which restores harmony.

However, the film gets its theology wrong (or, at least, it presents its highly sanitized version): in Kabbalah, God first withdrew into himself to open up the space for creation; then, he bungled the job of creation, making a deeply flawed and fractured universe—*this* is what we, humans, have to patch up. Happily, the story itself corrects this wrong theology: what if God's mistake was to create a flawless universe, and what if humans patch things up by introducing into it imbalance and disharmony? One might venture here another problematic speculation: this insight goes beyond the limits of Judaism and brings us into the central paradox of Christianity, which concerns the status of freedom: without the notion of a flawed divinity, we have a human subject subordinated to a substantial divinity, which secretly pulls the strings.

Hegel's famous guideline that one should conceive the Absolute not only as substance but also as subject generally conjures up the discredited

25. Roger Ebert, "Bee Season," November 11, 2005, http://rogerebert.suntimes.com/apps/pbcs.dll/article?AID=/20051110/REVIEWS/51019003.

notion of some kind of "absolute Subject," a mega-Subject creating the universe and watching over our destinies. For Hegel, however, the subject, in its very core, also stands for finitude, cut, the gap of negativity, which is why God becomes subject only through Incarnation: he is not already in itself, prior to Incarnation, a mega-Subject ruling the universe. Consequently, it is crucial not to confuse Hegel's "objective spirit" with the Diltheyan notion of a life-form, a concrete historical world, as the "objectivized spirit," the product of a people, its collective genius: the moment we do this, we miss the point of Hegel's "objective spirit," which is precisely that it is spirit in its objective form, experienced by individuals as an external imposition, constraint even—there is no collective or spiritual super-Subject that would be the author of "objective spirit," whose "objectivization" this spirit would have been. There is, for Hegel, no collective Subject, no Subject-spirit beyond and above individual humans. Therein resides the paradox of "objective spirit": it is independent of individuals, encountered by them as given, preexisting them, as the presupposition of their activity, yet it is nonetheless spirit, that is, something that exists only insofar as individuals relate their activity to it, only as *their* (pre)supposition.[26]

This is why Kierkegaard's critique of Hegel relies on a fatal misunderstanding of Hegel's fundamental insight. The first thing that strikes the eye is that it is based on the (thoroughly Hegelian!) opposition between "objective" and "subjective" thought: "Objective thought translates everything into results, subjective thought puts everything into process and omits results—for as an existing individual he is constantly in process of coming to be."[27] For Kierkegaard, obviously, Hegel is the ultimate achievement of the "objective thought": he "does not understand history from the point of view of becoming, but with the illusion attached to pastness understands it from the point of view of a finality that excludes all becoming."[28] Here one should be very precise not to miss Kierkegaard's point: for him, only subjective experience is effectively "in becoming," and any notion of objective reality as an open-ended process with no fixed finality still remains within the confines of being. Why? Because any objective reality, "processual" as it may be, is by definition ontologically fully constituted, present as the positively existing

26. See Myriam Bienenstock, "Qu'est-ce que 'l'esprit objectif' selon Hegel?" in *Lectures de Hegel*, ed. Olivier Tinland (Paris: Le livre de poche, 2005), 223–67.
27. Søren Kierkegaard, *Concluding Unscientific Postscript* (Princeton, NJ: Princeton University Press, 1968), 86.
28. Ibid., 272.

domain of objects and their interactions; only subjectivity designates a domain that is *in itself* "open," marked by an *inherent* ontological failure: "Whenever a particular existence has been relegated to the past, it is complete, has acquired finality, and is in so far subject to a systematic apprehension . . . but for whom is it so subject? Anyone who is himself an existing individual cannot gain this finality outside existence which corresponds to the eternity into which the past has entered."[29] What if, however, Hegel effectively does the exact opposite? What if the wager of his dialectic is not to adopt toward the present the "point of view of finality," viewing it as if it were already past, but, precisely, to *reintroduce the openness of future into the past*, to *grasp what was in its process of becoming*, to see the contingent process that generated to existing necessity? Is this not why we have to conceive the Absolute "not only as substance but also as subject"? This is why German Idealism already explodes the coordinates of standard Aristotelian ontology, which is structured around the vector running from possibility to actuality. In contrast to the idea that every possibility strives to fully actualize itself, one should conceive of "progress" as a move of restoring the dimension of potentiality to mere actuality, of unearthing, in the very heart of actuality, a secret striving toward potentiality. Recall Walter Benjamin's notion of revolution as redemption-through-repetition of the past: apropos the French Revolution, the task of a true Marxist historiography is not to describe the events the way they really were (and to explain how these events generated the ideological illusions that accompanied them); the task is rather to unearth the hidden potentiality (the utopian emancipatory potentials) that were betrayed in the actuality of revolution and in its final outcome (the rise of utilitarian market capitalism). The point of Marx is not primarily to make fun of the wild hopes of the Jacobins' revolutionary enthusiasm, to point out how their high emancipatory rhetoric was just a means used by the historical "cunning of reason" to establish the vulgar commercial capitalist reality; it is to explain how these betrayed radical-emancipatory potentials continue to "insist" as a kind of historical specter and to haunt the revolutionary memory, demanding their enactment, so that the later proletarian revolution should also redeem (put to peace) all these past ghosts. These alternate versions of the past, which persist in a spectral form, constitute the ontological "openness" of the historical process, as it was—again—clear to Chesterton:

29. Ibid., 108.

The things that might have been are not even present to the imagination. If somebody says that the world would now be better if Napoleon had never fallen, but had established his Imperial dynasty, people have to adjust their minds with a jerk. The very notion is new to them. Yet it would have prevented the Prussian reaction; saved equality and enlightenment without a mortal quarrel with religion; unified Europeans and perhaps avoided the Parliamentary corruption and the Fascist and Bolshevist revenges. But in this age of free-thinkers, men's minds are not really free to think such a thought.

What I complain of is that those who accept the verdict of fate in this way accept it without knowing why. By a quaint paradox, those who thus assume that history always took the right turning are generally the very people who do not believe there was any special providence to guide it. The very rationalists who jeer at the trial by combat, in the old feudal ordeal, do in fact accept a trial by combat as deciding all human history.[30]

Why, then, in an apparent contradiction to what we are aiming at, is the blooming genre of what-if histories hegemonized by conservative historians? The typical introduction to such a volume as a rule begins with an attack on Marxists who allegedly believe in historical determinism. Their conservative sympathies become clear as soon as one looks at the tables of contents of the leading what-if volumes: the favored topics oscillate between the "major premise"—how much *better* history would have been if a revolutionary or "radical" event were to be avoided (if King Charles were to win the civil war against the Parliament; if the English Crown were to win the civil war against the American colonies; if the confederacy were to win the U.S. civil war, aided by Great Britain; if Germany were to win the Great War; if Lenin were to be shot at the Finland Station; etc.)—and the "minor premise"—how much *worse* history would have been if history were to take a more "progressive" twist (if Thatcher were to be killed in the Brighton IRA bombing in 1984, if Gore were to win over Bush and be the president on 9/11, etc.).

So what should the Marxist's answer be here? Definitely not to re-hash the old boring Georgi Plekhanov ratiocinations on the "role of the individual in history" (the "even if there were no Napoleon, another individual would have to play a similar role, because the deeper historical necessity called for a passage to Bonapartism" logic). One should question the very premise that Marxists (and leftists in general) are dumb determinists rather than entertaining such alternative scenarios.

30. G. K. Chesterton, "The Slavery of the Mind," http://www.cse.dmu.ac.uk/~mward/gkc/books/The_Thing.txt.

The first thing to note is that the what-if histories are part of a more general ideological trend, of a perception of life that explodes the form of the linear-centered narrative and renders life as a multiform flow; up to the domain of the "hard" sciences (quantum physics and its multiple-reality interpretation, neo-Darwinism) we seem to be haunted by the chanciness of life and the alternate versions of reality. Stephen Jay Gould, a Marxist biologist if ever there was one, once remarked that if we were to wind back the film of life and play it again, the storyline of evolution would have been totally different. This perception of our reality as one of the possible—often not even the most probable—outcomes of an "open" situation, this notion that other possible outcomes are not simply canceled out but continue to haunt our "true" reality as a specter of what might have happened, conferring on our reality the status of extreme fragility and contingency, is by no means foreign to Marxism—on it relies the felt *urgency* of the revolutionary act.

Since the nonoccurring of the October Revolution is one of the favored topics of the conservative what-if historians, let us look at how Lenin himself related to it: he was as far as imaginable from any kind of reliance on "historical necessity." (On the contrary, it was his Menshevik opponents who emphasized that one cannot jump over the succession of stages prescribed by historical determinism: first bourgeois-democratic, then proletarian revolution, etc.) When, in his "April Theses" from 1917, Lenin discerned the *Augenblick*, the unique chance for a revolution, his proposals were first met with stupor or contempt by a large majority of his own party colleagues. Within the Bolshevik party, no prominent leader supported his call to revolution, and *Pravda* took the extraordinary step of dissociating the party, and the editorial board as a whole, from Lenin's "April Theses"—far from being an opportunist flattering and exploiting the prevailing mood in the party, Lenin's views were highly idiosyncratic. Many who knew Lenin and his work doubted his state of mind: Alexander Bogdanov dismissed the "April Theses" as the delirium of a madman, while Lenin's wife, Nadezhda Krupskaya, worried that he had gone crazy. Lenin immediately perceived the revolutionary chance that was the result of unique contingent circumstances: if the moment will not be seized, the chance for the revolution will be forfeited, perhaps for decades. So we have here Lenin himself entertaining an alternative scenario: *what if* we do not act now—and it was precisely the awareness of the catastrophic consequences of not acting that pushed him to act.

But there is a much deeper commitment to alternative histories in a radical Marxist view: it brings the what-if logic to its self-reflexive reversal. For a radical Marxist, *the actual history that we live is itself a kind of alternative history realized*, the reality we have to live in because, in the past, we failed to seize the moment and act. Military historians have demonstrated that the Confederacy lost the battle at Gettysburg because General Lee made a series of mistakes totally uncharacteristic of him: "Gettysburg was the one battle, fought by Lee, that reads like fiction. In other words, if ever there was a battle where Lee did not behave like Lee, it was there in southern Pennsylvania."[31] For each of the wrong moves, one can play the game of "what would Lee have done in that situation"—in other words, it was as if, in the battle of Gettysburg, the alternate history had actualized itself.

Thinking Backward

This brings us to the what-if dimension that permeates the very core of the Marxist revolutionary project. In his ironic comments on the French Revolution, Marx opposes the revolutionary enthusiasm to the sobering effect of the "morning after": the actual result of the sublime revolutionary explosion, of the Event of freedom, equality, and brotherhood, is the miserable utilitarian/egotistic universe of market calculations. (And incidentally, is not this gap even wider in the case of the October Revolution?) However, as we have already seen, one should not simplify Marx: his point is not the rather commonsensical insight into how the vulgar reality of commerce is the "truth" of the theater of revolutionary enthusiasm, "what all the fuss really was about." In the revolutionary explosion as an Event, another utopian dimension shines through, the dimension of universal emancipation, which is precisely the excess betrayed by the market reality that takes over "the day after"—as such, this excess is not simply abolished, dismissed as irrelevant, but, as it were, *transposed into the virtual state*, continuing to haunt the emancipatory imaginary as a dream waiting to be realized.[32] The excess of revolutionary enthusiasm over its own "actual social base" or substance is thus literally that of an attribute-effect over its own substantial cause, a ghostlike Event waiting for its proper embodiment. In his less-known *Everlasting Man*, Chesterton makes a wonderful mental experiment

31. Bill Fawcett, *How to Lose a Battle* (New York: Harper, 2006), 148.
32. For a more extensive discussion of what-if histories and the Marxist revolutionary project, see Slavoj Žižek, "Lenin Shot at Finland Station," review of *What Might Have Been*, ed. Andrew Roberts, *London Review of Books* 27, no. 16 (August 18, 2005): 23.

along these lines, in imagining the monster that man might have seemed at first to the merely natural animals around him.

> The simplest truth about man is that he is a very strange being; almost in the sense of being a stranger on the earth. In all sobriety, he has much more of the external appearance of one bringing alien habits from another land than of a mere growth of this one. He has an unfair advantage and an unfair disadvantage. He cannot sleep in his own skin; he cannot trust his own instincts. He is at once a creator moving miraculous hands and fingers and a kind of cripple. He is wrapped in artificial bandages called clothes; he is propped on artificial crutches called furniture. His mind has the same doubtful liberties and the same wild limitations. Alone among the animals, he is shaken with the beautiful madness called laughter; as if he had caught sight of some secret in the very shape of the universe hidden from the universe itself. Alone among the animals he feels the need of averting his thought from the root realities of his own bodily being; of hiding them as in the presence of some higher possibility which creates the mystery of shame. Whether we praise these things as natural to man or abuse them as artificial in nature, they remain in the same sense unique.[33]

This is what Chesterton called "thinking backward": we have to put ourselves back in time, before the fateful decisions were made or before the accidents occurred that generated the state that now seems normal to us, and the royal way to do it, to render palpable this open moment of decision, is to imagine how, at that point, history may have taken a different turn.

Such "thinking backward" is peculiar to Western thought: it is totally foreign to the Eastern notion of cosmic fate. This is why all those who try to demonstrate some deeper affinity between Heidegger and Oriental thought, mostly Buddhism, miss the point: when Heidegger speaks about the *Ereignis* (appropriating event), he thereby introduces a dimension that, precisely, is missing in Buddhism, that of the fundamental historicity of Being. Although the (wrongly) so-called Buddhist ontology desubstantializes reality into a pure flow of singular events, what it cannot think is the "eventuality" of the Void of Being itself. To put it yet another way, the goal of Buddhism is to enable a person to achieve enlightenment through "traversing" the illusion of the self and rejoining the Void—what is unthinkable within this space is Heidegger's notion of the human being as *Da-Sein*, as the "being-there" of the being itself, as the site of the event-arrival of Being, so that it is Being itself that "needs" *Dasein*—with the disappearance of *Dasein*, there is also no

33. G. K.Chesterton, *The Everlasting Man*, http://www.cse.dmu.ac.uk/~mward/gkc/books/ everlasting_man.html#chap-I-i.

Being, no place where Being can, precisely, take place. Can one imagine a
Buddhist claiming that the Void (*sunyata*) itself needs humans as the site
of its arrival? One can, but in a conditional way that totally differs from
Heidegger's: in the sense that, of all sentient beings, only humans are
able to achieve enlightenment and thus break the circle of suffering.

Perhaps the clearest indication of the gap that separates Christianity
from Buddhism is the difference in their respective triads. That is to
say, in its history, each of them divided itself into three main strands;
in the case of Christianity, it is, of course, the triad of Orthodoxy-
Catholicism-Protestantism, which neatly fits the logic of universal-
particular-individual. In the case of Buddhism, on the contrary, we get
a case of what in Hegel occurs as the "downward synthesis," in which
the third term, whose function is to mediate between the opposition of
the first two, does it in a disappointing-regressive way (say, in Hegel's
Phenomenology, the whole dialectic of observing reason culminates
in the ridiculous figure of phrenology). The main split of Buddhism is
the one between Hinayana (the small wheel) and Mahayana (the great
wheel). The first one is elitist and demanding, trying to maintain the
fidelity to Buddha's teaching, focusing on the individual's effort to get
rid of the illusion of the self and attain enlightenment. The second one,
which arose through the split from the first one, subtly shifts the accent
onto compassion with others: its central figure is bodhisattva, the individual who, after achieving enlightenment, decides out of compassion
to return to the world of material illusions in order to help others to
achieve enlightenment, that is, to work for the end of suffering of all
sentient beings. The split is here irreducible: working for one's own
enlightenment reasserts the centrality of the self in the very striving for
its overcoming, while the "great wheel" way out of this predicament
just repeats the deadlock in a displaced way: egotism is overcome, but
the price is that universal enlightenment itself turns into an object of
the instrumental activity of the self.

It is easy to locate the inconsistency of the Mahayana move, which
cannot but lead to fateful consequences: when the Mahayana rein-
terpretation focuses on the figure of bodhisattva—the one who, after
achieving enlightenment and entering nirvana, returns to the life of
illusory passions out of compassion for the suffering of all those who
are still caught in the wheel of craving in order to help them to achieve
enlightenment and enter nirvana—there is a simple question to be raised
at this point: if, as radical Buddhists emphatically point out, entering nirvana does not mean that we leave this world and enter another

higher reality, if reality remains as it is and all that changes in nirvana is the individual's attitude toward it, why then, in order to help other suffering beings, do we have to *return* to our ordinary reality? Why can't we do it while dwelling in the state of enlightenment in which, as we are taught, we remain living in this world? There is thus no need for Mahayana, for the "larger wheel": the small (hinayana) wheel is large enough to allow for the enlightened one helping others. In other words, is the very concept of bodhisattva not based on a theologico-metaphysical misunderstanding of the nature of nirvana? Does it not underhandedly change nirvana into a higher metaphysical reality? No wonder that Mahayana Buddhists were the first to give a religious twist to Buddhism, abandoning Buddha's original agnostic materialism, his explicit indifference toward the religious topic.

However, it would be an utterly non-Hegelian reading of Buddhism if we were to locate the fall in its development into the humanitarian "betrayal" of its original message enacted by the Mahayana turn: if there is a Hegelian axiom, it is that the flaw has to be located in the very beginning of the entire movement. What, then, is wrong already with the Hinayana itself? Its flaw is precisely that to which Mahayana reacts, its symmetrical reversal: in striving for my own enlightenment, I regress into egotism in my very attempt to overcome it, to erase the constraints of my self.

So how to bring these two orientations together? What both orientations, Hinayana and Mahayana, exclude is a shattering protoconservative insight: What if truth doesn't alleviate our suffering? What if truth *hurts*? What if the only peace attainable comes from immersing oneself into illusion? And is this conclusion not the secret underlying premise of the third big school, Vajrayana, which predominates in Tibet and Mongolia? Vajrayana is clearly regressive, a reinscription of Buddhism into traditional ritualistic and magic practices: the opposition between self and others is overcome, but through its "reification" in ritualized practices that are indifferent to this distinction. It is an interesting fact of historical dialectic that Buddhism, which originally dispensed with all institutional ritual and focused solely on the individual's enlightenment and end of suffering, irrespective of all dogmatic and institutional frames, ended up clinging to the most mechanical and firmly entrenched institutional hierarchic frame.

But the point here is not to make fun of the "superstitious" features of Tibetan Buddhism but to become aware of how this total externalization *does the work*, "delivers the goods": is relying on a prayer wheel or, more generally, on the efficiency of the ritual not also a way to achieve the "mindlessness," to empty one's mind and repose in peace? So, in a way, Tibetan Buddhism *is* thoroughly faithful to Buddha's pragmatic orientation (ignore theological niceties, focus just on how to help people, etc.): sometimes following the blind ritual and immersing oneself into theologico-dogmatic hairsplitting *is* pragmatically the most efficient way (as in sexuality, where sometimes the best cure against impotence is not to "relax and just let it go"—the moment one formulates this as an injunction, it turns into its opposite—but to approach sex as a bureaucratic, planned procedure, establishing detailed phases of what one is planning to do and so on). The logic here is the same as that of intelligent utilitarians who are well aware that moral acts cannot be directly grounded in utilitarian considerations ("I will do this because, in the long run, it is the best strategy to bring the most happiness and pleasure to me also"). But the conclusion they draw is that the Kantian "absolutist" morality ("do your duty for the sake of duty") can and should be defended precisely on utilitarian grounds—it is also the one that works best in real life.

What, then, is the Buddhist answer to the Hegelian question: that is, if we, suffering humans, are to be awakened into enlightenment, how did we fall asleep in the first place? How did the wheel of desire emerge out of the eternal Void? There are three main answers, which strangely echo the triad of Hinayana, Mahayana, and Vajrayana. The first, standard, answer is a reference to Buddha's practico-ethical attitude: instead of dwelling on metaphysical enigmas, Buddha's starting point is the fact of suffering and the task of helping people to get out of it. The next answer draws attention to the obvious cognitive paradox that such a question implies: our very state of ignorance makes it impossible for us to answer this question—it is only possible to answer the question (or even to pose it in a proper way) once one reaches full enlightenment. (Why then do we not get an answer from those who claim to have reached enlightenment?) Finally, there are some Tibetan Buddhist hints about dark demonic forces that disturb the balance of nirvana from within—and, of course, what remains in Buddhism a dark hint is only fully developed in modern European mysticism (Jacob Boehme) and then in Hegel's dialectics. So what we should do is read Buddhism in an openly anachronistic way, shamelessly reading its gaps as signs pointing toward the future: it is only Hegel who allows us to answer the open questions raised by Buddhism.

8

The Return of Mediation

John Milbank

Synthesis and the Event

In Alain Badiou's second *grand livre, Logiques des mondes,* which is also part two of his first "great book," *L'être et l'événement,* he divides reality into (1) mathematical "Being," (2) presubjective "appearance," and (3) "Event," within which subjectivity arises as "truth-process." Yet for him, Being as totally plural, utterly empty mathematical possibility only "is" through the determinate surplus of topological appearance (objectively given, presubjective phenomenal "worlds" that are always manifest within certain "logics" or algebraic geometries), while pure Being can, from one perspective, itself be understood as a kind of zero-degree of appearance.[1] Appearances, however, consist of contingent phenomenal "existences" that are semi-"fictional," since they are merely expressions of random mathematical—which is to say, ontological—combinations.[2]

This chapter originally appeared in a slightly altered form as "The Return of Mediation, or the Ambivalence of Alain Badiou," *Angelaki: Journal of Theoretical Humanities* 12, no. 1 (2007): 127–43.

1. Alain Badiou, *Logiques des mondes: L'être et l'événement 2* (Paris: Éditions du Seuil, 2006), 197.
2. Ibid., 234.

In this manner Being and appearance would appear reciprocally to engulf and abolish each other, in a way parallel to the defining symmetrical collapse that Badiou identifies in "modernist" (extended into "postmodern") thought between "differentiating process," on the one hand, and "presences," on the other. One can think here equally of Heidegger's Being and beings; Bergson's *durée* and spatialized Being; Derrida's *différance* and "presences," or "gift" and "economy"; and Deleuze's "nonidentical repetition" and "regimes of representation." In each case one has a fundamental unifying power that nonetheless "is not" (since it is in itself the ultimate Void) save in its problematic negative cancellation of the very existences that this power itself originally distributes and constitutes.[3] Concomitantly, these existences are authentically constituted only by the very moment that discloses that underlying potent nullity, which extinguishes their ephemeral insistence.

In Badiou's case though, in contrast to this "postmodern" paradigm that he ostensibly rejects, Being is not a forceful, distributing single power that nevertheless exclusively expresses itself in a plural manifold. Rather, Being as such is simply given as irreducibly and anarchically diverse, while appearances present arbitrary local logics of unification. "Difference," in Badiou, more emphatically precedes distributive process, while "unity" is more definitively localized and confined in its actuality to the regional appearing of a particular mode of organizing plural reality.

However, the problem of "mutual dissolution" between the One and the Many persists in Badiou's revision of the postmodern ontological paradigm. The local unities of appearance merely express ontological possibilities, while the latter, though fundamental, are only actualized through the phenomena. Each forever abolishes the other. But Badiou, passing here more emphatically beyond postmodernism, seeks to resolve this problem of twin-headed nihilism by introducing a "third" category of the Event, which both is and appears, and yet exceeds both Being and appearing. Therefore, despite his claim to have instituted a more radical pluralism than that of Deleuze, appeal to the Event seems to betoken a break with the philosophy of difference and a new elaboration of a philosophy of mediation.

In terms of the Event, an extraordinary existence of one self-defining singular instance of reality arises on the surface of a world of appearances normally obeying a closed logic. At the ontological level, this

3. Ibid., 403–11.

involves the instance of at least one element within a set that merely "belongs" to it in isolation and does not, insofar as it does so, present for cobelonging through "inclusion" any members of itself as a subset—this is in accord with Zermelo's "axiom of foundation," designed to secure limits to a set and prevent its dissolution into all the infinite subsets that it must inevitably contain. For Badiou, such a free-floating and yet necessary "element," in excess of belonging "parts," provides in its relative indetermination an "evental site" upon which, outside ontology as defined by the mathematical (for which no set can be a member of itself), an "Event" can historically emerge as an aberrant sheer singularity instanced purely by self-belonging.[4]

At the "logical" level of appearances, the indeterminacy of the evental site allows it to "directly appear" as such on the surface of appearances in terms of an intense stimulus for change and transformation that permits what is "unrepresented" and so "inexistent" in some apparent object (as, for example, the Muslim character of a supposedly "French Muslim" in France), now after all to be acknowledged. Because "worlds" are always instigated and sustained by such stimuli that are the dominant "points" (emphases of worlds that define them, one might say) that have the "power to localize" the merely mathematical by a kind of "force of decree," Badiou in *Logiques des mondes* qualifies the dualism that he presented in *L'être et l'événement* between a static sociohistorical "situation" that merely instantiates a stable ontological set, on the one hand, and the irruptive Event, on the other. For the latter book there is instead a much more dominant and continuous *changement*, which "diagonally" transforms different worlds and weaves them together through releasing the "decisional" power of points and proceeding "point to point."[5]

It is in fact the event as *changement* that now realizes a synthesis between Being and appearance and prevents them from collapsing into each other in mutually assured destruction. Normally, the various transcendental logics of appearing worlds that define them algebraico-geometrically in terms of dominant intensities, conjunctions, "enveloping" media, and excluded "minima" are "added back into" the world of sets by the process of "bundling," which means that merely mathematical quantities are also expressed as degrees of intensity (the "algebraic" aspect) and the interiors of diverse sets come to communicate with each

4. Alain Badiou, *Being and Event* (New York: Continuum, 2005), 81–89, 185–90.
5. Badiou, *Logiques des mondes*, 375–463.

other in terms of true mutually communicating conjunctures that are not simply further "settings"—where the elements do not interact—and so thereby establish real "sites" (the "geometric" aspect). Exceptionally, in the opposite direction, as we have just seen, an "underlying" rogue ontological element itself rises to the surface of the phenomenal. But in either case, the "real synthesis" between the ontological and the apparent-logical is brought about by the operation of the quasi decision of the transcendentally dominant object or objects that define worlds and are dubbed "points" by Badiou. And it is this decision or series of decisions that, when accentuated, becomes the full-fledged subjective ("human") Event.[6]

Thus it is *changement* and the Event that ensure that something both *is* and also *appears*, precisely because it is a dynamic process involved with radical alteration that exceeds as actual the mere potential of Being, and as dynamic equally exceeds the dependency of appearances upon a "bundling back" into the underlying mathematical repertoire. Beyond the postmodern shuttle between the real that is not and the unreal that always and inescapably dominates our lives, Badiou certainly appears to introduce a synthesizing third. He is able to do so because his mathematical "real that is not" is not a forceful "One," while his appearances are themselves but mere deposits of this emptily diverse "Being"—hence there would appear to be room for the merely emergent third nonetheless to *drive* the whole system.

Here, however, one can argue that Badiou is caught within an extreme aporia: on the one hand, his program is reductive, such that the real content of the Event or the "truth-process" that emerges from it must be the reirruption of the universal Void that is the empty basis of all mathematical sets exorbitantly (it would seem) taken by Badiou to compose Being as such. The consequence here would be, as he sometimes seems to imply, that the *only* mark of the true is its break with old systems and invention/discovery of a new mode of operation in art, politics, science, and love (the four categories that he sees as both defining our humanity and as composing in their interrelation the true subject matter of philosophy, as Socrates first realized). In this way, the "universality" of truth-processes would collapse back into anarchic manyness expressing only a nullity, and there would be no way to discriminate between one new eventful possibility and another (nor indeed did Badiou ever suggest any such way).

6. Ibid., 243–44, 277ff., 433, 462–71.

On the other hand, if only the Event causes Being to appear and appearances to be, such that, as Badiou says, the Event is "the fourth" that includes Being, appearance, and the Event, then his thinking seems to be incipiently somewhat idealist after all—even if ideas interpellate subjects rather than vice versa.[7] In this case, mathematical diversity would itself be upheld by quasi-subjective decisions in favor of unitary and unifying processes, while the more-than-liberal (meaning a formal agreement to differ, or to allot incommensurable spheres of influence) compatibility of these processes would also demand what Badiou does not provide—namely, an overarching truth process as such.

Indeed, Badiou frequently indicates that even mathematical truth is upheld only by decision and commitment—in a way highly reminiscent of Husserl's *Origin of Geometry* and *Krisis*, he recognizes that mathematics is also born from an event and sustained by fidelity to a truth-process.[8] Furthermore, if for Badiou the many different truth-processes are compatible with one another, then it does not seem satisfactory to say, as he does, that the public measure of their legitimacy is merely the noninterference of one process with another. For this lapse into liberalism, or what Badiou terms "materialist democracy" (for him this would embrace both Levinasians and Deleuzians), implies a permanent static appearing of a formal logic of noninterference and clearly demarcated distribution of boundaries of discourse to prevail over the unpredictability of a newly emerging Event, which must surely include the capacity to revise any such boundaries. Truly to escape such liberalism, it would seem that Badiou must consider the possibility of a "meta-truth-process" arising from an Event that is "the universal of all universals." He realizes, of course, that Christianity provides just such a possibility but seeks, perhaps incoherently, to confine its truth-Event to the full emergence of the very idea of a truth-Event as such, rather than as providing a needed overarching substantive horizon.

It would appear then that Badiou's materialism is subject to deconstruction in terms that he himself provides. His anarchic impersonal manyness turns out to be but the residue of unified quasi-subjective election of unifying truths. And his "underlying" hypermaterial plural atoms could be but the negative shadow of the light of ideal reason.

7. Ibid., 156.
8. Badiou, *Being and Event*, 23–81 and elsewhere.

Badiou's Platonic Flirtation

It becomes therefore natural to ask whether the "return to metaphysics" heralded by Badiou, which is inevitably in some measure, as he acknowledges, a return to Plato, should not consider more seriously the Platonic centrality of real constitutive relation and participation. They are refused by Badiou perhaps because he knows that an imprescribable mediation between the One and the Two in Plato already obscurely suggests a theistic ontological primacy for subjective judgment. However, in his interesting eagerness to avoid a materialistic immanentism of the One (Spinoza, Bergson), Badiou appears so much to wish to endow contingently emerging truths with the seal of absoluteness that his position can appear to be incipiently Feuerbachian, and indeed it is clear that his threefold scheme of Being, appearance, and event (which covertly structures both his "great books" in their interwoven meditations on mathematics, historical conjunctures, and the thoughts of individual writers respectively) has Hegelian trinitarian echoes.[9] It is as if all reality were upheld by a human projection of true ideas that, as he explicitly indicates, has the force of the Cartesian God's edict as to the truths even of logic and mathematics.[10]

Yet Badiou's primacy of the "true idea" over the person means that this humanism is not really possible for him. If his truth-processes are self-grounding and eternal, even though they arise within time, and if the subject is more the subject of the idea than she is the source of the idea, then it is impossible to see how Badiou can avoid saying that this is because these processes do, indeed, glimpse the eternal. It is as if at one end of the aporetic ambiguity of his entire philosophy, he flirts with full-blown Platonism.

This is confirmed in two further respects. First of all, Badiou's Event category is Kierkegaardian, not Hegelian. If it negates the usual norms of both Being and appearance and thereby mediates between the two, then this is because it involves a positive decided-upon surplus to either, which appeals to a horizon of actual infinity beyond the Hegelian identity of the infinite with the finite. Astonishingly, this means that his "Trinity" is in fact more "orthodox" than Hegel's One, since it is not at all the outcome of a negative agonistic struggle in Being but rather is

---

9. Ibid.: "This book, in conformity to the sacred mystery of the Trinity, is 'three-in-one'" (18). In light of Badiou's whole trajectory, this remark seems just as sincere as it is scornful.

10. Badiou, *Logiques des mondes*, 535.

the first positing of an in-principle peacable and creative play between mathematical possibility and topological actuality.[11]

Second, his account of truth-processes appears remarkably to reintroduce real relation and participation. Interruptive Events are always in some measure continuous with other interruptive Events and not *merely* de novo, such that they compose a "diagonal" across different sets, which forms a real connection between elements in diverse "paradoxical" sets (sets in which either the "situation" of the "belonging" of "elements" to an initial set is in excess to the "state" of "inclusion" of the "parts" of subsets, or the content and number of the latter are in excess of the elements) and not simply a new set of elements blindly indifferent to each other—as for example all the twos in the set of twos.[12] Badiou describes this diagonal as "the requirement of two" necessary for the time of truth, which seems to be for him also the ultimate truth of time. This "twoness" refers both to the link between Event and Event necessary for there to be any newly arising Event at all (in discussing Pascal, Badiou gives the example of the Incarnation assuming the giving of the law, and elsewhere he provides the example of the Russian Revolution assuming the precedent of the French Revolution), and the link between the first event and the "second event" of fidelity to the Event necessary for the emergence of any truth-process. One can infer that the linking of disparate Events and the process of fidelity lie close to each other, if they are not ultimately identical.

Later, in *Logiques des mondes*, Badiou further identifies this diagonal twoness as Plato's "Two" or "Other" in the Sophist, which permits, against Parmenides, the possible "is not" that guarantees the "is" of truth, only by admitting into ultimate reality a positive as well as negative alterity: the blackbird is not an eagle not just because it is a blackbird but also because there are eagles as well as blackbirds, and they can be compared generically, specifically, and ontologically. By reading Plato's "other" as a diagonal, Badiou *does* seem also to ascribe to a participation among the forms and a weaving by judgment in any specific instance of a blend of same and other, Being and not Being, unity and diversity.[13] It is clear then that his understanding of "twoness," since it already involves a real link of the one with the other, implicitly includes a decisional or judgmental "thirdness."

11. Badiou, *Being and Event*, 161–73; Badiou, *Logiques des mondes*, 153–65, 447–59.
12. Badiou, *Being and Event*, 210.
13. Badiou, *Logiques des mondes*, 132.

Badiou's understanding of diagonal twoness can be well illustrated by his reflection on the history of human art. He convincingly argues that, despite all cultural relativity, the painting of horses all the way from the Paleolithic grottoes of Chauvet to the depictions of Picasso, all operate in a shared strange area "between" actual horses and "the idea of a horse." In other words, one can conclude only that the site of the truth-processes of art *is* the site of participation in precisely the Platonic sense.[14]

Reduction or Elevation?

As I have already indicated, Badiou's thought appears, like that of his ultimate master, Sartre, aporetically to hesitate between materialist reduction and existentialist elevation of the human. Badiou himself nevertheless most often insists on the primacy of reduction. Yet it is hard to believe this. I would argue that in reality, on a careful reading, the balance of his thought bends toward elevation.

Nevertheless, I have already partially indicated the ways in which it does not: in terms of a seemingly vacuous account of change as self-validating and in terms also of the arguably still very "postmodern" relativism of sheerly diverse truth-processes that must simply "tolerate" each other in the public realm.

In both cases—in line with Badiou's own preferred reading of his texts—this is compatible with the idea that the subjective is possible in terms of the "holes" that open up within fundamental mathematical reality, according to various well-known paradoxes of set theory. These are primarily (1) the subset "diagonalizing out" of the initial set according to the "theorem of the point of excess" (there are more "parts" in the subgroupings of a set of five sisters, for example, than there are the five initial "elements"); (2) the diagonalizing excess even of an infinite subset over an infinite primary set, as shown by Cantor; (3) the undecidable excess or nonexcess of subsets over a "set of all sets," as shown by Russell, so proving that there is no "whole" of reality, which is rather infinite; (4) the need seen by Zermelo to posit at least one element within a set, none of whose own elements ("parts" of the initial set) at all belong as elements to the initial set, such that nothing is shared between the set and this member save the Void, and therefore a set is strangely founded by something radically "other" to itself—it

14. Ibid., 25–29.

is thus this axiom that precludes "self-belonging" and ensures that the Event lies "beyond [mathematical] being"; and (5) the "forcing," invented in the 1960s by P. J. Cohen, of sheerly indeterminable and so purely general mathematical parts within subsets into a kind of equality with the determinable elements of the initial one.[15]

The opening in Being provided by these paradoxes is then supplemented, in *Logiques des mondes*, by the intrusion of the parts of subsets or elements of the initial set not merely into or beyond the primary set but also, by virtue of what Badiou terms an obscure elective "affinity," into the algebraic-geometric arena of actual appearances.[16]

Here, normally, a "world" can only appear at all, because certain "objects" of appearance are dominant over others, such that some things appear only through other things (the leg of a chair "through" the chair), or else some things appear alongside others since they are both contained by a background "enveloping" reality (all the furniture in a room as surrounded by walls and covered by a ceiling). All this depends upon various degrees of "intensity" of individual items (the dominance of walls and ceiling within a room, for example) that express underlying mathematical atoms.

The prevailing objects of a world of appearances are, however, also for this reason typically, as we have already seen, "points" (echoing Leibniz's "metaphysical points" or "monads"), at which an underlying indeterminate potency tends to come to the surface. These "points" are precisely the hinge between appearance and Event, since they contain a capacity for radical change. (The walls of the room that alone snugly confine it are yet the very things that might be expanded, diminished, or altogether removed.) In proceeding from "point to point," a quasi-subjective process of decision emerges that vaults from world to world and yet sustains a continuity (like, for example, to begin at the most material level, a hedge that bounds a garden that turns into a hedge bounding a lane and finally a hedge bounding—more ideally—a county).

It is very hard to see how Badiou, for all his materialistic intellectual lineage, is *not* talking here about a "tradition" in something like a Gadamerian sense. For the procedure from point to point has its own unfolding integrity: it would seem to consist in the relating through time of one thing with another by a series of quasi decisions (which eventually become fully "human" decisions) that weaves, in Kierkegaardian

15. Badiou, *Being and Event*, 81–123; 173–201; 265–81; 327–441.
16. Badiou, *Logiques des mondes*, 272.

fashion (as Badiou indicates), its own specific character of nonidentical repetition, which nonetheless should command a universal assent as a process of truth.

One can now express the aporia concealed within Badiou's philosophy more radically. The way in which he links mathematical paradox and indeterminacy with the perplexities of the human existential condition is cognitively ecumenical, brave, and admirable. Yet the more he grounds the latter in the former, the more this merely redounds into a grounding of the former in the latter. Maybe subjects are indeed the scum of the Void floating to the surface, but Badiou equally declares that opting for the primacy of the Many is a mere decision that contrasts with what he claims was Georg Cantor's alternative *Catholic* decision for the eternal paradoxical unity of the One and the Many beyond the principle of noncontradiction, which Cantor's own paradoxes of transfinitude seemed to violate. Likewise, he declares that the postulation of an actual infinity is a decision taken within the course of Western culture.

And at this point Badiou's own decision regarding the immanence of the infinite seems yet more precarious than he will always concede: for to conclude that infinity, beyond the paradoxes of contradiction that collapse any finite or transfinite totality (after Russell and Cantor), is merely immanent and inaccessible rather than an eternally "actual" *coniunctio oppositorum*, is in truth to *evade* the demonstrated limit of finite logic rather than to embrace it.

Badiou's mere decision at this point is also supported by an inaccurate history: he claims that, in the Middle Ages, the Greek horizon of the essential finitude of Being was preserved, with God being a mere negative or eminent exception.[17] Thus the infinity of Being only emerges at the Renaissance with the infinitization of the cosmos. But this is false on two counts: first of all, Badiou reads medieval theology as if it were all Scotist and divided Being primarily into finite and infinite. And in fact even Scotus saw the infinite as primary and the finite as exceptional and secondary, whereas Badiou speaks as if, for the Middle Ages, it were the other way around. But more typically, the early to High Middle Ages, as with Aquinas, saw Being as such as infinite and saw finite existence as only participating in this. Aquinas, it is true, did not embrace an infinite cosmos or an actual mathematical infinite, but other thinkers of this period came near to doing so: Robert Grosseteste

17. Badiou, *Being and Event*, 142–70.

saw the creation as initially constituted by a Neoplatonic emanative series of transfinites that expressed the propagation of light. Finally, in the Renaissance period, Nicholas of Cusa's assertion of the infinity of the cosmos implied for him not immanence but rather the paradoxical and continuous passing over of the finite into its constitutively other and yet "not-other" transcendent infinite ground. Essentially the same construal was sustained by Blaise Pascal.

Thus Badiou's ultimate primacy of the Many over the One is a mere decision. Certainly, one can agree with him that, as already for Plato, and as in trinitarian theology (as he notes!) the One is later than the Many and emerges only as their unity—since if Being was originally really one, there would not "be" anything, as with Parmenides, and the One would have no content, as Hegel showed.[18] Nevertheless, because there is only ever any specific "set" of the manifold by virtue of its unity, one might still decide, in divergence from Badiou's fundamental option, to accord to unity a retroactive primacy (as indeed in the case of trinitarian theology).

Similarly, Badiou's preference for the sheer primacy of the manifold is undergirded by an arbitrary decision for the immanence of the infinite, which leaves it within an amorphous indeterminacy, in absolute dyadic excess of, and yet ultimately expressive of, the "anti-One" of the Void, which Badiou writes runically as $\emptyset$.

For this reason, it would seem that if Badiou's Being and appearance threaten to collapse into each other and cancel each other out (in the same fashion as Derrida's *différance* and presence), in the end the same thing is true of his Event as against his Being/appearance taken together. So while the Event is supposed to save the integrity of the actual and so rescue us from the postmodern shuttle of indeterminacy between the absent real possible and the illusory actual given (so inevitably seductive for Americans, as Badiou says) in the name of universal truth, then it seems to fail to do so because it is itself captured by a new nihilistic shuttle between mathematical Being and existential decision.

However, as we have already mentioned, Badiou declares that besides the triad of Being, appearance, and event there is a fourth—and that this is the Event! In which case, a Kierkegaardian positive mediation, which alone sustains a "Hegelian" double negation, is the "whole" of reality, constituting in effect Badiou's "absolute knowledge." And this would seem to be confirmed by the way in which, as we have seen, he

18. Ibid., 23–24.

says that even though mathematical entities compose "Being," Being can still be read as a minimal instance of appearance—indeed, only in this way does it exist at all.

The position presented here seems extraordinarily like that of the notion of "substantive relations" in orthodox trinitarian theology: the Father, though the source of all Being, "is not" without his generation of the Son, even though the Son only images the Father. Here one could argue that only the third person of the Trinity avoids "double abolition" (of the Son by the Father and vice versa) within the Godhead, by revealing that the Father as fully expressed in the Son nonetheless gives rise to a surplus potential beyond even "the all" of what is and what appears or is effective and effected (the Platonic *dynamis*). Only in this way are the Father's potency and the Son's actuality both "real"—precisely because they are upheld by the "Event" of the Spirit's dynamism. Badiou's granting of a fundamental role to *changement* as securing the "real synthesis" of Being and appearance seems astonishingly parallel to this latent theological topos—as he is most likely well aware.

Moreover, he *much more* stresses this role toward the end of *Logiques des mondes* than hitherto, in the course of making generous concessions to Bergson's and Deleuze's vitalism and subordination of finite Being to finite becoming. Yet he still in these pages wishes to avoid the notion of an "underlying" virtuality; rather, what is fundamental is the very "later" and always actual process of change—finally human historical change—itself.

If change as an actual process is now for Badiou fundamental, then it precludes any notion of a more basic virtual power that nourishes, unfolds, enfolds, and at the same time swallows up this actuality. Moreover, it also precludes the idea that such change is a subjective projection, since for Badiou the subject is constituted within consistent transformation and is in nowise its source. But if change directed toward truth is ultimate and self-grounded, such that, as Badiou says, it has the tonality of "eternity," then what is one to say? Surely that indeed this selective but ultimate temporality is *indeed* also eternity or, as it were, the underside of the eternal? It would seem to follow not merely that actual time as truth-process participates in eternity but also that it is included within eternity in exactly the same sense that, for Thomas Aquinas, the creation of the world is included in the paternal uttering of the Logos.

The profound paradox here is that Badiou, as a Marxist, in seeking a hopeful materialist ontology in the face of the current course of history and so in despair of historicism, veers ever closer not merely to Platonism but also to Christianity—as he is well aware, even if he has wagered on the success of formalistic advance raids upon alien beauties that will preclude any later yielding to their substantive charms.

For the more he rejects the unifyingly virtual as a foundational principle, the more he appears to break with a Bergsonian-Heideggerean emancipation of the possible from the primacy of the actual—an "emancipation" that always subordinates the Event to a merely forceful "power" of which it is an instance. Instead, Badiou seeks to render the import of the Event itself ultimate, precisely by conjoining it to the ultimacy of actuality—which is an Aristotelian and Thomistic thesis. He still wishes to insist on the immanent primacy of becoming, yet arguably, to yoke this to the self-grounding of the actual is barely coherent: an event that manifests only its own actuality as universal truth must be, as he says, an instance of "grace."[19] But once he has declared that the Event and the truth-process arrive in their actuality as a "gift," then it scarcely matters that he does not affirm their arrival from an "elsewhere." For indeed, they do not come from an elsewhere in any ontic sense; but if they arrive and reveal the eternal, then how is this not the arrival in time of the eternal? To speak of grace without God can only mean to speak apophatically of God—unless the Event is entirely hollowed out by the Void or is simply a human projection. But we have seen how there are elements in Badiou's writings that seem to prohibit those renderings.

Even the most reductive moment in Badiou's thought, namely the mathematical ontology, appears precariously materialist, since his radically "nominalist" atoms, which collapse beyond even individuality into pure multiples of multiples, are also, by that very token, idealized. As Ralph Cudworth noted in the seventeenth century with respect to Thomas Hobbes, materialism seems to demand atomism, but the most rigorous atomism reverts into intellectualism.[20] So to say that numbers are the ontological alphabet runs dangerously close to saying that elements of thought are the constituents of Being.

And sure enough, as we have seen, it turns out that the mathematical atoms only "are" through actual existing appearances of contingently diverse "worlds," which themselves are only given to possible appearance by exhibiting "transcendental" logical structures (transcendental for

19. Badiou, *Logiques des mondes*, 534.

20. Ralph Cudworth, *The True Intellectual System of the Universe*, vol. 3 (1845; repr., Bristol: Thoemmes Press, 1995).

the objective situation, not for a subjective observer) that are in excess of the specific content of appearance. These "logics" have, therefore, once again an ineradicably intellectualist and abstract aspect. It follows that while, certainly, one can concur, against the Husserlian legacy, with the realist bias of Badiou's phenomenology and its freedom from any *époche*, it is still difficult to elide from this revisionist phenomenology, as he appears to wish, the view that reality, as it objectively exists or appears, is *also* a reality that can only be defined as presenting itself to the human mind in a certain way and may sometimes appear to different persons in incommensurably different ways.

Finally, if Being only appears, and appearance only is, through the point-to-point procedure of eventful processes, which give rise to and yet also consist in, quasi-subjective "decisions," then not merely the logical but also the intellectual consistency of the material cosmos seems to be now trebly confirmed. It is hard to avoid the conclusion that Badiou's *changement* is not in some sense psychic—rather like the world-soul in Russian thought from Solovyev onward.

This is further underlined by his refusal to read the aporetic character of the relation of past, present, and future in terms of Bergsonian *durée*, Heideggerean *ecstasis*, or Derridean *différance*. He denies that presence vanishes in the face of the direct passage from past to future and instead affirms, with Kierkegaard, that past and future are synthesized in the instantaneous "moment" of the present that can occupy no real measured time and therefore coincides in some fashion with the eternal.[21] For Badiou, time is the Cartesian *creatio continua* that binds moment to moment through an extrinsic intervention, which for Badiou is that of the ontological Void. Yet he also seems to point beyond such extrinsicism, whether divine or nihilistic. For if the series of replete temporal presences or Events are primary (so redeeming the integrity of humanly significant "instances") rather than any temporal power of flux, then the flow of time must surely flow into time ahead of itself from eternity rather than from a latency of time itself—which, be it noted, must always, even in Bergson, spatially denature temporality.

Badiou's Bias toward Transcendence

The above analysis concurs with the fact that, throughout Badiou's thought (in this connection oddly at one with Emmanuel Levinas), he

21. Badiou, *Logiques des mondes*, 377–419, 447–59.

seems to prefer the thinkers of transcendence to the thinkers of immanence: Paul to the Stoics, Descartes and Pascal to Spinoza, Kierkegaard
to Nietzsche. His aim, of course, is always to plunder the valency of
transcendence for the confirmation of dialectical materialism—yet it
can be argued that the real thrust of his thinking demands rather an
outright *theological materialism* (and then that this alone can overcome
"materialist democracy").

This is above all because any favoring of the primacy of the actual,
the relational, and the participatory cannot be readily divorced from
some mode of metaphysical Platonism and also what can be regarded
as not just its modification but also its *more emphatic and effective
restatement* by Christian theology. For in the latter case, the Absolute
itself is conceived, in trinitarian theology, as substantially relational,
and the creation, since it is at once ex nihilo and emanatively *ex Deo*
(in Aquinas, for example), is regarded as only existing at all within an
entirely asymmetrical relation of dependence on God that now renders
participation more extreme, since there is no longer, as for Plato, an
ontologically original matter that both "imitates" the eternal and receives a "share" in the eternal.

So in considering the "logic" of Christianity, one can read trinitarian
relation as radicalizing the "weaving" by judgment of the One with
the Many in Plato that begins to suggest the ultimacy of "spirit" even
in the realm of the forms. Likewise, one can read creation ex nihilo as
radicalizing the notion of *methexis* in terms that fully express rather
than compromise the idea that existence is a personal or hyperpersonal
gift.

To complete this brief picture, one can understand the doctrine of
the Incarnation as radicalizing the Platonic teaching of recollection,
as Kierkegaard so brilliantly realized in his *Philosophical Fragments*.
For Plato, recollection was triggered by certain events of historical encounter, which in the later "theurgic" gloss on his work by Iamblichus
and Proclus was read (perhaps correctly) as also the descent of divine
powers into physical reality. Christianity, in effect, as later Greek fathers
like Dionysius and Maximus came to realize, proffers the most extreme
example of "theurgic recollection" imaginable; for here the encounter
of all human beings with the life of one man who is personified by the
descended Logos itself "reminds" the whole of humanity of the forgot-
ten trinitarian God and its own true lost life, which consists in gradually
entering into the eternal Triune rhythms. In this way "incarnation"
means that participation in the divine relational life is restored. The

truth is recovered not by a "more precise human gaze" but rather by a repairing of the asymmetrical relation to God of the creation by the action of God himself. Truth, which is itself relational, is relationally restored.

So if, for Badiou, the Christian Event is the Event of the arrival of the logic of any universal truth-process as such (albeit in a false "mythical" form), then one can suggest that this is implicitly because it radicalizes the Platonic notion of recollection. For here the "trigger" of recollection and what is recollected precisely coincide, such that, as Kierkegaard put it (although he read "recollection" in over-Kantian terms), truth is now a matter of "nonidentical repetition forward" and not simply (instead of Kierkegaard's "rather than") "recollection backward."[22] In this way, the truth has become a historical project for the first time, since it is tied to the "participation-in" (imitation through sharing) the extraordinary yet ordinary life and resurrection of one human being. Just for this reason, as Badiou rightly says, truth as a project becomes also for the first time with Christianity something truly universal, since this imitation is possible for all humans, not just the learned, and can be diversely and yet consistently expressed in myriad diverse cultural idioms. In this manner Badiou espouses (albeit formalistically and athe- istically) a Christian paradigm that construes "truth" as emerging from a singular event of a mysterious "gift" or "grace," and a "further event" as he describes it (in a transparent allusion to Pentecost) of continuous fidelity to the original Event that can only be a relational weaving of witnesses through the course of time.[23]

My argument here then is, first of all, that Plato (and Aristotle in his wake, to some degree) favored the primacy of the actual and the rela- tional and that this stress, under the impulse of "revelation," is much accentuated by Christianity. Second, Badiou's formalist favoring of a Christian paradigm is connected to those moments in his thought— grounded in the supremacy of the Event rather than the supremacy of the Void—when he too seems to favor the primacy of the actual and the relational.

22. See John Milbank, "The Sublime in Kierkegaard," in *Post-Secular Philosophy: Between Philosophy and Theology*, ed. Phillip Blond (London: Routledge, 1998), 131–56.

23. Alain Badiou, *St. Paul ou la naissance de l'universalisme* (Paris: Presses Universitaire de France, 1999). See also John Milbank, "Materialism and Transcendence" in *Theology and the Political: The New Debate*, ed. Creston Davis, John Milbank, and Slavoj Žižek (Durham, NC: Duke University Press, 2005) for a further discussion of Badiou, Deleuze, and politics that at points, however, reads Badiou, as I now realize, in too simplistically dualist a fashion.

Badiou's Latent Christian Metaphysics

But to what extent is this favoring of the primacy of the actual and the relational really the case? As we have already seen, read one way, and perhaps the most "obvious" way, Badiou's work entirely denies this: what matters is the abstract potential of mathematical elements and the purely monadic (multiples of multiples) basis of relational illusion, such that apparent relational ties are (by a "preestablished harmony") only the trace on the surface of the relative weights of phenomena determined quite independently of each other. Thus, for example, we might see a large house as dominating both its garden and its surrounding wall, yet the fact that they have been constructed and conceived within this pattern of relation is really (on Badiou's view) subordinate to the way these items embody respective degrees of intensity of appearing. (This, of course, seems to raise the problem of how such "degrees" could have any meaning outside the relational context.)

Yet if the mathematical possesses for Badiou no Deleuzian force, it is hard to sustain this reading. Instead, the more primary hermeneutic key to his thought appears to be the thesis that the Event is the fourth that is "the all" in such a manner that the later, the emergent, and purely contingent is bizarrely fundamental. It is for this reason that, as we have seen, Badiou can say that human beings "create the truth" in exactly the same way as Descartes' God—who, beyond any medieval voluntarism, ordains even the laws of arithmetic and logic. Yet here one can suggest that his humanist appropriation of divine voluntarism and of the divine *causa sui* (also first affirmed by Descartes) is not really consistent with Badiou's view that subjects are only subjectivized within the truth-process, for this implies that if, indeed, human beings create the truth, it is inversely the case that humanity only emerges at all within this creating of the truth. (Since this happens in language, Badiou's explicit rejection of the linguistic turn as "finitistic" also seems questionable—for he fails to see that in its most radical form this turn *breaks* with transcendentalism and phenomenalism and points back toward metaphysical speculation, since, if language is always already given, its "transcendental" instance is as much ontological as epistemological and therefore precludes any "critical" certainty about what is merely subjective and merely confined to the phenomenal and finite.)

Despite his Cartesian voluntarist affirmations, human beings appear to be "compelled" by events and truth-processes for Badiou, just as for Aquinas God the Father is "compelled" by the truths of the Son-Logos, which he nonetheless utters. This gives a notion of expressive creating as being "sur-prized" and "led out" by the very truth to which it gives rise. In this way Badiou's *verum-factum* would appear to be more like Giambattista Vico's scholastic modification of Descartes in his *Liber Metaphysicus (De Antiquissima Italorum Sapientia)* than like Descartes himself. However, the Vichian model is less easily given a "Feuerbachian" treatment than the Cartesian one. For perhaps a finite being could create infinite norms of truth. But if a finite being is "compelled" by the norms it creates and projects them to an infinity whose end it can never actually reach and that it also projects as "actually beyond" any mere "always one more step" (as Badiou clearly affirms), then it would seem that the "compelling" and universal character of truth "arrives" to human beings indeed as a gift, so that its "as if from an elsewhere" is really indistinguishable from "indeed from an [ontological not ontic] elsewhere." The latter would not follow only if human beings were in truth actually infinite and eternal—then certainly their being compelled by what they make would be identical with their own self-compelling (if not Cartesian "self-causation," since God always "is"). But if human beings, though "eternal" and "divine" for Badiou, are always merely in the process of being deified (as he also clearly thinks), then even though on earth they inaugurate the infinite, they are also here drawn forward by an actuality that must be inaccessibly "already" and that they can never entirely command.

What I am trying to suggest, therefore, is that Badiou, read in terms of the supremacy of the Event, is drawn despite himself ineluctably toward a more-than-formal espousal of Platonism and Christianity. To be able to claim this, one has to make reference to the following statements in *Logiques des mondes*:

> First of all, as we have already twice seen, mathematical Being can, for Badiou, itself be regarded as a zero-degree of logical appearance.
>
> Second, as we have also already seen, the "worlds of appearance" can themselves be seen as the fixed deposits of eventful processes pivoting about points: "Points are metaphorically the indices of the decision of thought."[24]

This second position is much less clear in the book than the first, because Badiou admits the existence of "atonal" worlds without the

---

24. Badiou, *Logiques des mondes*, 443.

prevalence of overridingly significant "points," or else conversely, "over-stretched" worlds saturated with such points, as in the case of a scenario of constant crisis where every day one must make crucial and ambivalent decisions—Badiou cites the experience of the Maquis in France during World War II.[25]

However, just as one can understand pure Being in terms of an exceptional negative instance of appearing that is nonappearing, so likewise one could regard an atonal world without points as presenting a zero-degree of the Event, where all commitment to the pursuit of noble ideas has been abandoned in favor of a nihilistic anticommitment to the leveling of all values that is characteristic of contemporary "anti-ideological" liberal postmodernism (that is dubbed by Badiou "democratic materialism"). Has the latter not arrived as a kind of negative truth-process (rather than its mere refusal or subversion according to Badiou) emergent from certain "antievents" and "antifidelities" (like the defeat of trade unionism in the 1970s and a merely "liberationist" construal of the significance of 1968)? As for the overstretched world that is saturated with points, thereby almost compromising the significance of any of them, this seems to concern an excess of Event and transformation rather than its absence.

In these ways, the existence of atonal and overstretched worlds without Events does not disprove a reading of Badiou according to which all reality is actually emergent from Events. For how, indeed, can appearing worlds arise at all save through some sort of radical change that elects the dominance of certain privileged points over others, which then settles into a constant logic of fixed comparative ratios between inner-worldly objects? This seems to imply that there exist Event-processes within prehuman nature that would be dealt with by physics and biology. Badiou says almost nothing about the latter two disciplines, yet if he excludes their role, he would then seem to espouse an extreme Cartesianism that declares nature may be exhaustively described and accounted for in terms of mathematics and algebraic geometry. This, though, appears to conflict with the fact that he refuses any Cartesian dualism of mind and matter by locating within the material the mysterious and paradoxical grounds for the emergence of subjectivity. For if, on the one hand, the subjective is rooted in material nature and, on the other hand, the Event is the all, then surely one requires a mediating category of forceful physical processes of eventful change and not

25. Ibid., 442–47.

just modification of a basic scenario. A certain degree of Bergsonian vitalism would have to be incorporated—and indeed, Badiou shows signs of moving in such a direction.

If one reads Badiou's philosophy from the vantage point of the Event rather than from the vantage point of the Void, then the Void appears to be only the negative shadow that the Event works with, like God working with nothing in order to create. Similarly, appearances become the deposits of the Event, laid down in the past from a future anterior, as *natura naturata*. For we know that Badiou does not ascribe the latter to the workings of a Spinozistic virtual *natura naturans*. But if phenomena are the deposits of the Event before they are the manifestations of the mathematical noumena (reduced to the raw material that is pure potentiality), and if the Event is what produces the human rather than being commanded by the human, then how can there not be a "divine shaping" or a kind of "world soul" at work here?

If, furthermore, the logic of appearances is read in terms of the primacy of the Event, then Badiou's thesis of a preestablished harmony would surely have to be abandoned. For one thing, how can mutually constitutive relations (like the garden defined by its boundary and the boundary that is only visible as the boundary of the garden) be the apparent upshots of variegated intensities of objects if these intensities merely express abstract mathematical atoms that in reality do no work?

Badiou also affirms that the mark of every apparent relation is that it can be envisaged from a standpoint outside the relation, such that this standpoint can in turn be envisaged in relation to the poles of the first relation and so on ad infinitum. Yet if relative intensities can only *exist* in appearances and so are only existing-through-manifestation via comparison, then are they not in reality *constituted* through this comparison (rather than by preestablished harmony) such that they truly *depend* on an infinite implied gaze that is forever withheld from their view?

Badiou takes it to be a confirmation of "materialism" that a world can be "inaccessibly" closed by its own transfinitude because, through the process of "exposure" of one relation from a third vantage point that sets up two new relations (of this new point to each of the poles of the first relation), one can, by imagined endless triangulation, project this process into the infinite.[26] However, if the diagonal path of eventful transformation, rather than the atomic insistence of the Void, accounts for relations, then it would seem to follow that the latter are *constituted*

26. Ibid., 329–38.

beyond and yet between themselves by an infinite gaze that is really actual. The "materialist" closure appealing to the paradoxical infinity of the finite would turn out to be equally a "theological" closure—where immanent transfinitude is closed in its transfinitude only by the always further lure of the positive actual infinite.

So it has now been seen that worlds of appearance may be regarded as themselves the deposits of consistent processes of fidelity to events in such a manner that the ecology of a specific world sustains, as a coherent logic, the outworking of certain evolutionary interruptions. Furthermore, I have also argued that these processes are constituted through real relation and do not merely express on the surface various intensities of underlying atomic possibility.

This is finally confirmed by the dominance of the Event. For Badiou, as we have seen, the Event as "a member of itself" exceeds the mathematical elements that only qualify as mathematical insofar as they can be arranged in sets as always members of an overarching category. (The *mathematical* one is not radically singular but is rather defined as lying within the set of all ones, the series of one, two, and three, as subincluded in the set of all twos and so forth.) The identity of *changement* beyond the bare facts of its instances can therefore be sustained only by a process that "point by point" deems it to sustain a consistency with the original Event and indeed to other Events to which it alludes.

It then follows that relationality must be original and can in nowise be reduced to preestablished intensities. For the Event and its sequence do not hang together for Badiou like a mathematical set or like a topological arena that only appears to view in terms of a fixed pattern of relative intensities (else we would only be presented with a blank or a blur). To the contrary, "the pattern" of the truth-process seems to be inseparable from both its *actual* occurrence and the *relational* reference back and forth through time of one thing through another. Indeed, this is exactly why Badiou thinks that Pascal's typological argument for Christianity is to be taken as exemplary: here foretype and fulfillment are *both* necessary (and therefore inextricably related) because the Incarnation is only "true" as the miraculous fulfillment of Old Testament prophecies in terms of which it alone makes sense and yet is also true as their utterly *surprising* fulfillment—for otherwise the prophecies alone would have sufficed for human salvation.[27]

27. Badiou, *Being and Event*, 212–23.

And even at the ontological level, Badiou's "preestablished harmony" seems to be negated by his own maneuvers. For although relations are supposed to be the accidental effects of the expression of intensities, so that they are but illusorily there for a series of triangulated gazes projected into the infinite, we have seen that in reality worlds are constituted as the deposits of the interweaving of the actual and original relations through space and time of the process of *changement*. In this way, one might say that the Event is always superadded to worlds that nevertheless paradoxically first exist in terms of this very extra—rather as, in Aquinas's theology, the creation is sustained only as orientated through humanity to deifying grace.[28] In that case, the relations within worlds are real and constitutive and not mere secondary quasi illusions. But furthermore, if such relations compose worlds and the logic of worlds is, as Badiou says, "retroacted" back into Being, then it would seem that real relations invade even the mathematical-ontological level. For the mark of retroaction, as we have seen, is the forming of secret "tunnels" between the aberrant members of one set and those of another, such that diverse "interiorities" are combined. While Badiou appears to wish to read the conjunction of two topological areas in a "Leibnizian" fashion as the preestablished transcendental conjunction of their two interiors, this seems to be negated by the fact that "site" can be "added back" to set only if one assumes that apparent constitutive connections (as between one end of a drawn line and another, or the four points of a square at the very simplest level) are indeed irreducible.[29]

And at the phenomenological level also he is surely wrong. To take roughly his own example, the back garden that might link a house with a lake does not merely reflect, as he suggests, the "preestablished" link (which would appear to be but weakly metaphorical) between the tranquility of a domestic interior and that of a lake but also tends to imply "for the first time" through strong metaphoric transference that this house is indeed a pool of tranquility and that the closed water of the lake is indeed a tamed wildness, while at the same time the "openness" of the lake is linked with the house, and the secrecy of the house confirms the "closure" of the lake. Finally, the garden establishes an interchange between the house's interiority but penetrability and the lake's openness and yet impenetrable depths. It is more the case that it

---

28. See John Milbank, *The Suspended Middle: Henri de Lubac and the Debate concerning the Supernatural* (Grand Rapids: Eerdmans, 2006).

29. Badiou, *Logiques des mondes*, 433–36.

is the garden that "gives" through transition this lake and this house, than it is the case that the house as a house-in-general and the lake as a lake-in-general give the garden.

At this point in my argument a possible misunderstanding must be headed off. To insist, with and yet against Badiou, on the primacy of ontological relation is *not* to propose a modern, post-Kantian—as opposed to Badiou's neo-Cartesian—philosophy. The latter might appear to be the case, were one to accord with the view of a writer strongly influenced by Badiou, namely Quentin Meillassoux, that premodern thought is characterized by the primacy of substance taken as independent of knowledge, whereas modern thought is "correlationist" or critically idealist, such that while thought is always here taken to be thought "of" something, "somethings" are only those things that can be thought— such that outside this correlation one can only be agnostic.[30]

Meillassoux is surely wrong on two counts. First of all, the "relation" of thought to appearance in Kant and his successors is only an accidental, not a constitutive, relation: it concerns how Being appears for us and not the way in which human knowledge is in some measure truly disclosive of Being as such, and thereby "really related" to it. Still less does it concern a fundamental teleological orientation of Being toward being known.

Second, since in classical and medieval "realism," both of these circumstances *were* affirmed, it is wrong to see this realism as defined by a kind of inert substantialism, which was surely *invented* by Descartes with respect to his primary qualities (whereas Meillassoux sees the latter ontology as simply one example of an inherited realist paradigm). On the contrary, it is the older realism that is more radically "correlationist." Thus for Plato temporal formations only exist as participating in (as related to) the eternal forms, while these themselves are relationally defined through mutual comparison and "intermixture." Aristotle may by contrast have newly stressed the integrity of substance, but he also regarded all temporal substances as relationally constituted by the lure of the first mover and understood the act of human knowing to be a further relational realization of the very Being of the known existing thing. All four of these emphases were confirmed and exaggerated by Christian thinkers and in particular Aquinas, for whom the doctrine of creation renders even matter itself relationally dependent and the

---

30. Quentin Meillassoux, *Après la finitude: Essai sur la nécessité de la contingence* (Paris: Éditions du Seuil, 2006), 13–69.

doctrine of the Trinity newly suggests the possibility that sheerly relational Being (Being that is relational without remainder) characterizes Being as such. Participation in this sheer relationality by creatures lays new weight in his writings upon mutual dependence, temporal becoming, productive expressiveness, and the ecstatic character of knowing and willing.[31]

Therefore, outside antique materialism, there was no notion in traditional realism of a "substance" indifferent to the relation that is awareness. Rather, the highest substance was typically understood as also knowing, and the economy of finite existence was assumed to require the presence of created intelligence both as its author and as its interior culmination. It follows that "correlation" is scarcely the typical mark of modern thought; rather, it is the replacement of (Aristotelian) "knowledge by identity" with "knowledge by representation," which leaves substance and understanding indifferent to each other and knowledge as a merely accidental event that might or might not befall existence.

The difference between ancient-medieval and modern thought can then be better understood as one between constitutive relation, on the one hand, and accidental relation, on the other. In these terms Descartes falls firmly on the modern side of the divide, while the denial of the objectivity of primary as well as secondary qualities is, after all, pace Meillassoux, simply a further evolution of the paradigm Descartes helped to establish. (It is hard here to see why Meillassoux is so convinced that the prehuman past is more of a problem for this model than is physical space without a human presence; surely in either case, on the "modern," nonrealist paradigm—which I am not assenting to—one is simply speaking of a projected reality that we are forced to describe "as if" human beings were there: the prehuman past is neither affirmed nor denied, because we simply cannot know whether, outside our human perspective, temporal perspectives in our sense have any meaning. And one should add here that Badiou's "realistic" primary mathematical elements do not seem to be tied to any "actual" past time or to any "actual" spatiality.)

To return to Badiou, it has now been seen that eventful relations finally leak back even into Being itself. But in that case, what are we to make of Badiou's comparison of the belonging of elements to sets to

---

31. See John Milbank and Catherine Pickstock, *Truth in Aquinas* (London: Routledge, 2001). I am indebted to Adrian Pabst of Cambridge University for his doctoral work on relation and participation.

the link of things to forms in Plato and his assertion that this belonging is an equivalent of Platonic participation?[32] He means this surely in a subversive sense, since this belonging is the mere randomness of possibility. The more serious participation in ideas happens in the course of *changement*, but here ideas are supposed to be purely immanent. Yet we have seen how this is hard to believe, and now we can also see that these ideas as diagonals percolate back via appearances all the way into the empty font of Being as such by virtue of its ineliminable gaps, aberrations, and paradoxes. Does this not mean that the manyness of sets is also and "originally" the dyad and triad of the other, which is the diagonalizing event? In that case, the participation of elements and parts in sets is really also a participation in the One and the Two and the mediation between them. Or, indeed, in the Father, the Son, and the Holy Spirit, who might be read as null origin ("prior" to relation), manifestation, and eventful donation.

It has now been seen, in the first place, that Badiou appears to refuse relation and participation and to be stuck, like most of postmodern thought, in an aporetic shuttle between the One and the Many—in his case, between the manifold settings of the Void and the universal imperative of the Event. However, we have also seen, in the second place, that, read in a particular direction, Badiou appears to reinstate relation and even participation. If we take the Event as dominant over the Void, then, since the Event *is* a category of (non-Hegelian) mediation between Being and appearance, he appears to more than flirt with a Christian metaphysics of primary actuality, real relation, and participatory sharing in the eternal. The possibility that he points toward a new fusion of the Christian and the Marxist traditions cannot be quickly dismissed.

The Overreductionism of Badiou's Ethics and Politics

Yet we can now add, in the third place, that in terms of Badiou's *ethics* this fusion is by no means clear. Certainly he understands subjectivity in terms of collective participation in a truth-process and not, like Levinas, in terms of the encounter of one individual with another, and this is all to the good. However, at times he construes this in terms of the adhesion of an individual to an abstract generality deciphered mathematically in terms of the un-Leibnizian "forcing" of the indeterminable, and so as individualized *only* as universal into the realm of determinations them-

32. Badiou, *Logiques des mondes*, 317.

selves as "another" member paradoxically locatable only as nonlocatable and so as specifically general. This is the most acute instance of the way in which Badiou consistently associates the diagonalizing excess of "the state" or "representation" of parts of subsets over the "situation" or "presentation" of elements of an initial set with the *political* "state" and the political or economic processes of "representation," where a set of persons is treated in terms of their manifold ways of being such and such—citizen, woman, worker, shareholder, and so forth. This excess of the parts over the whole is for him, it should be said, at least two steps away from the Event or from *changement*: this requires in addition the excess of the singular *element* over its parts (a reverse excess after Zermelo) to give the "evental site" (for his later work, also ontologically intrusive within appearance) and the more-than-mathematical or logical irruption of the Event itself as "self-belonging."

It is, however, in terms of a certain ambivalent celebration of the first excess of parts over elements and so of "state" and "representation" that Badiou too readily seems to endorse Rousseau's "general will," which is specifically and immanently universal because it is not merely the abstract empirical outcome of representative democracy, nor is it universal as mediating the transcendent but rather as realizing the supposedly "objective" emergent essence of all human beings taken as "citizens."[33]

According to this endorsement, Badiou also defends the French revolutionary terror and the Maoist cultural revolution on behalf of such objective essences (ignoring the questionably "radical" character of even the aims pursued in both cases). One should presumably construe this dark side of his thought as believing that one requires the initial emergence of the "specifically general" (according to the "point of excess" and of "forcing") as a destructive clearing of the way for the emergence of the Event, rather in the way that for Marx the provisional Socialist state must prepare the way for full-fledged Communism. But why this residually agonistic dialectics and supposed ontological need for an initial tragedy and beneficial purging? For if, as Badiou affirms, the mediation provided by the Event is in Kierkegaardian surplus to Hegelian determinate negation, then why cannot this medium be self-sustaining from the outset? Then there would be no need for participation in truth-processes to imply a moment of what Levinas might have rightly described as surrender to "totality."

33. Badiou, *Being and Event*, 344–54.

Instead, as with Badiou's account of the painted horses, one could speak of a universal truth grounded in an event as *not necessarily* prepared for by an independent and terroristic moment of specifically general "forcing" but rather as always already overtaking this moment in terms of a hovering "between" the remotely ideal, on the one hand, and all the diverse local and individual perspectives, on the other. Politically, this would allow that radical movements and processes do not always need to commence with a "revolutionary" seizure of the state in the name of a provisional abstraction, but, like many cooperative socialisms or current movements in Central and South America, may simply sidestep the state and "representative" revolutionary forces in order directly to institute newly just collective practices. Indeed, Badiou's usual and correct disdain for representative democracy—as indifferent to truth and so bound to betray the objective interests of what the representatives claim to represent—should allow him to acknowledge this. He needs surely to jettison a residually "negative dialectical" element in his thought that leads him to suggest—in accordance with the priority of the Void—the necessity of this sociopolitical moment in which the "representation" of the "power set" or set of subsets (as normatively for set theory "larger" than the initial set) "diagonalizes out" of the initial set in terms of both the number of elements "included" in excess of those "presented" (as, for example, the functions of a populace are in excess of the number of a populace) and also the excess of the indeterminate specified as general over the presented determinate elements (such that you only ever vote "qua citizen" as such and not qua yourself as unique person).

For if, in accordance with the alternative priority of the Event, it is the Event itself that actualizes among appearances the diagonal excess, then representation can be always already overtaken by a substantive procedure (based on the excess of the more singular and yet open initial element over the more determinate and yet abstract parts) that seeks to pursue—not by voting but by action—the objectively ideal interests of a variegated populace. These, however, are not (as for Rousseau) any longer reduced to their interests qua citizens or to the abstract technological coordination of their myriad social functions but rather are seen as embodied only within an actually realized "between" of collaboration in pursuit of true ideas. This collaboration must involve also a coordination of functions not merely in the interests of power and utility but architectonically, in terms of a human metafunction that is a kind of construction of a vast collective work of art proffered beyond humanity itself as a spectacle for eternity. (In Italy especially, one has the sense of a huge continuous collective work of liturgical art being assembled from the time of the Etruscans to the present.) This would mean that, beyond Rousseau, the true "general will" must allude to a true transcendent telos for human nature as such.

Then indeed, the truth would not be *in excess* of the interpersonal exchange of unique expressions. So read in one direction against Badiou himself, Badiou's philosophy turns out to imply the paraontological primacy of the good—if not, certainly, the good as beyond Being, then actual Being as supremely the good, though equally (in contrast to Levinas) supremely the true. Indeed, Badiou's last word in *Logiques des mondes* is that the Event itself is the gift and that this gift is sustained only by the generous and coordinated interchange of human beings across time.

If one reads Alain Badiou in this seemingly perverse and yet, I consider, accurate fashion, then one can see that he has helped to indicate, in a remarkably original way, how we might restore the European tradition of universality in terms of a concealed underlying homology of socialism, materialism, Platonism, and Christianity.

Author Index

239

Subject Index

241